My Godawful Life

Sunny McCreary

My Godawful Life

BOXTREE

First published 2008 by Boxtree

This edition published 2014 by Boxtree
an imprint of Pan Macmillan, a division of Macmillan Publishers Limited
Pan Macmillan, 20 New Wharf Road, London N1 9RR
Basingstoke and Oxford
Associated companies throughout the world
www.panmacmillan.com

ISBN 978-0-7522-6559-9

Typeset by SetSystems Ltd, Saffron Walden, Essex

Visit **www.panmacmillan.com** to read more about all our books
and to buy them. You will also find features, author interviews and
news of any author events, and you can sign up for e-newsletters
so that you're always first to hear about our new releases.

The author wishes to thank
Jeremiah, Bruno, Premee, Neil, Emi, Dusty, Andrew and Will
for helping to lighten his sorry burden in this Vale of Tears,
or trying to.

The reader is cautioned that, as this is an unflinching account
of the most Painful, Miserable and Tragic life ever,
it is at times crude and shocking both in
content and language.

1

I am born, a terrible mistake in retrospect

I was born, by breech birth, in a run-down shack, after having been choked on the umbilical cord for half an hour, and was promptly dropped on the floor by the doctor, and when he went to pick me up inadvertently kicked across the room. It was to set the tone for the rest of my life.

This I do not remember, of course, but have been subsequently informed by doleful relatives, all of whose existences have been very nearly as dreadful and downtrodden as mine.

I do however have a distinct memory – gained decades later while undergoing regression during my many years in therapy – of my first attempt to suck on my mother's nipple. Alas, I bit down somewhat hard and pierced the sac of her saline implants, which burst and nearly drowned me.

Perhaps this was the reason for my mother's subsequent hatred of me. She eked a degraded living as a pole-dancer and whore, and after the accident, left with one breast 50 inches large, and a small deflated one that I had popped and which she could never afford to get fixed, she was only ever able to attract the occasional fetishist, the hardcore asymmetry freaks, or of course the desperate, such as lepers. The pole-dancing was over because her balance and centre of gravity had been thrown so far out that the first time she tried to whirl around a pole the centrifugal forces sent her flying off and she landed on a table halfway across the room, breaking her spine. Paralysed from the neck down, she was nevertheless still able to earn a living servicing her few remaining customers, but as soon as I was old enough I was given the chore of moving her limbs while she was being fornicated with so as to give the illusion of passion. It was some years before I discovered that moving my mother's nerveless hand up and down a john's back was not a normal part of many people's childhoods.

I do not remember ever eating food during my child-hood, or indeed having any clothes, toys or friends, apart from the nice man up the road who used to give me a penny for being allowed to put his finger up my bum. Our meagre income all went on crack cocaine for my mother and nails for my stepfather to pound into my flesh, his favourite pastime.

I could not find it in my heart to grudge him this, his only creative outlet. In an ideal world, I suppose, he would have had a job that involved hammering nails into children, for he was very good at it, but as fate had decreed that he be a small-time pimp I was his only canvas. I felt that by taking part in his hobbies we were in some measure brought closer together. I still remember the day he finally succeeded in pounding a dozen five-inchers completely into my skull in an exactly equidistant ring, the sense of accomplishment we both felt and the proud way he took me in to show me off to my mother and her client with fridge magnets playfully plastered all over my head.

I sometimes wonder, however, if there were long-term side-effects to this little game, and if this is the reason for the searing headaches I have suffered from all my life, and the strange syndrome that has baffled a succession of neurolo-gists whereby whenever a TV remote control is used in my vicinity I flip over. (VCR remotes have an even more unusual effect, causing me to move either backwards or forwards very quickly or freeze motionless. Incidentally, when I try to watch television myself, I am only ever able to pick up reruns of *Celebrity Squares*. When other people think of television, they probably think 'Entertainment and escape' or 'A gateway to the world'. I think, 'The box of torment'.)

At other times, though, our relationship was not so good. My real father could have been any one of seven, all of whom were eaten by a shark before I was born, and I believe my stepfather resented this fact and took it out on me. He was adamant that I must earn my keep and at the age of eight put me to work tilling the back field. With my limbs tied together and several long nails strategically hammered into my nose I made a simple but effective scratch-plough or harrow as he dragged me back and forth behind the mule.

His notions of discipline were oppressive in the extreme. With a view to teaching me to knock before I came intox the shack, he rigged the door with a series of ingenious booby traps. If I remembered to knock he would disarm it for me, if he was in a good mood. If I forgot or he was feeling tetchy, I would walk through to find an axe swinging down towards my head or a javelin hurtling towards my chest, or the handle of the door itself would give me an electric shock.

This has resulted in a crippling fear of doors that has lasted all my life. For preference I will always use a ventilation shaft to move about a building wherever possible. To this day, if I am forced to pass through a door I do so in a crouching waddle with my hands over my head, or hurl myself through in a flying leap and then roll for cover. To other people, I suppose, doors represent opportunity and adventure. To me, they evoke the swish of descending axes and the twang of crossbow bolts, and I often vomit when I see one.

For most of my childhood I was rarely allowed in the shack anyway, except when I was needed to move my mother's limbs or to try out one of my stepfather's nail designs, and was kept in a pigeon loft in the yard and made to sleep there. The pigeons hated me and would peck me all day and night in well-organized shifts. I believe pigeons are bullies at heart and can sense weakness, although if I ever tried to stand up to one of them they would all go for me in one big mob. There were endless squabbles over the seed we were fed and I never got my fair share.

When my stepfather was going through a mood of artistic frustration, believing that he would never really be any good at expressing himself through pounding nails into children, and would probably never even get an Arts Council grant for it, he would leave me locked in the pigeon loft for months on end. I often spent more time in the company of pigeons during my childhood than I did with humans and as a result took on many of their traits. To this day, I tend to walk with my hands behind me, thrusting my head forward and back. And whenever I see a statue I feel a strange urge to shit on it. I am in fact only able to defecate from a great height and when using the toilet am forced to squat on the cistern and wave my elbows like wings. Furthermore when I see food I often forget to eat human style and simply peck sharply at the plate; I have broken my nose in restaurants twice. As a child I came to be able to speak pigeon-language, mostly to find they were all swearing at me and insulting my personal appearance. This still affects my speech patterns nowadays and I find I use the exclamation 'Coo!' more than

4

is usual. On the upside, I am good at finding my way home from places. On another downside, I am only able to sleep in a small box.

Nevertheless I am grateful for my upbringing. I have always been an optimistic person, no matter how many times life has squashed it. I believe that whatever doesn't kill us makes us stronger. The trials of my childhood had strengthened me so as to be able to endure the utter horror of my youth.

2

My first love; my first tragic loss

They say that your first love never dies. This is literally true in my case as my first love, Sally-Ann Larouche, is now a cryogenically frozen severed head in a vault somewhere, awaiting the day when the disease that slowly ate the rest of her body can be cured. For me there has never been anyone else but her, nor is there ever likely to be, especially as my dick gets chewed off by a rabid bat in chapter 15, and a baboon's arse is grafted on to my face by a mad scientist in chapter 7.

I first met Sally-Ann in the sludge-fields at the back of the chemical plant that abutted our shack. I was fleeing some children who were throwing stones at me because I had declined to show them my vestigial tail, when she appeared out of nowhere and came to my rescue. A feisty little tyke, she had soon driven them off with fists, sticks, and well-aimed handfuls of chemical sludge. I thanked her humbly and found she was staring at me wide-eyed.

'You – you are covered in boils!' she gasped.

Lowering my eyes, I allowed that this was so. I had lately contracted a rare disease, the first of many in my life and, to the doctors' bafflement, thought to be caused by swallowing large amounts of pigeon-shit (for the malicious birds would take it in turns to defecate in my mouth while I slept). It manifested itself as a crop of spectacular green buboes across my skin.

'I love boils!' she cried. 'May I – may I pop them?'

Smitten by this gorgeous creature, I nodded shyly and she set to work with relish, squeezing, pinching and poking my ripe, bursting bubbles with a greedy glee. The touch of her fingers made me catch my breath with mingled pain and ecstasy. It was springtime, the sun reflecting in rainbow colours off the scum-pool beneath the factory drainage pipe, and it came to me that the gunk spurting from my huge verdant blisters was like sap rising within me or the spores floating off the wasteground dandelions.

'I have never seen so much pus!' she exclaimed. I felt a thrill of pride.

'There are more on my chest,' I said, taking my ragged T-shirt off and delighting in her gasp of admiration at the rich bubonic splendour I revealed.

From then on we were inseparable. I was able to keep the disease going indefinitely by scratching the infection and putting the pigeons' arses in my mouth and squeezing them so they would shit down my throat, and each time we met I had a fine new crop of buboes to offer her. We would make ourselves cosy dens amid the toxic-waste drums and talk, pinch, and extrude long purulent strings of diseased lymph matter all the endless carefree afternoons.

At last one day she permitted me to kiss her and admitted she was my girlfriend. I taught her pigeon-English and we would bill and coo at each other for hours on end.

She was my only friend, the only ray of sunshine in my dismal life. I had never been popular at school for any number of reasons. There was my strange head-jerking pigeon-walk for one thing. For another there was the awkward matter of my name. When I was first (and belatedly) sent to school I made the embarrassing realization that I didn't have a name as my parents had never bothered to give me one. 'They must call you something,' the teacher pressed. I tried to think, and innocently volunteered that my stepfather called me variously, in ascending order of menace, Son, Sonny, Sonny-Boy, and Shithead. The slightly wandering old teacher, misinterpreting or perhaps thinking she was doing me a kindness, wrote down 'Sunny-Boy' in the register and called me 'Sunny', saying it was a lovely, cheerful name that suited me, not caring or not knowing that it was more usually a girl's. My schoolfellows, meanwhile, opted for the more gender-neutral 'Shithead', perhaps because I was perpetually covered in pigeon droppings.

I was bullied mercilessly and horrendously throughout my school life. Apart from all the other things that singled me out I was teased and picked on because my mother was a whore, and when I huffily retorted that the preferred term nowadays was 'dick-technician', and that I had never heard any of their fathers complaining about her easy payment terms and value-for-money, it didn't help much.

From morning until hometime I would be insulted, punched, kicked, shunned, and used as a puck in impromptu games of playground head-hockey. I was desperately unhappy and was only able to keep my sanity thanks to the solace of an imaginary friend, Scary Jack, a ten-foot bipedal horned platypus with huge teeth and fiery eyes who would tell me to burn the school down with everyone locked inside and call me a wimp when I refused. But when he wasn't sulking about this we would play tick or hopscotch together, sometimes I-Spy, although this was hard for me as Scary Jack was half in a different and very horrible dimension and would spy things like Brain-Eating Laser-Buzzards and Skull-Headed Deathbeasts.

Sally-Ann was never there to protect me: her father had a responsible position at the factory and she went to a posh school miles away. But as soon as the last bell had rung I would flee to her eager arms and she would make me forget it all.

It was not to last, and nor was she.

I remember we blithely ignored the first ominous hint that something was terribly wrong.

We had lingered over a farewell kiss one day and I made her promise never to leave me.

'No,' she vowed solemnly, 'I will never leave you.' Suddenly she glanced down and frowned. 'Oh no,' she said, 'my toe has fallen off.'

With the resilience of youth, we shrugged this off and thought no more of it. I said it must have been a baby toe and a new one would grow in its place which would be even prettier. I made her give me the old one as a keepsake; impulsively she tied a bit of ribbon around it in a bow and I kept the blackened thing under the bit of old sacking that served me as a pillow, the happiest boy in the world.

However, a week later we were on a sketching expedition to the slagheap which was abruptly curtailed by a rainstorm. Hurriedly we gathered our belongings and were about to flee when I perceived she had overlooked something.

'Hey, Miss Scatterbrain, don't forget your foot!' I called with indulgent remonstrance.

She frowned, hopping with impatience, as I proffered the rotted thing to her. 'Oh – you carry it, please.'

Slyly, I forgot to give it back to her and took it home and kept it in a shoebox.

Two weeks after that we were returning from a day at the swamp when I felt moved to ask:

'Didn't you have two legs when we set out?'

Tutting, she checked the picnic hamper, glanced back

the way we had come, then shrugged. 'I expect it will turn up.'

That evening I devotedly retraced our route and found the errant limb stuck on a barbed-wire fence we had crossed. I chased off the dogs that were worrying at it and brought it home to keep enshrined in my treasure crate along with my conkers and bubblegum cards. Every morning I would take it out and kiss and nuzzle it. I think I still have it somewhere.

It was when her hand plopped off in the middle of detonating a bubo I had been proudly cultivating on my forehead that we were forced to realize something was amiss.

'How – how can I pop your buboes – without hands?' she gasped in horror, pale and stricken, staring wide-eyed at the stump, and collapsed.

'Sally-Ann!'

Tear-stricken, heart pounding, I carried her to her home. Doctors were consulted. The news was not good.

As the disease spread to her internal organs she was in an horrific amount of pain. I could only watch helplessly as teams of specialists failed to fight its advance. She was brave and defiant to the end. Her heart had always been set on a musical career. Realizing she would probably never be able to play the violin again, she learned to play the mouth organ without hands. When the doctors grimly broke the news that she would soon have no lungs to blow it with, she resolutely taught herself percussion, gripping a drumstick between her teeth and determinedly bashing out tunes on triangles and cowbells I held over her head. When they sadly explained that she would eventually have no mouth, it came as a hard blow. But two days later she had learned to play bulb-horns with her nose like a circus seal. Her plucky rendition of Beethoven's 'Ode To Joy' by this method was perhaps the most stirring musical experience of my life. The medics, weeping at her misplaced courage, were forced to spell out that by the time she lost her lungs and mouth she would, most likely, be dead. Not one whit deterred from her dream, she instructed me to put her ashes in a pair of maracas and play them every day.

At the eleventh hour a rich grandfather, long estranged from the family, intervened. The specialists he flew in from all over the world availed no more than the ones who had already been consulted. But he was determined she would not die and resolved to confer on her a dubious immortality he had long had planned for himself. At the last moment, when her poor tormented body could take no more, her head would be whipped off and stashed quickly in a waiting freezer, there to while away the long chilly centuries in who knows what dreams of frostbite until such a day as a cure could be found.

By this point she had been reduced to little more than a slowly disintegrating torso. I beg the reader will excuse me if I do not dwell on our last tragic hours together. My editor tells me I must, but I really cannot face rehearsing the tormented cries, the vomit, the diarrhoea, the stench of rotting flesh, the fevered ravings, the undignified inch by inch erasing of a personality I had loved, so please do not ask me. For those who are curious, however, it happens that I taped her final agonized screams and gurgles for posterity, and may release them as a separate CD or put them on my publisher's website as a sound file.

I was with her until the end. We were unable to hold hands, as she no longer had any, but I gripped her gently by a shoulder stump as we gazed into each other's eyes.

Surrounded by doctors, technicians and her grieving family, for privacy's sake we had recourse to pigeon language to express our final tender farewells.

'Coo,' she said, which means 'You were my one true love, my destiny, the ring around my foot, the loft I will always home to, and I will never forget that fated Tuesday in the fields at the back of the chemical factory', provided it is inflected right.

'Proo,' I responded, a pigeon endearment which translates as 'From this day forth every statue I shit on will be to the glory of thy name.'

'Now, Sunny,' she said in human, 'it's time.'

For as if my agony was not unendurable enough already, she had asked that I be the one to cut her living head off.

I would fain spare you this grim scene; but both my editor and the sales team assure me that nothing should be hidden. I suppose that shedding light on this Gothic episode may be of great comfort to someone somewhere, and that any of my readers who have also known the horror of being forced to cut a loved one's living head off will have the solace of knowing they are not alone. For the fact is I have never been able to find a support group devoted to this trauma, except an online one written in Transylvanian.

'Quickly,' she said, 'do it quickly.'

I nodded and fumbled for the junior hacksaw I had been provided with. It had to be quick, for medical reasons. Nervously I glanced up to where a string of doctors, who were also expert basketball players, were standing by ready to catch her severed head when I threw it to them and relay it quickly between them to the freezer at the other end of the room.

I looked down to where I had already drawn a dotted

line across her neck in felt-tip. I wiped the sweat from my brow and energetically started to saw.

Ping! went the blade of the junior hacksaw as it snapped.

'Gurrrrg!' said Sally-Ann, as her arterial blood jetted up and splashed into my eyes.

'I knew he'd do that,' said my scowling old woodwork teacher, Mr McGurk, who had been brought along to coach me through it. 'Every bloody time. It's in the wrist, son, how many times do I have to tell you? Slow and even and keep the blade straight. He'll not learn.'

'Give me another!' I cried, frantically putting my hands over her ragged neck to try to keep the blood in. 'Quick!'

Muttering to himself he passed me another saw. This time I got to the bone before the blade snapped.

'Shit!'

'You saw like a fairy.'

'Gurrrrrrrg,' gurgled Sally-Ann.

There was pandemonium. Suddenly everyone in the room was crowding in on me, all yelling at once and trying to make me get out of the way or tell me what to do. 'Give it here, you wet bugger,' said a capable old grandmother, grabbing the broken saw off me and trying to push me aside. An uncle offered me his open penknife, which I seized in a panic and started to slash desperately at the still-attached flesh with. 'Too much blood loss!' screamed a doctor. There was blood pumping everwhere. Frantically I stuck my index finger into one of the exposed arteries to stem the flow. 'Don't worry, it's all under control,' I told Sally-Ann. 'Another saw, quick!'

'You've broken them all,' said McGurk in satisfaction, arms folded. 'That's the tenth one this year, we can't budget for any more.'

'Shut up! The axe! The axe!' I pointed desperately with my free finger. There was a fire-axe in a glass case on the wall. A dynamic young surgeon smashed the glass and grabbed it.

'Stand back!' he cried. Everyone got out of the way. He stood over her and dramatically raised the fire-axe right over his head, neatly embedding the back of it in the skull of Mr McGurk who was standing behind him. Meanwhile I had one finger stuck inside an artery and with the other hand was yanking at Sally-Ann's hair desperately trying to pull her half-severed head off, smiling nervously into her open staring eyes and mumbling loving reassurances as she gurgled at me.

The doctor messily extricated his axe from McGurk, who slid to the floor lobotomized and was a much less grumpy man afterwards. 'Stand back!' he cried again, and again did his barbarian axe-man move.

It was at this point I discovered my index finger was completely stuck inside Sally-Ann's jugular vein. I screamed as the axe descended, neatly lopping off Sally-Ann's head and taking my finger with it.

The head rolled off the table and landed on the floor with a thud. Everyone rushed to grab it and in the confusion it was kicked around the room. Lurching round in agony screaming at the spurting stump where my finger had once been, I inadvertently stood on her. I tossed her to a medic, he slammed her in the freezer, and everyone heaved a big sigh of relief.

I stood pressed against the freezer for so long my face and hands stuck to it, and boiling water had to be poured over me to get me off.

Part of me will always be with her, namely my finger.

★

Without Sally-Ann my life at home and school was bleaker than ever. But that was all about to end anyway.

An observant teacher asked me why I was always covered in pigeon-shit and tended to peck at my food. My casual answers alarmed him and the social services were sent to investigate my home conditions. Once they had discreetly established that my parents didn't have any religious or cultural reasons for torturing me I was swiftly taken into care. As I was RC on my mother's side my case was taken by an organization run by the Catholic Church. I was adopted by a family in Ireland and placed in a church school.

That was when my sufferings really began.

3

I have the shit kicked out of me by nuns

Through some sort of mix-up that may have been due to my name I was enrolled to be taught by the sisters at the Blessed Black Heart of Torquemada Convent School for Wicked, Wicked Girls and Horribly Doomed Young Ladies. The baggy gym-knickers and dowdy skirts and blouses were the least of my problems.

To people who were never taught by them, I suppose, nuns are angels of mercy or an appealing sexual fetish. But to this day, whenever I see *The Sound of Music* I scream and wet myself.

'You are all here,' said Sister Heinrich Himmler, a spectacled nun with beady eyes and five o'clock shadow, tapping a South African police-issue sjambok against the palm of her hand menacingly, 'because you are wicked, wicked, haythin' little girls. That will be beaten out of yis and the love of Jaysis beaten in, so it will, so it will, at all at all.'

I raised my hand. 'Please, Miss, I'm not a girl.'

'Jesus O'Reilly! A tomboy, is ut? The Good Lord hates a tomboy, to be sure, to be sure! Whoy a little girl's petal is her crowning glory, so ut is, so ut is, so long as you don't look at it, or touch it, or allow some Prodestant pervert to go down on it, bejabers! Go and report yourself to Sister Reggie Kray, the dharlin', dharlin' woman, and be electrocuted.'

I can still remember the clammy hand of fear that would grab me during the long lonely walks along the draughty corridor to Sister Reggie Kray's office.

'Top of the mornin' to ye!' Sister Reggie Kray would say menacingly. 'Now whativer have you done to be sent to me, at all, at all, tooraloora acushla?'

'Please, Miss, Sister Heinrich Himmler said I was to be electrocuted because I told her I wasn't a girl.'

'Ah Jaysis, Mary, Mungo and Midge! Did you iver hear the likes of ut? Now I'll be putting the electrodes up your arsehole, will I?'

As I trudged back along the corridor rubbing my bottom, Sister Graeme Souness the sports mistress would come lunging out of nowhere and fell me cruelly with a flying tackle below the kneecap.

'Bejasus and begorrah!' she would say, moustache bristling fiercely, as I rolled around on the floor clutching my leg in agony, 'whativer are you doin' out of class, at all, at all!'

'Please, Miss, Sister Heinrich Himmler sent me to Sister Reggie Kray to be electrocuted because I'm a boy,' I sobbed.

'A loikely story! Go and take yourself to Sister Judge Jeffreys to have your ears cropped and your nipples twisted.'

So I would trudge to Sister Judge Jeffreys's office.

'Please, miss, Sister Graeme Souness sent me to have my ears cropped and my nipples twisted.'

Sister Judge Jeffreys punched me brutally in the face and then kicked me in the ribs when I fell to the floor.

'Sure and she niver did! Nipples are not a fitting word for a young girl. Go and take yourself off to Sister Scorpius Out Of Farscape to be tortured in the Aurora Chair.'

Sister Scorpius Out Of Farscape, a pale and calculating nun in leather bondage outfit, said:

'John, the wormhole technology in your brain … I

mean, top of the mornin', acushla, now whativer have you been afther doin', me bonny proud colleen?'

'Please Miss . . .'

So then Sister Scorpius Out Of Farscape sucked my mind out in her Aurora Chair and sent me along to report to Father Rasputin for a good hard fucking.

Father Rasputin sat me on his knee and started to tickle my chest.

'Ah, my choild, that's a foin pair of budding little dumplings ye have there. Will you not be needing a bra soon?'

'I'm a boy!'

'Are ye now?' he said, slightly but not crushingly disappointed. 'Still, ye're wearing the knickers and all, and we must make do with what the good Lord sends us. Bend over the table now.'

So it went. Nothing I ever did was right and I was always in trouble. To the ill-educated nuns the teachings of the Catholic Church had absolute authority, but even at an early age I was able to see through their simplistic doctrine and reject it.

'We believe in one God, the Father, the Almighty, maker of heaven and earth, of all that is seen and unseen. We believe in one Lord, Jesus Christ, the only Son of God, eternally begotten of the Father, God from God, Light from Light, true God from true God, begotten, not made, one in Being with the Father, through him all things were made.'

I raised my hand. 'But please, Miss, how can Jesus be both God and the son of God? God has the attributes of being both eternal and indivisible, ergo if Jesus was created by Him he cannot be God.'

'Sure and ye're afther denying the dhivinity of Christ, now!'

I quaked but stood my ground. 'I would rather formulate that Christ was *Homoiousion* (of like substance) with God rather than *Homoousion* (of the same substance). There can only be one God and He cannot be divided.'

' "Tis a heretic ye're afther bheing! Isn't it as plain as the nose on your face that the Holy Trinity is to be considered as one in *ousia* and three in *persona?'*

'Nevertheless even though Christ is the *Logos* or Word that was in the beginning, if he was made by God then there was a time when he was not.'

'Sure and you're not as green as you're cabbage-looking! However, both time and materiality are alien to the Divine Essence and therefore the state of Divine Sonship can be as eternal as the Divinity itself. Did you iver think of that now, at all at all at all? Now go and ask Sister Ilsa The She-Wolf Of The SS to rape you with a sthrap-on.'

Nor did I find much comfort at home with my adoptive Irish family. In poverty-stricken Ireland children who lacked the gift of the gab were strictly culled by starvation and only potential poets and memoirists were allowed to survive. Da would beat us and deprive us of food if our language wasn't lyric and fanciful. In these circumstances it was hard to report that the nuns were abusing me.

'Top of the evenin' to ye, me little carragheen, and how did ye fare at school today?'

'Sister Ilsa The She-Wolf Of The SS raped me with a strap-on.'

'Flatley preserve us! Sthrap-ons, is ut? Now there's a thing, isn't ut?' Da twinkled and winked approvingly. 'That's my bhoy, you're learning, lay it on thick now, you'll be a hit with the prosaic tongue-tied Anglos one day, so ye whill.'

'No, really, she did, a monstrous vibrating strap-on dildo as big as my arm.'

'Ah, 'tis a joy to listen to yer blarney! Come and hear the hyperbole on the young one, mother mavourneen, he could charm the birds from the trees with his shoite, so he could.'

People forget nowadays how hard times were in Dublin during the IT boom of the early '90s. Da would come home intoxicated on lattes after a hard day of Computer Aided Design, fetching with him a humble takeaway supper of Japanese-Peruvian fusion sushi and finger-foods, which we were forced to eat with our bare hands. To make ends meet my foster-mother had been forced to resort to the shameful expedient of earning a living thinking up new surcharges for Ryanair. My three stepbrothers had been taken away by the English to work on the stand-up circuit and my poor sister was running a shamrock bar in St Tropez. Every morning I would have to take an old newspaper and make my way shivering across the icy yard to the outdoor shithouse where we kept the recycling bins, and then come in again to crap on an uncomfortably heated toilet. We were the scandal of the street because our au pair girl was only Lithuanian when everyone else owned a Pole.

But home was at least a welcoming refuge from the depredations of the nuns, a snug and cosy haven full of tay and taters and the ould peat fire and simple little diversions like the Gamebhoy machine. That is, until Uncle Finster came to stay with us.

To the world he was a lovable old rascal, fond of a drink, always up for 'the crack' or indeed any other drug that was going around, with a fund of merry IRA songs like the one with the rollicking refrain that went, 'Oh, the bomb of Enniskillen, it did go a-bang.'

He was also blind, hiding his disability behind a pair of

dark glasses and a smile and an uncanny sense of direction that enabled him to find his way around in his perpetual darkness as a sighted person could in the light – as I was to find to my cost, for from almost the first moment he entered the house he started to molest me.

At first this took the form of disingenuous fumbling as he affected to be groping his way about the house. 'Christ and where's the door now . . . now the whall must be over here so it must . . . oh Jaysis and that's the little one isn't ut? . . . I do beg your pardon, me little muldoon, I mistook you for the door . . .' Fumble fumble fumble, and a whisky-breathed whisper: 'Sure and yer little dumplings will be growing in soon, won't they?'

'I'm a boy!'

'So ye are,' he admitted, slightly but not crushingly disappointed.

However, that did not damp his ardour, and the next time he mistook me for the door, he also mistook my genitals for the handle.

That was only the beginning. That night he made his way to my room and raped me.

It is horrible to be raped by blind people. They are very tactile and fumble a lot, and their guide dogs pant and slobber over you horribly. I have been raped and molested by many types in my life and can honestly say blind people are the most distressingly inept, apart from spastics.

Naturally my adoptive parents were horrified when I told them and beat me senseless for my evil lies. 'A poor helpless blind man that can't see at all!' sobbed my foster mother, crossing herself and stamping repeatedly on my face.

Da shook his head sorrowfully as he took his belt off.

'There's blarney, there are things you tell the American tourists, there are James Joyce tales for the academics and then there are wicked, wicked lies. Yis have crossed a line, son.' He looped the belt around my neck and hung me from the door for a while.

No matter how much I protested they would not believe me. I was scared to go to bed. Every night without fail there was the tap, tap, tap of Uncle Finster's cane along the landing and the scratch, scratch, scratch of his guide dog at the door.

I was sometimes able to decoy him by putting a side of meat in my bed (hiding crouched nearby, nail-biting and scarcely daring to breathe while he humped it) but meat was hard to come by and sinful to waste in a Dublin overrun by fusion sushi.

Another time I gained a temporary respite by leaving a skateboard on the landing and had the satisfaction of hearing him crash down the stairs. The house was roused and I was beaten almost to death and the next day sent to make my confession to Father O'Toole at Saint JFK's.

'Bless me, Father, for I have sinned . . .'

'Tell me, choild. Do ye have sinful and lascivious thoughts? Do ye wear silk knickers and flaunt yerself loik a jezebel? Do ye trollop yerself down Montgomery Street takin proid in how much yer little dumplings have grown?' There was an urgent intensity in his voice.

'I'm a boy,' I said.

'Sure and that's a slight disappointment (but not a crushing one). Tell me your sins then. Do ye mastherbate now? Do ye wear tight leather shorts and flaunt your arse to sailors? Do you grease yourself up with oil and . . .'

I tried to call to mind the things that other people had told me were my sins.

'I left a skateboard out for a blind man to step on and

made him hump a side of beef. And Sister Heinrich Himmler says I flirt with the Arian Heresy.'

A hairy old hand smashed through the wooden partition and grabbed me by the throat. I was pulled through to the priest's side of the confessional and summarily buggered.

There is a special horror and agony in being raped by priests. This is not much talked about but the reason they are not allowed to marry is that they all have barbed cocks like tomcats, and it is excruciatingly painful.

Back at home that night things took a turn for the better. In the middle of Uncle Finster's exertions his guide dog suddenly flung itself on the side of beef I had put in my place and started to wolf it down. Unable to restrain it, Uncle Finster was alarmed as he felt the chewed flesh.

'Oh Christ, Parnell is aytin the child. I'd best scarper for a while.'

He vanished in the night. However, it was too late to save me.

'We cannot cope with your wicked ways,' Da told me. 'Now Uncle Finster has fled because of you. There is nothing else for it. We have asked the nuns to take care of ye. You must go to live with them as a boarder and hope that they can reform ye.'

So I was sent to the convent school full time, and it was then that the horror really started.

If I had thought things were bad as a day pupil, for the boarders it was much worse. Black death was rife in the dormitories, for they were overrun with rats, which we would try to catch to supplement our meagre rations, ordinarily a few biscuits with weevils, except on Fridays, when the weevils would be picked out and replaced with silverfish. It was freezing cold in the draughty dorms at night, our night-dresses were flimsy rags and there weren't enough bedclothes to go round, and when I was made blanket monitor I was in effect forced to choose which of the girls would live and which die of pneumonia by morning. I am afraid this went to my head somewhat and I am remorseful now to think I usually gave the threadbare squares of blanket to whoever lent me hair-ribbons or agreed I was the prettiest.

In the evenings we were put to work like slaves. Our hands were tied behind our backs and we were forced to Riverdance on a treadmill. Sometimes a girl would fall into the gears and be cut to pieces while the nuns laughed.

What we feared most of all was to be pulled from our beds in the middle of the night when the nuns were having one of their riotous parties. They would get drunk and make us play Russian Roulette for their entertainment. Those who did not survive were buried in mass graves or simply eaten by the Bishop or Val Doonican. This is an open secret in Ireland which no one wants to talk about.

On top of all this there was the pervasive sexual repression, apart from when we were being pimped out to priests or raped with strap-ons or they were laying on charabancs for people to come and gang-bang one of us. A girl caught with a tampon was bricked up in the walls with a nest of ants; my best friend Theresa was killed horribly for having an innocent picture of Donny Osmond pinned up above her bed. When most people see Donny Osmond, I suppose, they merely shrug and think 'That non-threatening Mormon crooner.' But to this day whenever I so much as hear a few bars of an Osmonds song I sweat horribly and have a flashback to a convent garden and a young girl being tied between a pair of bent pine trees and torn in two while the whole school watched.

But it was this repressiveness that was to be my means

of escape and eventual salvation, although at the time it seemed more likely to mean my death.

One morning our class was given a Sex Education lesson, or what passed for it.

The nun in charge drew a phallus on the blackboard and crossed herself. 'This, girls,' she said glaring at us, 'is a penis. It is the fires of hell. You must learn to recognize it and shun it at all costs.'

She put two large posters up in the classroom. One, entitled 'Know Your Enemy', was modelled after Second World War aircraft spotting posters and featured silhouettes of different types of penises labelled for handy recognition: 'the curvy banana', 'the untrustworthy viper', 'the crusty baguette', 'the modest fleur-de-lys' and so forth. The second bore the legend *Watch Out Watch Out There's A Penis About!* and featured a foolhardy girl about to venture into a dance-hall while a man-sized penis, sinisterly disguised in dark glasses, bowler hat and a mackintosh with the collar turned up, lurked in the shadows nearby watching her menacingly.

Pamphlets were passed among us entitled 'The Most Surprising Men Have Penises', which featured black and white drawings of offices, street scenes, shopping arcades and so on, featuring bankers, bakers, candlestick-makers, shopwalkers and policemen, all with penises or portions thereof subtly protruding from their trouser-flies (or in some instances their waistbands, and in a couple more the bottom of their shorts or less often their trouser legs, or in one case, a ruddy-cheeked self-satisfied bourgeois solicitor, peeping slyly out of his waistcoat buttons next to his fobwatch), labelled 'Can you spot the hidden penises in this picture?' We were given points for each one we could identify and scribble out and the winner was to be given the prize of an engraved nutcracker.

I had started to feel somewhat uncomfortable. I could see two girls in the front row with their heads together whispering.

Suddenly one of them, the dorm snitch, stood up and put her hand eagerly in the air. This hateful chit had always been jealous of the way Theresa and I would play hopscotch and hand-clapping games together and plait each other's hair.

'Please, Miss,' she said, 'Sunny McCreary has one of those, I saw it, so I did. She hides it in her knickers and takes it into bed with her.'

The entire class gasped in horror and turned to look at me.

'Whaaaat?' The nun picked up her studded mace and threatened the girl with it. 'What kind of a tale is that, at all at all at all? Go and wash your mouth out with soap at once! There are no penises in my school!'

She stood firm. 'Please Miss, it's true, so it is! It gets all inquisitive when we go in the showers and sometimes in the night she feeds it Kleenex.' She pointed at the silhouette poster. 'Just like those, a little fleur-de-lys I think it is.'

'It's not!' I bridled. 'It's a bloody fer-de-lance at least.'

'Come to the front of the class, Sunny McCreary,' the nun hissed icily. Swallowing, I complied. 'Now take down your knickers.'

I did so and she collapsed clutching at her heart. (A reaction I have to say I have never had since.) Then she came to and fled screaming while the rest of the class shrieked and cried and jumped on their desks.

Within a minute Sister Heinrich Himmler marched in and pointed a peremptory finger at me. 'You. Come with me.'

The word had spread like wildfire and as I followed her

sweating through the corridors the whole school had emerged from their classrooms to watch, whispering to each other incredulously as I passed. 'That's the girl who smuggled in a penis!' 'Sunny McCreary has brought a penis into school!'

I quaked and trembled. Surely the Pope himself would rape me for this infraction.

The only thing that worked in my favour was that the enormity was so outrageous no one knew what the proper punishment was.

Sister Scorpius Out Of Farscape fainted when she heard while Sister Reggie Kray cried 'The divil! The divil!' and knelt down and started to tell her rosary.

Knouts, bastinados, gallows, guillotines and iron maidens were produced and discarded as too good for me.

At last, Sister Heinrich Himmler came up with the answer.

'We will sell her to the child slavers, so we will, and they will take her for to be a soldja.'

4

My life as a child soldier

In Vietnam, the average age of combat personnel was nineteen. In Umgawa, it was eleven and three-quarters.

The degradation started as soon as I arrived, for the first ordeal was the picking of sides. Our captors were selling children to both sides in the civil war even-handedly, and we were lined up in the marketplace of Umgawa City and captains from the rival factions would take it in turn to choose one of us. I had never been very athletic and I knew I would have to endure the humiliation of being the last to be picked. It didn't help that I was still wearing the girl's blue gym knickers I had been dressed in at the convent school.

Sure enough, before too long there was a fat asthmatic, a boy with a metal leg calliper and me left. I tried to stick out my chest and surreptitiously unscrewed the cripple's calliper to make him fall over, but to no avail. My ears burned with shame as the captain of the Northern Army finally drawled, 'Looks like we're stuck with the weed then', and I trudged over to join them. Inwardly I vowed to perform some feat of military prowess that would make them glad to have got me.

Initially this seemed unlikely. I was a clumsy and unco-ordinated soldier. Once when I was dramatically yanking the pin out of a grenade with my teeth I somehow got the bomb itself stuck to my tongue. My comrades and the enemy alike dived into the undergrowth as I lurched round in panic pleading incoherently for help. Fortunately the trigger mechanism was still depressed, giving me time to free myself by hacking the end off my tongue with my machete, also severing the tip of my nose in the process. I then hurled the grenade into the bushes, where it unfortunately detonated in the midst of my own platoon.

Another time I was responsible for routing one of our own attacks by firing a bazooka in the wrong direction. Imagine my surprise to see the enemy jumping up and down and cheering, and my embarrassment to turn round and find my comrades scattered over a large area of jungle in smoking pieces. The upside was that, as on these occasions, my fellow soldiers rarely survived my blunders, so I was often able to return to camp and claim I had been the only survivor of a glorious Pyrrhic victory. By inadvertently killing my own men I soon rose through the ranks and became a trusted lieutenant. Due to the exaggerated caution and dramatic way of hurling myself into rooms caused by my Fear of Doors I was at least adept at storming bunkers, and as I had been the hopscotch champion at the convent school I was also good at getting through minefields.

I was in the international brigade, a motley crew made up of children and young men kidnapped from all over the world. I idolized the godlike figure of my captain, Rupert Henley-Pryce, who had been taken from Eton. He could throw a grenade further than anyone with a flawless googly action, shoot the eye out of a sentry from two hundred yards and hack a prisoner's arm off with one stroke of his machete. He exuded a breezy nonchalance and would constantly exhort us to 'play up' and 'hit the rotters for six'. Once when a patrol boat we were on was caught in a crossfire from the riverbank he led us all in a rousing chorus of 'Jolly boating weather'. Looking back it is a wonder we never fragged him and it was something of a relief when he was taken prisoner. I later heard he had a rough time of it in one of the enemy's notorious POW camps and was held in disgrace post-war by those who said he had co-operated too closely with the commandant, helping him to build a model railway.

Our sergeant major was an intimidating Scot with a voice like thunder. We quivered in terror as the parade ground echoed with his harangues: 'Wait for it . . . *Byyy* the left . . . pick those trotters up, McCreary, you horrible little man, you parade like a Joey . . . don't cry for your mother, boy, I *am* your bloody mother, I cry myself to sleep every night out of shame for my girly son who lost a fight to John Inman . . .'

'Did NOT!' I protested.

'Did TOO!' he roared. 'John Inman beat you up and stole your bike, but he gave it back because it had stabilizers on.'

With the infants' unit, however, he was as tender as a parent and would change their nappies and sterilize their dummies. We mostly used the infants as scouts and messengers, and also trained them to defuse landmines as they crawled close to the ground anyway and knew no fear.

There were various young French and Italian conscripts who we naturally just used as sandbags. There were also several youths who had been press-ganged from nearby Nigeria. I got to know one of them, a boy named Solomon. He told me his life-story, which was quite heartbreaking:

'Greetings and blessings of Christ be upon you! I am the Reverend Solomon Mbeki MD. My father was the Honorable Joshua Mbeki BSE who as interior minister amassed a sum in excess of $80,000,000. In 1989 he and my mother and my sister were executed in a coup and I was forced to flee for my life with full velocity. In order to obtain these monies I will require a foreign bank account and a trusted confederate to whom I would cheerful stipulate an honorarium of 15% of monetary value with godspeed. Do not reply to this address.'

He was full of involved plans to regain his family fortune with my help but, alas, he was destined never to do so, for several weeks later our platoon was ambushed and he caught a bullet and bled to death in the bushes. His death cries still ring in my memory:

'Urgent assistance required! Can you help me??? Please respond quickly.'

We all ignored him.

Atrocities and war crimes were widespread. I personally witnessed troops of my own side pulling pigtails and giving Chinese burns to innocent civilians, and shooting people who had their fingers crossed and were saying 'Barley'. We took gory trophies and wore strings of human ears and genitals as necklaces. The aim was to collect a full set of different shapes and sizes and after each massacre we would eagerly trade spare parts, going, 'Got, not got, got, not got . . .'

Brutal and merciless guerilla warfare was our only choice. We were hampered by the top brass, who had no notion of how to fight a modern war. Our colonel was a bluff old stager of seven whose mind was still stuck in an era of catapults and pea-shooters. 'Back in '92 . . . behind Leeds gasworks . . . that was a war, by God . . . now Basher Sugden's gang had set an ambush . . . pinned them down and made them cry uncle . . . breach of their human rights nowadays . . .' he would rumble while we furtively rolled our eyes. He would insist on reviewing elaborate cavalry drills where we were all mounted on wooden hobby horses, and ordered that a regimental comb-and-paper band should lead us into battle. On Sundays the officers and more experienced men were put to the ordeal of attending the regimental tea-parties organized by his lady, a six-year-old girl. Grizzled veterans of the jungle would sit there uncomfortably, being required to pretend to sip delicately at little cups containing imaginary tea and nibble at cakes made out of rocks, and make polite conversation with her dollies and teddy bears. If any of us made a faux pas she would scream, 'You didn't do it right! Now we'll have to start again.' She also doubled as our nurse and I do not believe she knew the first thing about medicine. No matter what you reported to her with, a septic finger, dysentery, shrapnel in the ribcage, she would bandage your right arm and your entire head and say 'It will be all better in the morning.' Then she would ask to see your willy.

She was the only female company for miles around although at Christmas the girls of the St Winifred's school choir were helicoptered in to entertain us. We were lonely and missed our mothers and sweethearts. Once one of the boys in my platoon got a heartbreaking Dear John letter. It read:

> *You are not my boyfriend any more Barry is now*
> *You smell like a PIG*
> *PS. I want my pencil-gonks back*

Most of our wounded didn't even make it back to be killed by the nurse. More often they were abandoned where they fell. Hard choices were necessary. Once on our way back from a raid on an enemy Tuck Shop the captain drew me aside and said:

'Noticed anything odd about Evans?'

'No, sir.'

'Look at the way his nose is running.' It was true, he had candles of snot running down his face which he surreptitiously wiped off on his sleeve.

'You mean—'

'The dreaded lurgee.' I gasped. 'Charlie must be using biological weapons. Pass the word.'

I nodded and started the whisper: 'Evans has got the lurgee, pass it on.'

The word spread like wildfire, the men in the platoon surreptitiously moving away from the doomed Evans and going 'Tss' and giving themselves pantomime injections.

I went back to Rupert. 'What shall we do?'

He chewed his lip but hesitated only briefly. 'Shoot him, of course, I have the other men to think about, besides with the lurgee it's probably kinder. I think I'll shoot Jones, too, I've heard he's a Gaylord.'

So we shot the pair of them and burned their bodies. Back at camp we examined each other for symptoms of lurgee but it seemed we had stopped the infection in time.

I suppose looking back we were going stir crazy. We were trapped in the middle of the jungle isolated from the outside world for months at a time. Soon I found I couldn't do without the adrenaline rush of combat. On a rare period of R&R I found myself pacing my room restlessly, unable to switch off, endlessly swigging at PX alcopops and longing to be back out there. I prayed for a mission, any mission. For my sins, they gave me one.

'I need a volunteer for a suicide mission,' the Intelligence major announced.

'Bags not me!'

'Bags not me!'

I was too slow.

Upriver, a Colonel Bunter of the Greyfriars Battalion had

gone out of control. He had taken over a large tract of territory as his own private kingdom. He had the power of life and death over a quarter of a million people and was taking everyone's cream buns. He was treating prisoners horrendously, sitting on their heads or making them the centre of games of All Pile On involving thousands of people.

I was ordered to terminate with extreme prejudice, which I took to mean I should call him a Fatty before shooting him. A patrol boat took me as near as they dared to go. I smeared my face with mud and swam to shore under cover of darkness, hampered by leeches and the fact that I could only manage a modified doggy-paddle with a great deal of thrashing. My orange armbands were spotted and I was captured and locked in a cage.

After baking in the sun for two days I was hauled out and thrown in a hut. There was a figure sitting in the darkness. I was in the presence of the dreaded Colonel Bunter.

There was a porky face like a waxing moon, half in and half out of the shadows. Disjointed sentences reached me, more as though he was talking to himself than me. His voice was hypnotic but mumbling: he had a mouth full of gob-stoppers.

'How do you presume to judge me?

'I remember,' he murmured, 'we were on a hearts-and-minds mission, some nothing village in the middle of nowhere, handing out Panini stickers and bubblegum packs with free rub-on-transfer tattoos. All the kids put the tattoos on their arms. A week later we came back through. Charlie had been there. Every single arm they had found with a tattoo on, they had taken it and they had written 'I am a spaz and the council cuts my hair' on it in indelible felt-tip. And they'd taken all the Panini stickers they hadn't got and in return left nothing but a pile of duplicate triceratopses and the Leeds United badge, which everyone in the world already has. And then they drew nobs on everyone's pencil cases.

'It hit me, like being shot with . . . a stick of rock between the eyes, the genius of that, the absolute crystal clarity . . . How can you fight something like that?

'The horror . . . the horror . . .

'So, anyway, I thought I'd get the hell out of it and start nabbing cream buns.'

Personally I thought he had a pretty good set-up there. I persuaded him to cut me in and became his second-in-command and the two of us had a high old time of it until the enemy mounted a massive offensive and we were forced to flee.

I journeyed for several days through devastated land-scapes and burned-out, corpse-strewn villages. Back at HQ things were sombre. The war had turned against us and the enemy were closing in. Most of my old comrades had been lost to attrition and I had to search for some time before I found a familiar face, a hardened teenage veteran from my platoon named Animal, who was now our acting com-mander. He gave me the news: Umgawa was lost, but our mercenary overlords were withdrawing the remnants of our forces and redeploying us to another warzone. He was expecting news of our destination any minute and speculated happily as to what it might be as he assembled his kit and cleaned his weapons.

Just then a junior handed him a piece of paper and whispered in his ear. He paled.

'No!' he cried. 'No! I won't go! They can't make me!' In a moment he was gone, crying that he would take his chances with Charlie. I picked up the discarded paper.

They were sending us to South London.

Fortunately before they could do so we were liberated by grown-ups from the UN. I was carefully deprogrammed of my military training and repatriated.

*

It would take me some time to readjust. At an age when other children were doing homework or being taken to visit their gran, I was firing machine guns and massacring small villages. I suppose there was a downside too, but all in all it was bloody ace and looking back my biggest regret is that I didn't get to use flamethrowers enough. It was a dangerous and arduous existence, but certainly compared to the rest of my dreadful life it was something of a high point.

In fact, the very next week I would be missing the jungles and minefields of Umgawa, for due to a mix-up I was sent back to live with my mother and stepfather.

5

I am reunited with my parents. They pimp me out to truckers.

The reunion was unemotional. My mother barely grunted when she saw me again, although the client who was on top of her said I was looking well and could I come and put her hand between his buttocks. My stepfather seemed to have missed me more but was equally taciturn, although this may have been because he was holding a lot of nails in his mouth. Wordlessly he led me to his workbench; I could tell by the light in his eyes he had an idea for a new composition and I knew better than to interrupt. Within minutes he had hammered all the nails into the soles of my feet, a radical new direction in his art. I congratulated him on the break-through he had made and he gruffly admitted that having to make do with pigeons just hadn't been the same.

Soon it was as though I had never been away. I went back to school and was given my old room back in the loft. The pigeons were as malevolent as ever but were a lot less cocky with a few nails through them.

Then one day my parents came to a big decision. My stepdad said:

'Time you started earning your keep. It's time for you to join the family business.'

'You mean – I can become a pimp? Father, I am so proud. Already I have thought of many ideas for making Mother more profitable.'

'No,' said my stepfather, 'that would be a case of too many chiefs and not enough Indians in the organization.' My stepfather had lately started taking management courses to improve his pimping skills and their precepts and cliches would turn up in his speech. 'You're a free rider, son. A poor investment. A non-liquid asset. There's no such thing as a free lunch.'

'It's time you went on the game,' said my mother.

'But . . . I do not have a vagina.'

'Think outside the box, son,' said my stepfather.

I was horrified.

'But what about my education? I hope to go to college and then university one day.'

My father snorted and looked up from the geometric string-and-nail pattern he was making on my chest. 'Do you know how many university graduates are unemployed? Supply and demand. There'll always be money in giving blowjobs to truckers.'

'But—'

But there were to be no buts. I was dolled up in pink satin hot pants, halter top and an orange wig.

'Make me proud, son,' said my mother. 'Remember, men won't respect you unless you haggle.'

My stepfather dropped me off at a motorway service station frequented by lorry drivers. It was a freezing night.

He appeared to have a tear in his eye. 'You're a man, now, son.'

I looked down at my marabou halter top, pink satin hot pants and white stiletto knee-high boots. 'Yes,' I said.

'It seems like only yesterday you were crawling round my feet gurgling and puking.'

'It was,' I pointed out. 'You drove a nail through my oesophagus.'

'Well, you know what I mean.' He looked reflective. 'I envy you this opportunity. I always wanted to see the world.'

For the first time, I suddenly saw my stepfather as a real person, rather than a maniac dispenser of nails through my head. It didn't help much.

An 18-wheeler lorry pulled up and a squat and hairy man in denim and cowboy boots got out.

'Go get him.'

My stepfather shoved me forward and brandished his hammer at me angrily when I hesitated.

'Hello,' I said to the lorry driver, tottering forward on my high heels and trying to look sexy. 'That looks like a powerful rig.'

He looked me over appreciatively. 'Turbocharged four-stroke.'

I put a hand on my hip. 'You must burn a lot of rubber.'

'I sure do.'

'I'd like to blow your air-horn,' I said ingenuously.

He smirked. 'I'll bet you would.'

'Is it an articulate lorry, Mister?'

He laughed indulgently. 'You silly boy! You mean "artic-ulated". Articulate means good with your tongue.'

'Of course,' I said knowingly. 'My teachers say I am very articulate.'

'Is that so?' he said meaningfully.

'Yes, it is.' I licked my lips and fluffed my orange wig. 'You must get lonely on the road.'

'Sometimes, but you get to make new friends. Very good friends.'

We smiled at each other.

I said:

'I hear the road tax and fuel duty charges are really iniquitous for someone in your profession.'

'Yes, it's unfair, in effect lorry drivers from the continent are allowed to compete with us at an advantage because—'

My stepfather stepped forward and rapped me smartly on the back of the head with his hammer.

'Can I be your bitch?' I said.

The lorry driver smiled. 'That's a 10–4. Why don't you get in and see how far I'm going?'

'Keep your eye on the ball, son,' my stepfather called encouragingly, waving, as the diesel engine roared and he receded into the distance in the door mirror.

★

After the lorry driver had dropped me off I phoned home.

'Dad? I'm in Oslo.'

'Ung. What did you get?'

'A Yorkie bar.'

'I get half.'

'How do I get back?'

'Pick up another lorry driver.'

★

'Dad? I'm in Vladivostok.'

'What did you get?'

'A potato.'

'Sweet.'

'I've met a man who's a deckhand on a boat, he says he can give me a lift. Can you tell school I probably won't be in on Monday?'

★

'Dad? I'm on a factory trawler in the Bering Straits. I'm being passed round the sailors for a frozen herring a time.'

'I get half.'

'Can you tell school I probably won't be in this year?'

'Ung.'

'If they want to send me any extra homework, my next landfall is Fort Walrus, the Aleutian Islands.'

'Ung.'

'Especially French. I think if I could speak French I could get my price up to two herrings.'

'Smart thinking, son.'

'Could you cancel the *Beano* for me? And glurble wurble wurble furble wurble.'

'I think you're breaking up, son.'

'No, the radio operator just stuck his cock in my mouth.'

*

'Dad? I'm in Mongolia. The chief of the village wants to make me his wife.'

'Is he a good provider?'

'He has seven yaks.'

'Get a pre-nup.'

*

'Dad? I'm in a transport caff off Spaghetti Junction.'

'What happened with the Mongolian chief?'

'He divorced me because I couldn't have children. I got a yak in the settlement but customs confiscated it.'

'Bummer.'

'And I got mugged outside Luton. They stole all my herrings.'

'Bastards.'

'I know, all those French verbs for nothing. Can you come and pick me up?'

'No.'

'OK, I'll hitch another lift, then. See you soon.'

*

'Dad? I'm in Tierra del Fuego. My arse is really sore.'

'Business is good, then?'

'No, I got the squits somewhere in Mexico.'

'Your mother wants to talk to you.'

'Happy birthday, son. I bought you a train set.'

'Gosh thanks, Mum! Glurble wurble wurble furble. Not now, Hernando.'

*

So it went. Perhaps my stepfather was right to envy me. Over the following months I suppose I did see something of the world, even if it was mostly truck stops and lay-bys. If I neglected my homework, my education was on the streets, and in Little Chefs. If I missed out on the innocent joys of childhood, which of my schoolfellows could say they had been buggered in a factory trawler's freezer compartment on top of a pile of frozen herrings? In time I came to feel there was a kind of bohemian glamour in my new calling.

I learned a lot quickly – which tricks were worth pulling and which were best avoided unless you were desperate. Peterbilt drivers were generous, Mack truck drivers stingy. Fuel tanker drivers are appropriately volatile; bin lorry drivers tended to treat you like rubbish; milk-float drivers are slow and cautious but deliver in pints. Morris Traveller drivers demand elegance and sophistication and will only let you in if you're wearing pearls and a cardigan.

Even just trolling along the motorways of England I met clients of a dozen or more different nationalities. I liked the French lorry drivers best, who took a long lunch hour and had good things to eat, and would always give me a bite of an onion to take away the taste of their cock. Polish lorry drivers I learned to avoid except when I was in a fatalistic mood. Their despatchers know they are almost suicidally brave and will undertake delivery to any destination at any time with a complete disregard for their personal safety. However, this is because they are all consumed with overwhelming melancholy because of the Nazi destruction of Warsaw during the Second World War. Deep down they don't care whether they live or die, they exist only for revenge on the butchers of their homeland, and several times in the dark reaches of the night I had to wrest the wheel away from one of them to prevent him from crashing us into a German car.

Of the Germans themselves, the Bavarians are fat and jolly and like you to wear lederhosen and sing rousing drinking songs in the cab; the Prussians wear monocles and have duelling scars and are very cruel; and I will not even say what a driver from Düsseldorf wanted me to do once. The Swiss are cold and aloof and have cocks shaped like Toblerone.

Spanish drivers are temperamental and prone to jealousy. Two of them once played a game of chicken in 18-wheelers over me, which I found quite thrilling.

There was a mixture of comradeship and rivalry among the lay-by whores and Little Chef Lolitas. They were suspicious of me at first but once I had earned my stripes by pulling a train for a Saga coach tour (notoriously demanding and poor tippers) they accepted me as one of their own.

Things really took off when I was able to buy my own CB radio and got a call-sign. Few people outside the business realize that truckers' CB radio slang is actually a specialized Polari and all the transmissions are lorry drivers arranging assignations with rent boys or the rent boys gossiping about their clients. I soon got the hang of it. A 'bear' is a man with a hairy back. A 'chicken inspector' is a social worker. A 'rubber duck' is a penis in a condom. A 'whip antenna' is a long willy. A 'rig rip' is something quite painful. 'Get your ears on' means to dress up as a rabbit for those who are into that sort of thing. 'Cut some Zs' means to dress up as Zorro.★

Despite the sense of belonging and my small triumphs

★   Some more – 'Come back' is an occupational hazard for rent boys who don't allow full penetration. 'Do you copy?' means 'Do you take short-hand?', used by truckers who like to dictate letters or memoirs while getting a blowjob. 'Breaker breaker' – help, my penis has snapped off. 'Dust my britches' – dress up as a French maid. 'Drop the hammer' – whip me in the face with your schlong. A 'dead pedal' is a limp, drained cock. 'Hell bent for leather' – self-explanatory. 'Foxtrot Oscar' refers to a notorious twenty-stone Walsall-based haulage contractor who liked to put on a ballgown and dance along the central reservation of the M6 in the middle of the night. 'Full bore' means bum sex. 'Full throttle' is a form of homoerotic asphyxia-tion involving a very long penis being wrapped around someone's throat. 'Gas jockey' is someone who is prepared to beat you with a riding crop and fart in your face. A 'Grease monkey' is a nude, oiled, shaved chimpanzee – we rent boys hated them as they would do anything and had no union rates. 'Greasy spoon' – to frot while slathered up in engine oil. An 'Eighteen-legged pogo stick' is an arcane form of clusterfuck in which eight people pile on top of someone very well endowed who is bouncing up and down on his penis. 'Hang a Looey' – to flaunt a Vuitton handbag, or alternatively an SM game involving a portable gallows and someone dressed as an army lieutenant, difficult in a small cab. 'Highball' – a young rent boy with an undescended testicle. 'Hit the cobblestones' – a vigorous handjob. 'Kojak with a Kodak' – a bald man who wants to take pictures. 'Kojak with a Kodiak' – a bald man who wants you to perform sex with a bear (a real bear). 'Mile marker' – erection. 'Motion Lotion' – KY jelly. 'Rake the Leaves' – I am looking for someone to read me Whitman's poetry. 'Rubbernecker' – fetishist who doesn't want to go too far on a first date. 'Souped Up' – naked apart from a soup bib. 'Tighten up on the rubber band' – pretty self-explanatory perversion. 'Twin huskies' – either two chunky rent boys at once, or an Inuit trucker's fondest fantasy. 'Mayday' – codeword to announce the convening of the homosexual lorry drivers' secret picnic, held once a year in the woods behind the Newport Pagnell Services, where they hold ribbons and skip round a maypole. Really, it's a wonder anything ever gets delivered.

and the undoubted counter-culture glamour and enviable authenticism of being beaten, abused and infected with diseases, I was terribly unhappy most of the time. I thought I might feel better about myself if I was at least allowed to wear a different uniform: while my parents took great care to reassure me about the important social and economic role played by dick-technicians, I couldn't help feeling my get-up was somewhat undignified. Couldn't I go to work in an ordinary suit, or at least jeans and T-shirt?

'Certainly not,' replied my stepfather. 'How you dress is a product identifier. To vary it now would confuse the clientele. You need to own the pink satin hot pants brand.'

I supposed he knew best but continued to nag. Eventually he relented to the extent of introducing a dress-down Friday where I was allowed to wear arseless leather chaps and nipple-tassels.

My stepfather was deeply into his management courses now. He would often accompany me to the truck stop in the cause of market research and maximizing efficiency. He used to encourage me to speed up my flash-to-bang time, and once experimented with a system of parallel processing, which meant giving two handjobs at once.

He wrote up a mission statement for me, which he nailed to my coccyx for anyone who cared to read it. I vaguely remember:

> . . . committed to bringing you the best in underage boy-whoredom via a mixture of traditional cocksman-ship and innovative bleeding-edge perversions . . . the client's satisfaction always comes first . . . Our corporate philosophy is both customer-centred and Stoic . . . If you find the same utter lack of human dignity anywhere else cheaper we will refund the difference . . . never be beaten unless you want me to be . . . real and genuine

commitment to diversity and inclusion and will never turn away lepers or even Belgians . . . blue-sky thinking and pink satin pants . . .

He instituted a loyalty card scheme for my customers, which he called Arse Miles. Anyone who clocked up a certain number of 'Arse Mile' points was entitled to a free rimjob or an attractive set of crockery.

I don't know how long I would have gone on like that if I hadn't met Tarquin.

Tarquin was class. I could tell that the first time he walked into the Little Chef in his silk dressing gown, breezily saluting the waitresses with his cigarette holder, and delicately ate the beans out of his all-day breakfast with a silver toothpick. That had to be his 22-wheeler out there, with the elegant custom exhaust stacks I later learned had been modelled on the chimney of the Sistine Chapel; they said he sent up a puff of pure white smoke every time he chose a new catamite. All of the boysluts wanted him, crowding round his table like flies on honey as he lazily darted epigrams at his fellow hauliers. I didn't even try to join the feeding frenzy. But I was the one he pointed to as he left.

His cab was decorated with Aubrey Beardsley prints and a small Caravaggio; there were first editions of Firbank and Forster under his logbook, and delicate objets d'art stood on his ormolu dashboard. Soft music played on his gramophone as I lay down on the chaise longue at the back of the cab and stared at the painted cherubs on the ceiling, circling the chandelier.

After the first time he said, 'This isn't really your thing, is it?', and I admitted I preferred girls. He sighed and never touched me again. But he kept me with him.

On long straight stretches of motorway when the cruise-control had kicked in he would paint delicate pastel nudes of me as Pan – 'the vestigial tail really works' – or a pagan water-sprite – 'Where shall I ever find such webbed feet again?' He had a very small baby grand piano in the glove compartment on which he would soulfully pick out tunes with his toothpick when in a melancholy mood.

On our third trip he introduced me to his mother, a faded but still glamorous former actress who lived upstairs in the cramped sleeping compartment above the cab but was careful to give him his privacy. There was clearly a lot of love between them; whenever he invited her down they would hit the gin and exchange affectionately barbed repartee, and she would regale us with anecdotes of the great figures of the golden age of the theatre. A couple of times at weekends he would stop off in Shaftesbury Avenue to pick up some of their theatrical friends, who would crowd into the cab in a giddy whirl of tuxedos, bon mots, cocktail shakers. The piano or gramophone would come out and he would put the seats down so people could dance. We would go all night, the party getting more and more raucous until people were swinging from the chandelier, and then he would pull up at Knutsford service station and we would all pile out for breakfast.

He opened up a whole new world to me. He had an extensive library lining the cab, although the look of the books often seemed to be more important to him than their content, and I started to make up for my lost education. For the first time I saw that my upbringing had been neither healthy nor usual and that a different world existed elsewhere. He made me see that I could choose to change my way of life.

'Why do you go on with it if it makes you so unhappy?

If I had listened to what my father wanted I would be some dreadful art historian stuck out in the middle of Florence or somewhere.'

I could never quite understand what he saw in me. He mentioned something about the appeal of a tragic, haunted, horribly doomed look, and having a fetish for tails.

Whatever the reason he seemed to like having me with him. There was even some talk of him adopting me as his son. But then tragedy struck.

A rare Fabergé gearstick-nob was coming up for auction; he had to have it. He signed up for a dangerous but lucrative nitroglycerine run. He wouldn't let me go with him.

He had named me as his next-of-kin. It was six months before someone found me and gave me his twisted and blackened cigarette holder and the news that I had a modest amount of insurance money awaiting me at a solicitor's in London. In the meantime I had assumed he had abandoned me and done my best to forget him and all he had told me. But just the night before, hobbling down the M6 in a broken heel and a rabbit costume, I had remembered the mental window he had opened and had a moment of clarity. It didn't have to be this way.

I collected a few belongings from the shack and got on a bus without looking back. I didn't actually have any money for the fare so I had to bargain with the driver. Fortunately I had brought my pink satin hot pants.

6

My new life; my not-so-brilliant career

A new life! I lingered on the steps of the bus station, gawping frankly at the spectacle of the big city before me. I was eighteen and eager to begin to live. I would put the unhappy past behind me and make a fresh start. The world was my oyster and it would yield me its pearls. I would lay siege to this city like an army with banners; I would take it like a lover and it would crown me as a king. The bustling crowds drew me. I too belonged in that busy tide of life, pursuing happiness, success, and limitless freedom. I had a lot to make up for and no time to lose. Let it start now! Joyfully, I stepped out on to the pavement and fell down an open manhole.

I will skip over the two years I spent wandering trapped in the sewers after the manhole cover was belatedly replaced. It was all very humdrum and depressing and I have no wish to try your patience. When you have heard one story about wrestling a giant crocodile you have heard them all, and the anecdote about being hunted down by a tribe of blind albino cannibal troglodytes who worshipped a psionic monster grown out of an imperfectly aborted flushed foetus is surely of interest to no one but my therapist. The remarkable story of my eventual escape is already public knowledge and can be found in the newspaper archives, but I would like to apologize again to Mrs Beryl Frodsham for the heart attack she suffered when my hand reached out of her toilet and grabbed her.

After six months living in a hostel gradually acclimatizing my eyes to daylight (and fighting to keep my name off the sex offenders' register) I started again.

I will perhaps spare you the painful disappointment I was doomed to feel if I tell you at once that my attempts to make a career for myself were not to be a rip-roaring success.

Due to my various afflictions, for most of my life I have found salaried work hard to come by and hard to keep. My tragic Fear of Doors has been especially hampering. Employers, I have found, are reluctant to hire a person who starts whimpering and crying when asked to pass through a door, and co-workers do not take easily to someone given to entering rooms via ventilation shafts and ceiling cavities, no matter how brightly you smile at them. (Moreover I was born with a freak muscular condition of the face which meant I was physically unable to smile in the normal way – not that I have ever had much cause for it. Whenever I wished to indicate to anyone that I was smiling at them, I had to put my fingers in the corners of my mouth and pull my lips up, something which alarmed my colleagues even more.)

An equally debilitating condition that struck me down just as I was setting out in the world made things even worse: namely, premature incontinence.

This was the one lasting side effect of my years spent living in the sewers: wading waist-deep in water with a constant trickling sound in my ears, I found it hard to fight the urge to urinate almost constantly, and, as I was wading through effluvium anyway, didn't bother stopping myself, and eventually lost the ability. When I got back to civilization I fought to overcome this but was unable to do so completely. Various forms of stress made it worse and several job interviews I attended were blown by my having to mumble excuses and dash out in the middle of questions, or worse, my failing to in time. My opportunities appeared to be limited to employers who didn't frown on the wearing of rubber trousers, or shouty egomaniacal tyrants who quite liked to see their employees wet themselves with nerves when they ordered them to do things.

Fortunately I actually encountered more than one of these last, who were also impressed at the way I would cower and whimper outside their door with my hands over my head, one of whom finally started paying me an impressive salary just to be called to his office when people he wanted to show off to or intimidate were waiting in his anteroom.

But the jobs never lasted. I would irritate people, I would spend too much time off with one or other of the painful diseases and improbable injuries that were to plague me throughout my life (the plague, come to think of it, was what led to me losing my job as paid cowerer with the tyrant, when I surprised him and not a few of the medical profession by turning up with it one day), things would go spectacularly wrong. This was partly just a natural accident-proneness, but partly I suspect the result of the strange electromagnetic condition engendered by the various nails lodged in my head and elsewhere that also affected my TV-watching. At any rate, machines have always hated me, almost as much as (as I will narrate in fuller detail soon) animals do. (Of my attempts to get on with people, you have already seen and will continue to see. But to look on the bright side, my relations with the plant kingdom have always been strictly business-like and impartial – in fact I would go further, there was once a small potted fern that absolutely thrived under my attentions and seemed to perk up every time I approached, until a cat ate it to spite me; and funguses of all kinds positively adore me, and many of them have chosen of their own free will to grow about my anatomy over the years, and have flourished.)

I would shred vital documents, fax incriminating ones, cause my boss's intimate e-mails to his mistress to be displayed on electronic advertising hoardings in Piccadilly Circus. Lifts would go flying out of the tops of buildings when I summoned them; I would try to use a vending machine and cause it to rain scalding coffee over the entire office via the sprinkler system. Once, working as a janitor at MI5, I inadvertently activated a self-destruct sequence when trying to enter my keycode to get into the building in the morning. I decided to say nothing and come back later and act as surprised as everyone that the place was now a smoking hole in the ground.

I would eagerly fetch a managing director his favourite fountain-pen so that he could sign a prestigious multi-million-pound deal, and trip on the carpet and stab him in the eyeball with it so that he would go staggering round the office screaming 'My eye! My eye!' with a pen sticking out of his head and eventually collapse on the floor frothing at the mouth while Japanese tycoons politely pretended not to notice anything was amiss. (I did not have much better luck with ballpoints; I once clicked one and the retractable pen portion went flying across the room like a harpoon and embedded itself in a light circuit, sparking off an electrical fire that burned down the whole building.)

During a stint in the civil service I made an amusing mix-up as a result of which a hundred foreign murderers and rapists were given knighthoods rather than being deported. Fortunately we were able to pass this off as just another

Human Rights Act requirement. However, not long after I made a much graver error, and put people forward for honours without making sure that their cheque to the Labour Party had cashed, and I lost my job.

As time went on usable testimonials from former employers became fewer and further between. Even the ones I had not maimed or injured tended to couch their praise for my skills in ambiguous terms such as 'I rue the day he ever set foot in my business', or 'Shoot on sight'. So I was forced to leave gaps in my employment history when applying for new positions and rely heavily on my early freelancing experiences. Unfortunately neither 'trucker whore' nor 'subterranean crocodile wrestler' look very good on a CV, although they do provide openings for small talk if you get as far as the interview.

So I took what I could get. Stints washing up in kitchens, temporary packing jobs at minimum wage, once a gig as a roller-waitress at a drive-through burger joint (dusting off my pink satin hot pants for the sake of the extra tips), which ended when I skated out into traffic and caused a major pile-up. It was often a struggle to get by and there were lengthy periods of unemployment.

At one point I ended up destitute and living rough. I had no money even for basic necessities and was forced to sell my eyebrows to make ends meet. This was a heart-rending decision as they had always been my pride and joy. I supposed they had been transplanted on to some rich person who had none. Several times afterwards I would see someone with shapely eyebrows passing in the street and think 'Are those my eyebrows?' and follow them for a while. I would search for them hopelessly in crowds, as De Quincey searched for Ann of Oxford Street.

Worse was being forced from then on to enviously

watch other people express surprise or quizzicality and never be able to do so myself.

(In later years with the help of a private detective I tracked them down. The owner had not taken care of them and had allowed them to grow wild and bushy. He only used them for frowning, and curtly summoning barmen. I no longer recognized them and left without introducing myself. Inadvertently, however, my investigations enabled me to smash an eyebrow-trafficking ring who stole eyebrows from Hungarian children, but that's a different story.)

I was living in the back of a car at this point. The owner didn't know and I had to keep my head down when he was driving to work and so on. Once there was nearly a nasty accident when he pulled up abruptly at some traffic lights and my gas stove and sausages went flying. By the time he finally discovered me I had successfully established squatter's rights. Then I was able to put curtains up and bring in a few potted plants in hanging baskets and there was nothing he could do about it. He tried to force me out with petty meannesses, such as driving around at high speed all the time so the postman could never cycle fast enough to give me my mail. But in the end he sold the car to a stock-car driver to get back at me, and all my good china was smashed in a four-way pile-up.

Back sleeping on the streets again, I was taken up by a modern artist and installed in a gallery as a conceptual work of art. I was at least warm and well cared for, but one night I was stolen by art thieves in a daring heist and sold to a private collector, who kept me in a vault and took me out to gloat over me every evening. Cunningly I started to speak in a posh voice until he came to have doubts about my authenticity and got rid of me.

Then it was a return to living rough, dossing on benches, rummaging in bins for left-over food, hearing the pigeons mutter, 'Look at that scrounging bum.'

But then I got my lucky break.

If any youngster was to say to me, 'How could I get into the rhinoceros porn industry?' I would have to reply, 'The same way I did, the same way anyone does, by being tricked into it. There are no short cuts.'

Reading the help-wanted columns one day after living rough for weeks, I was curious to come across an advert saying 'Rhinoceros Masturbator Needed'.

All my life I have had a deep love for the animal kingdom; alas, this has not been reciprocated, as I have a rare syndrome whereby I exude a hormonal smell which causes 90 per cent of living creatures to attack me on sight. You already know of how the pigeons treated me, and in due course you will hear of the vampire bat which chewed off my genitalia. At other times of my life there have also been ants that quite painfully colonized my nasal cavities and attempted to bore through to my brain, and a bald eagle that pursued a ten-month vendetta against me and in the process almost left me bald, and a movie stunt chimp that contrived to run me over in a pick-up truck. And the woodworms who ganged up to send a sixty-foot oak tree crashing into my bedroom, and the snail that, with infinite patience and cunning, gave its own life to overbalance a radio into the bathtub with me. One should not, I know, anthropomorphize the instinctive behavioural patterns of nature, but it is hard not to take it all personally.

So while I would have been thrilled at the idea of working in a zoo, I had to admit that I might not be the ideal candidate. But there were not many other opportunities available to me, and I thought it at least possible that the rhinoceros would come to love me, or at least feel some basic gratitude.

However, upon reaching the address given in the ad I found not a zoo or safari park but what appeared to be a film studio in a dingy warehouse. My boss explained that his group had a behavioural research grant to study the effects of sexual stimuli on captive rhinoceroses and that I should sign a release form. As no other applicants were forthcoming, and as my co-star, Wilfred, was peaceably chewing straw and showed no signs of attacking me, to my joy and gratitude I was given the job by default, and told to get in there and start yanking.

One thing led to another and soon I found myself in a female rhinoceros costume and after that leather chaps. I suppose in some ways I was quite naive in not asking to see their scientific credentials sooner. By the time I found I had been duped – the day I was stopped in the street by a family of Japanese tourists who excitedly asked me to sign a DVD case – I had become used to the steady income.

Obviously there was some degree of discomfort and humiliation involved, but I was simply pleased to be earning a living again and among people who accepted me. I had a place in the world: a locker, a parking space, even my own canvas chair marked with the words 'Rhino Gimp (disinfect before touching)'. Perhaps I had not after all come far from my trucker-whore days; but Wilfred was much more polite and less demanding than the lorry drivers and would never ditch me penniless in the middle of Silesia.

The rhino-porn business is, I suppose, generally looked down upon by outsiders as one of the less-glamorous fields of human endeavour. Yet when I think back on those sweaty afternoons with Wilfred, it is with something like affection.

In many ways, that period of being humped by a rhinoceros twice a day was the least unhappy time of my life. Of course, that isn't saying much. But in comparison with the hard road that lay ahead of me, those were definitely my salad days. Every life has its springtime.

7

I become addicted to helium

We now come to the unhappiest part of my life so far, the saga of torment and degradation that were my years of helium addiction.

Of all the many ways of getting high a man can resort to to make this vale of tears more bearable, helium abuse is easily the most self-destructive and degrading. Reader, I knew it was wrong, but do not begrudge me a few small moments of escape from the unrelenting hideousness of my life. It was not to last and a terrible price would have to be paid. Soon I was no better than a savage animal with a squeaky voice.

I was first turned on to helium while I was in hospital being treated for weeping sores on my anus, a condition which had sadly led to me being forced to resign my job with the rhinoceros. (It may, indeed, have been a rhinoceros clap I had contracted.) At the time this was the most painful ailment I had ever suffered, although now when I review the catalogue of diseases I have endured in my life I look back at it almost fondly.

One afternoon there was a small leaving party on the Embarrassing Ailments Ward for one of the nurses. That night I was woken by a high-pitched giggle and found an orderly avidly sucking on one of the left-over balloons. My curiosity got the better of me and I asked him to give me a hit. In a voice like Pee-wee Herman's he warned me I was booking a ticket to hell, but I persisted and he shrugged and showed me how to do it.

'I don't feel anything,' I said in a shrill falsetto.

Suddenly my face contorted and an alarming noise burst from my throat. I thought I was going to die.

'Jesus,' I squeaked, 'what was that?'

'You were laughing.'

'So that is what laughter is like,' I said thoughtfully, for I had never experienced it before, and rarely have since, apart from a bout of lunatic cackling that time I had rabies.

I felt light-headed and dizzy, but I felt good. I took another hit.

From that moment on I was hooked. When I was on helium everything finally made sense. For the first time in my life I felt like a man, even if I sounded like a mouse. I didn't want to do anything but helium. The orderly introduced me to his connection and within two days my apartment was filled with pressurized cylinders. From morning to night I would be floating, often literally. My new friend taught me the technique involving sphincter control by means of which the expert helium fiend can take the gas into the stomach and intestines as well as the lungs and thereby rise above this sordid world. The pair of us would drift lazily around the room like Goodyear blimps, soaring like angels, squeaking like bats.

I was to come back to earth with a bump, however. Soon all my money was gone. I was homeless and couldn't afford my next fix. I was wracked with agonizing withdrawal symptoms and felt leaden and heavy all the time. I was reduced to stealing balloons from children at the funfair and was arrested several times. There seemed no end to my degradation. One night the orderly sneaked us into the incinerator room of the hospital and we scored a surgical balloon that had been up someone's bum. We didn't even wipe the excrement off before sucking on it hungrily.

To this day, when I see balloons I taste shit. Perhaps that is why I do not like parties. (Mind you, I am never invited to any parties anyway. And even if I was I would probably not be able to go, because I am allergic to crisps. When other people see a packet of crisps, they think 'Yum.' I think 'A packet of death.')

Worse was to come.

At a low ebb after ten days without helium and five without food, some masochistic instinct prompted me to go on a pilgrimage to visit the frozen severed head of Sally-Ann Larouche, my first love. At the cryogenic clinic the technician showed me to her vault and then tactfully left me alone. I fell to my knees and wept.

'Well, Sally-Ann,' I said, 'I am no longer the carefree boy whose buboes you used to merrily pop in the sludge-field behind the chemical plant not so long ago.'

Suddenly I stopped. Nestling in the inside of the little refrigerating unit that preserved her head I had spied a gleaming metal cylinder. Like a frantic animal I disconnected it from the pipe leading to Sally-Ann and ripped it out.

But it was not, I saw, helium, but super-cooled nitrogen. Cursing, I sucked on the valve just to be sure. My tongue froze and my teeth shattered and fell out. Guiltily I reconnected it to Sally-Ann and left.

I could sink no lower. There was nothing else for it.

Home, to paraphrase Robert Frost, is the place where, when you have to go there, you can expect to have nails pounded into your head. But I had no choice.

Tremendously mixed feelings assailed me as I trudged up the familiar path at the back of the chemical works leading to the shack where I was born. All was as I had left it, the old rope swing dangling from the tree just as it had been on the day my stepfather had used it to hang my puppy. I had taken some knocks here, but now that I had come full circle I did not want to focus solely on the bad memories. There had been good times too, like the summer he taught me to swim by throwing me into the septic tank.

Moving back in wasn't so bad. I was older and tougher now and my stepfather found it hard to hammer nails into me without clamping my limbs in a vice. To my surprise, my mother greeted me almost enthusiastically, giving me a pallid smile from around the head of the leper who was humping her, and offering me my old room in the pigeon loft back.

'I reckon I can forgive you now,' she said. 'I finally saved up enough to get my other breast fixed.'

My stepfather kicked the leper off her so I could see – her previously burst and shrunken tit now matched the swollen fifty inches of the other.

'How could you afford that?' I wondered. 'That amount of saline must have cost a fortune.'

'Not saline – helium!'

Helium.

My mother had had her breast reinflated with helium.

I wrestled with what remained of my conscience all that night. 'No,' I said, 'I can't.'

But I did. In the dead of night I stole into my paralysed mother's room and siphoned all the helium out of her tit.

The next day, I was confronted with the evidence of my crime.

'Son,' said my mother mournfully, 'did you steal the helium out of my tit?'

'No!' I squeaked indignantly, bobbing near the ceiling. 'How could you accuse me of such a thing?'

Growling, my stepfather drove a nail into me and I flew three times around the room and crashed out of the window, squealing as I deflated.

Sometimes, there is no going home.

But the tragic end of my saga of addiction was now approaching. Returning to the filthy squat I had last occupied, I was greeted excitedly by my friend the orderly. He had come into some money, I prefer not to think how, and had just scored from a new connection who had drifted into town.

'He said it was prime stuff.' I helped him lug a large unmarked pressurized cylinder up to his room. With trembling hands we fitted a tube and inhaled deeply.

But a few moments later we were exchanging suspicious glances. 'Anything?'

His voice was as deep as ever. I frowned. I felt satisfactorily giddy and, standing on point and tentatively launching myself into the air with a good stomachful of the stuff, I was able to achieve a reasonable lift-off and float briefly a few feet off the floorboards. But there was something missing, not least the telltale squeak you got with the real thing.

'We've been burned.'

As I subsided back to earth I sighed and lit a cigarette. It was then that I realized exactly how he had been ripped off and how unfortunately apt my choice of word had been. For the gas in the cylinder was not inert helium but highly flammable hydrogen.

As I lit my cigarette, jets of flame thirty feet long burst simultaneously out of my mouth and arse.

The agony was indescribable, despite the best efforts of my literary coach, and luckily I lost consciousness before the ambulance arrived. My alimentary canal had been completely burned out. I now have copper intestines, which gurgle every time I swallow. My face had also been burned off in the explosion. A few years earlier I would have been left like that. Fortunately I fell into the hands of a surgeon who was pioneering a brilliant new technique of baboon's arse face-grafts. In a seventeen-hour operation I do not have the technical expertise to describe, and to the astonishment of the surgical profession, he triumphantly grafted a baboon's arse on to my face. I understand this was a medical first, and indeed last, for he was forced to give up medicine shortly afterwards.

On the plus side, the hydrogen blast finally if painfully cured the weeping sores on my rectum, which is one of the reasons I always say every cloud has a silver lining, even if my arse now has a lining of copper.

8

Prison and rehab

I was given no time to brood about my new copper bowels and baboon's-arse face, for as soon as I was released from hospital much worse suffering was to come my way as I was ordered to undergo rehab for my helium addiction.

First, though, I had to serve a jail sentence of several months (or it may have been a few hours, I forget, but it felt like longer) for a crime rampage I had gone on while under the influence of the chemical (or it may have been a parking offence, but let me tell the tale) which had ended in me being chased by two, no three hundred armed cops and shot down off a skyscraper by biplanes (although to my puzzlement the records show I was placed under a citizen's arrest by a community support officer on a bicycle).

I am reluctant to make too much of my time in the Big House and rehab, but my editor insists that people may be able to profit from it. Some names, dates, locations, facts and laws of physics have been changed. But if I am to be tied down to petty matters of objective reality, Essential Truth will never emerge.

My cellmate was a vicious ice-pick killer I befriended by punching in the face, who sobbed his heart out when I read him *Little Women* and went on to do a doctoral dissertation on Mallarmé. There was a wise old Negro who played the harmonica and a lifer who had become an expert ornithologist. There was a sadistic prison guard named Bellick, and a bald sweaty Turkish one who strung me up by the ankles. And a Nazi doctor who tortured me dentally asking, 'Is it safe?' There was a big tough muscular Pole named Danny who was great at digging tunnels and a man who used to play baseball in solitary every time he was caught trying to escape. There was a gay mafioso who befriended me, who was secretly digging a tunnel from his cell behind a poster of Judy Garland. (After I got out of rehab he took me into the Gay Mafia with him for a while. Whenever any of his lieutenants got out of line he would leave a bloody horse's head on their nice clean bedspreads and wipe his hands on their curtains.) And I fell in love with a Tart with a Heart of Gold but then she got TB and died in my arms after a final aria. At least, that's how I remember it, which is valid.

The worst thing about rehab apart from the agonizing pain is being surrounded by Goddam Phonies who have never known Authentic Suffering.

9

Eating disorders; other neuroses; suicide attempts

Slowly I started to put my life back together. By a lucky break I got a good new job with a company who had been criticized for not hiring enough minorities and people with disabilities of various kinds, and who calculated that being able to point to a man with a baboon's arse face on the payroll would make everyone shut the fuck up. (Indeed this coup enabled them to steal the moral high ground to great effect; their rivals tried to headhunt me, and when this failed forced one of their own junior executives to have elective baboon's arse face surgery just so they could look enlightened.)

My material worries were over and I had put substance abuse behind me. But at this point I descended into a new circle of hell when my battle with eating disorders began.

To most people, I suppose, food is one of the great joys and solaces of life. They look at a big plate of sausages and mash and think 'Mmm, yummy!' For most of my life I have tended to think 'That has about eight million calories but will make a really spectacular puddle of vomit.'

In retrospect my eating problems may have had their roots in my childhood. Very often I had to fight the pigeons for scraps. When my stepfather did feed me properly, he was fierce on teaching me to take small, delicate mouthfuls rather than bolting my food, and to this end would hide tacks in my gruel. He also wanted me to learn to ask for the condiments to be passed rather than grabbing them for myself, and rigged up the salt cellar as a lever to activate a trapdoor under my chair leading to the scorpion pit he had constructed under the shack. While I think of it, there was also the ritual where he would shoot me in the chest with a blunderbuss after saying grace; if I had remembered to put on the bulletproof Kevlar napkin, all would be well, if not, I would have absorbed a valuable lesson, to say nothing of buckshot. I have to say my table manners are impeccable today, although I tend to twitch somewhat whenever I sit down for a meal. The fare at the convent school was if anything less appetizing, especially after the day I was drafted in to help out with the catering under Sister Sweeney Todd.

However I mostly attribute the onset of my anorexia to my poor self-image and the years of unhappiness and rejection. Perhaps I believed people would fancy me more if I looked like a malnourished survivor of Belsen. I thought I was hideously overweight. I would look in a mirror and shriek, 'My face looks like an arse!' Of course, my face *was* an arse. But at that point I thought it had cellulite.

I partly blame society. The media constantly bombarded me with images of David Bowie and Gandhi. I wanted to be skinny like that. Moreover the government kept launching campaigns urging people to cut down on snacks and sugary foods, saying we were turning into a nation of big fat slobs and that we should all try to be svelte and wonderful like them. I took it all to heart.

I embarked on a series of crash diets. The GI Diet, the SS diet, the counter-intuitive Stuff Your Fucking Face With Cream Cakes Fried In Batter And Mmm, Bacon Bits Diet, the Diet of Worms, something I heard about in passing which turned out to be not a diet at all but a historical treaty

– nevertheless I followed it for several weeks and lost two stones, although my lawn suffered.

Then I began to starve myself mercilessly and would go for an entire week eating nothing but earwax and pencil shavings. I would feel guilty and rush to the scales after licking a stamp. Soon my face was no longer a healthy plump ruddy arse but all skinny and wrinkled like an old man's catflap.

Twice I collapsed in the street from malnutrition and once I got stuck down a grid. I was so thin the ambulance-men simply rolled me up into a scroll for easy carrying and at the hospital I had to be reinflated with a foot pump.

Then I snapped. Overnight I went to the opposite extreme. I gave in to the overwhelming craving for food and ate for three days solid. It felt good. I never wanted to stop. I didn't stop. By the end of a week I was twenty stone and rising.

The pockets of my clothes were all filled with chocolate bars and fried egg sandwiches to tide me over between snacks. My colleagues at work complained when they came in one Monday and traced a bad smell to my filing cabinet and opened it to reveal a stash of emergency food alphabet-ically filed – I think it was the veal scallops in the V section that were the last straw. I slept on pillows stuffed with chicken wings in case I got hungry in the night. I got up every morning and dived head-first into a bath filled with cream cakes. It got so I lacked the motivation to move an inch without the reward of food at the end of it and when I went shopping used to unreel a string of sausages behind me so I would be able to eat my way back to the house. I made sporadic attempts to stop myself but even the doctors couldn't help. At one point I gained so much weight so fast that a baffled medic tentatively diagnosed a hitherto unknown late-onset variant of Prader-Willi syndrome, a chromosomal deficiency normally manifesting itself in childhood (not to be confused with Prada-Willy syndrome, a letch for expensively dressed women). I lost all self-esteem and sense of personal appearance and my face would light up with glee whenever I discovered a half-eaten chocolate eclair trapped between the folds of my fourth and fifth bellies or a lost pork chop nestling under my seventh chin.

Then suddenly I flipped and started to starve myself again. Three days later and with the aid of some auto-liposuction using a kitchen knife and the hoover I was down to five stone.

The binge–purge cycle grew faster and faster and more perilous. I would eat and eat and eat like a big fat greedy pig. Then I would stick my finger down my throat to throw it all up. In a second I would change, and eat my own finger. Then I would puke that up, and then fry all the puke up in an omelette and eat it. Then I would go and binge at some burger chain, then come home and have another puke omelette just to take the taste away. I needed help.

I attended support groups, but some of the members seemed to be there for mutual competition and to affirm their illness as a lifestyle choice. There were even those on the fringes who had turned it into a New Age religion with an elaborate invented mythos, worshipping a tragic willowy goddess called Anorexia, whom Zeus had amorously jumped on one day and unfortunately snapped. Similarly the fanatical overeaters had developed a cult centred around a gargantuan divinity named Hippopotoma, who among other exploits ate the area currently occupied by the Mediterranean Sea in a fit of peckishness and later destroyed Atlantis with a belch.

In the end I was hospitalized. I caught a supervirus in an unclean ward and watched as huge chunks of my flesh were bitten out of me by an unseen enemy. Something about the experience of being devoured by a mindless appetite snapped me out of my madness and I resolved to start pulling myself together. Besides, I decided I was pretty much my ideal weight at the end of it, if somewhat asymmetrical and riddled with bloody great holes.

★

With hard work I started to get my eating problems under control. However, it seemed that some self-tormenting energy still required an outlet and presently other neuroses began to emerge. As if there had not been enough pain in my life already – and there had, lots – I started to inflict it on myself.

I was filled with self-loathing and started to act it out. I would look at the baboon's arse that confronted me in the mirror and be filled with disgust. I wrote out lists of all the things I hated about myself, e.g.

1. *My face (baboon's arse)*
2. *My arse (wobbly, and clangs like dustbin when I sit down due to metal intestines)*
3. *I think I smell like stale Horlicks*
4. *My knees (pointy bony kneecaps)*
5. *My belly button (bitten off by a weasel)*

And so on. (It was later confirmed that I do, in fact, smell like stale Horlicks due to a rare mutation of the sweat glands.)

I made lists of all the horrible things I had done:

1. *Haven't visited severed head of first love in two years*
2. *Herded small tribe into church and burned them alive when child soldier*
3. *Parked on double yellow lines last Tuesday*

4. *Had sex with a rhinoceros purely for financial gain*
5. *Haven't called him since*
6. *Stole helium*
7. *Crucified UN peacekeepers when child soldier*
8. *Don't recycle enough*

I blamed myself for everything that had happened to me. My stepfather had been right to fire javelins at me every time I came through the door. Kids needed discipline and I had been an evil one. The bizarre accidents and so on: there were no accidents, I had made them happen.

I would punch myself and then flush my head in the toilet. I would pinch myself really hard on the arm and deliberately stub my toe against the furniture. I once spent an entire evening slamming my own head against the living-room wall until I broke through to the other side and my next-door neighbour complained.

I started self-harming in earnest. I mail-ordered a set of three dozen attractive Staffordshire figurines commemorating seventy years of weather forecasting. And then deliberately broke the head off Ian McCaskill so they would be valueless. I tried to reason with staff in call centres. I visited the Turner Prize shortlist exhibition hoping for some aesthetic pleasure. I tried to climb into the lion cage at the zoo, and defended American foreign policy in front of Harold Pinter. I read political manifestos and expected them to have some relation to reality. I briefly took up dairy farming for fun and profit. I just wanted to be punished.

With therapy I gradually managed to overcome this. But as if to fill the void I then started to manifest symptoms of obsessive-compulsive disorder.

I filed all my clothes in alphabetical order, cross-indexed for colour and material. I developed an uncleanness phobia and every time my hands became dirty would undergo an elaborate purification ritual involving carbolic soap, burnt offerings and water from the River Ganges. I coated every object in my house in plastic shrink-wrap, quarantined all my mail for six months, and hoovered under my foreskin twice a day.

I was prey to absurd superstitions and developed a series of elaborate rituals I dared not deviate from. Every time I made a cup of tea I had to put in exactly two and three-quarter spoonfuls of sugar, add water before the kettle had finished boiling, stir seventeen times anticlockwise, sacrifice a chicken and recite a cycle of medieval canticles while jiggling my leg. Every time I left the house I had to put on my right shoe first, tuck a sprig of mint into my buttonhole, then ring up a full page of B names from the telephone directory and ask them all to wish me luck. (If any of them swore at me, I stayed at home.)

My OCD meant a new set of eating problems. I reached a point where I would only eat baked beans on toast for lunch and dinner, and when I did so felt compelled to clean the tomato sauce off first, draw smiley faces on them all in biro, and then meticulously arrange them on the toast in ascending order of size. I believed if I did not do this an Albanian would die for every bean I ate. This process took forever and involved a magnifying glass, and meant I usually had to eat in because few restaurants would cater for this requirement. (Later, however, I won a discrimination lawsuit against an establishment that refused to do so, so that has all changed now.) Eventually I was partly cured of this obsession when some Albanian neighbours made unkind remarks about my baboon's-arse face. I went right home and guzzled every bean I could find straight from the tin, cackling to myself. The next day I avidly read all the papers expecting news of a really big earthquake or chemical leak in Albania, but was shocked to find the place was still intact. Still part of me thought maybe God was killing them all quietly and a few at a time and I continued to feel guilty on and off. Finally I was referred to an eminent Harley Street psychologist about this neurosis and he leaned across the desk and slapped me repeatedly.

Due to my various tics and fears I would often not leave the house for weeks at a time and came to develop an acute agoraphobia. Before I was eventually cured of this it got to a point where I hated open spaces so much I would not go out without a pair of binoculars clutched over my eyes, to make things which were far away look reassuringly close. Then I gave up going outside altogether. When I ran low on provisions I would stand at an upstairs window with a fishing rod and try to snag food from the shopping baskets of passers-by. Once I reeled up a six-pack of beer with a very large man in a string vest still attached to them, who punched me in the face.

During these times I made various half-hearted suicide attempts that were really just cries for help: I jumped out of a ground-floor window, I threw myself in front of parked cars, I lay down on a railway track when a Great Western train was due. (This last was quite dangerous, actually, as I nearly died of thirst and exposure before I was found.)

Despite all my tribulations I have very rarely felt seriously suicidal, perhaps because of the stabilizing influence of my relatively happy childhood. Even in my darkest hours I have had certain fond memories to cling to – my mother's laugh when once on her birthday my stepfather brought me into her room with lighted candles around my head standing in Rawlplugs he had driven into my skull, a surprise we had been planning for weeks; the unforgettable look on Sally-

Ann's face as we finally succeeded in slamming her severed head in the freezer; the swell of pride I felt the first time medics told me I had a previously undiscovered disease that would probably be named after me – anyone who has experienced such moments knows in his heart that life isn't all gloom. Moreover I have always felt curious to see what is around the next corner, and, while it has invariably been something really awful, usually worse than anything that has come before, the hope always remains that one day it will be something comparatively not that bad after all. (In concrete illustration of this tendency, I am suddenly reminded of the time I was walking down the street and saw a five pound note fluttering on the ground halfway up an alley. My lucky day, I thought, and went to pick it up. However, as I drew near it suddenly seemed to be blown further away from me. Every time I almost had it in my grasp, off it would flutter again. I eventually realized it was attached to a thread of cotton being pulled by someone around the corner. Oh well, I thought, as the money was yanked off in that direction with a last tantalizing rustle, may as well see what it's all about, and followed after it curiously. I imagine you have guessed what happened next. Yes, sure enough, no sooner had I rounded the corner than I was hit on the head with saps and kidnapped by white slavers, and shipped to Buenos Aires, where I was kept doped to the eyeballs, kitted out in a low-cut pink satin ballgown and forced to dance the tango in a seedy nightclub for two years. My shoes never fitted and it was hell on my arches. On the upside, though, I ended up as an ace dancer, and on my return to civilization won several trophies in the All-England Tango Championships (Female Impersonators with Baboon Parts Category). So you see, perhaps you should always venture around that next dim-lit corner after all.)

It has been my pride to face everything life has flung at me with, if not quite courage and fortitude, at the very least a drudge-like endurance and numb resignation. But I hope the reader will not judge me harshly when I say that I have been of genuinely suicidal intent on two occasions. One of them, which I will relate in its proper place, cannot really be counted against me, as I was not in my right mind at the time, and ended by curing me of any such inclinations forever. The other came a few months after the half-hearted attempts I have just related and I may as well mention it here.

The immediate cause was the injury to my feet. I had always been very proud of my feet. They were the one part of my body that had somehow escaped deformity, disease or mishap. Other people, I suppose, regard their feet as unexciting and, literally, pedestrian organs that enable them to get from A to B. I used to think 'Oooh, you little beauties!' Sometimes at night to take my mind off the pains and heartaches of the day gone by I would lie there and admire them. Unlike the rest of me, they were perfect. I would lie on my back and hoist them into the air and wiggle all twelve of my toes in turn, admiring the play of light through the little webbed bits in between.

But pride comes before a fall. Or, as in this case, an industrial steam-press accident.

The pain, of course, was hideous, and afterwards my beautiful feet were horrendously squashed and mangled. Worse, at the hospital two of my toes were amputated, leaving me with the freakish total of ten. (This compulsory decimalization was not even symmetrical – I was left with six on one foot and four on the other, forcing me to wear shoes in vastly different sizes.)

Coming on top of my various other afflictions I decided

it was the final straw. I got back in touch with my shady underworld contacts from my helium days and purchased a gun.

I made no farewells, no prolonged ritual of leave-taking, simply closed the door when I got home, put the gun to my head and pulled the trigger before I could change my mind.

They say suicide is painless. It wasn't in my case. With the possible exception of my bowels being burnt out it was the most excruciating agony I had yet known (it was surpassed later but probably remains in the top five). Every nerve ending in my body appeared to be on fire. The doctors later pieced together the improbable chance that had saved me. The bullet had been stopped by one of the nails that my stepfather had left in my skull. However, this nail itself had thereby been driven deeper into my brain, penetrating among other things the pain centres and making it feel like my whole body had been horribly damaged. But that wasn't the bad part. The bad part was that, when I staggered to get help, I found I was talking Welsh.

It was a nightmare. Everything I was saying made sense to me but my neighbours merely flinched and stared at me in alarm. Several thought I must be choking on something and pounded me on the back. Most just slammed and bolted the door, although a few found the non-gurgly bits pleasantly musical.

I was presently conveyed into the hands of the police, who initially assumed I was in the grip of some drug and pinned me down. After several other possibilities had been eliminated I was at last taken to the station's Welsh Community Liaison officer. She was an amiable old woman sitting at a spinning wheel in a cosy stone-flagged parlour off a back corridor, wearing a tall black hat, apron and red shawl. As I frantically tried to explain what had happened and pointed at the bleeding wound in my head, she bustled about smilingly setting out tea and cakes while making sympathetic noises. To my relief, she understood me.

'Look you, he have put a tidy big bullet into his brain, now,' she explained to the policemen.

'Gogogoch!' I nodded urgently.

Dr Oliver Sacks himself excitedly flew in to examine me. Scientists had long been anxious to isolate the part of the brain that, when inflamed or damaged, causes the speaking of Welsh, and thanks to my ordeal he could now pinpoint it. He was eventually able to cure me and thereby offer hope to an entire nation. Still I could easily have been stuck like that for the rest of my life, and I put this story down as a stern warning for anyone ever foolish enough to contemplate suicide.

*

Looking back I suspect my eating disorders and other neuroses were at least partly a product of the relative prosperity I was enjoying at that period of my life. I had a good job with a steady income and, did I but know it, no real problems.

At any rate, it is certain that their more extreme manifestations disappeared overnight when genuine suffering came into my life again. One day my boss called me into his office to announce a sweeping reorganization in the company that would have a terrible consequence for myself. Though I wept and begged and clung to his knees he was inflexible, and everything was changed forever.

The most awful thing that had ever happened to me or would ever happen to me in my life was about to happen.

10

I am forced to live in Northumberland

We come, now, to the absolute low point of my life, when the thing which every sensitive person fears, the most painful thing that can happen to anyone, happened to me. Yes, reader, I was forced to live in Northumberland against my will. (As if anyone would ever live there voluntarily.) The more squeamish among you should skip to the next chapter immediately. I only wish I could do the same.

I do not, actually, intend to dwell on my dreadful experiences in that godforsaken place for overlong. Even my publisher is ambivalent about including this harrowing chapter. It will undoubtedly have a tawdry commercial appeal among those morbidly drawn to Gothic horror, but he has some morals after all, and worries that this book may fall into the hands of children. The sales department, pale and trembling themselves, but awed by their own daring, like men plotting an outrage against God, point out that the opposition have already sunk to dabbling in memoirs of forced exile in Northumberland, and say that there is no choice but to follow them into the same fetid morass. At which my editor draws himself up and harangues them, saying that when Ebenezer Boxtree founded this noble imprint 150 years ago he did so with the stated aim of Inspiring, Uplifting and Edifying, and built the business by putting out tomes of merit and worth guaranteed not to offend the most delicate sensibility. Would he have stooped to the vulgar sensationalism of bringing out travelogues of That Place? To which they retort that the problem of people being forced to live in Northumberland is one that confronts us all, and it will not be made to go away by ignoring it. How proud will he feel, they urge, when politicians are finally shamed into action, when a parliamentary committee or UN taskforce is at long last convened? Do not hide behind social concern, he responds, you whose concern is only to pander to the lowest common denominator in order to maximize profit – and are you so sure that it will not backfire? What if the book is condemned to be kept behind the counter and sold in a plain brown wrapper? What if shops are burned, booksellers lynched?

'I will leave it to you, Sunny,' he decided at last, torn between greed and ethics. 'I will not force you to it. God knows there is not enough money in the world to make the proposition appealing to you. But if you can bear to relive those days – oh, may heaven have mercy on me –'

Do I dare to try? I am not even sure myself if it is morally justified. I do not even think I have the excuse of reaching out to those who have undergone the same thing, for the sad fact is that statistics show that 90 per cent of those who survive Living in Northumberland kill themselves within a year of escaping, and of those who do not the overwhelming majority are functionally catatonic. There are probably only three of us in the country who have gone though that horror and are still in a condition to be able to talk about it, and if we wished to offer each other solace we could meet in a pub somewhere. And even for us, what would there be to talk about? There are no words to adequately describe what we have been through, and there can be no comfort, *none*, until death releases us from our awful memories. All we could do would be to hold each other's hands and gaze mournfully into one another's terror-blighted eyes and silently affirm I *know*. I was *there*. And then, I have no doubt, we would come to a sudden unspoken decision, rise with one accord, and make our way out to the car park and set fire to ourselves.

So if I try, if I try, if against my better judgement I try to give you some inkling of what it was like, do not ever fool yourself, do not try to sympathize, do not ever dare to dream of thinking that you can imagine how it must have been. You can never really know, and for that you should give thanks every day of your lucky life.

Where to begin . . . ? What horror to dwell on first . . . ?

The place was full of uncouth figures in muddy wellies, and a fearful number of Christians, and Christians in muddy wellies talking loudly about Jesus, even at Christmas, and saying that latte machines were only a theory they didn't believe in. I was scared. They had all manner of weird beasts like 'horses' and 'cows' and 'sheep' and said things like 'pet' and 'marra'. There were lost tribes of Tories performing sinister ritual dances in archaic costumes called 'dinner jackets'.

The poverty and degradation were unbelievable. I met one poor woman who was forced to lived in a five-room hovel with three children and a husband and an au pair and only a £70,000 book advance to tide her over. And she had to get the builders in. And she was surrounded by scary walls her children might fall off, which she regarded as her enemies and apostrophized viciously. And inanimate objects like Agas and hedges that talked to her. And she had to kill some flies, it was awful. And once she couldn't find her TV remote control. I wonder who will play her in the film.

This woman had been brought to Northumberland from

London by her own husband – which must rank as the ultimate betrayal – and forced to live there without homeopath, nutritionist, therapist, or of course any ray of hope or dignity.

(I later heard of another woman who was brought by her husband from the Philippines to Teesside, which is very near to Northumberland. She was forced to kill him to escape, and who can blame her? I expect the woman who was dragged there from London will have to do the same sooner or later, and not a court in the land could find her guilty. No one has ever suffered as much as me, but she comes close.)

There were—

But no, I cannot bear to go on with this. Already I am starting to sweat and tremble all over, and besides there is no point in ruining your life as well as mine. A full description of my travails in Northumberland would be too shocking even for this account of the most Painful Life Ever. I will draw this chapter quickly to a close and pass instead to a much happier period of my life, the time I was raped by Cossacks.

11

I am raped by Cossacks

On a camping holiday by the Black Sea I was raped by a band of Cossacks. It was pretty awful.

Still, I thought happily, as my piles burst under their ministrations, at least I am no longer in Northumberland.

12

I am taken in by a cult. They torture me horribly, pimp me out, and put me on a really unfair washing-up rota.

For a time I drifted. My life had reached a plateau of a manageable amount of low-level misery. I was lost and confused, and also had a stubborn throbbing boil on my leg. I wanted to build some sort of life for myself but didn't know how to start. I regretted that my education had been interrupted by the necessity of providing blowjobs for truckers, for I felt the lack of a formal philosophical system or worldview that would enable me to put my tribulations into perspective and help me weather the storms of mischance. Moreover I felt lonely and in need of some sort of comradeship and support network.

Then one day I thought I had found what I was looking for.

I was wandering through the marketplace in the town where I was then living when I saw two rather pretty young ladies accosting passers-by and attempting to hand out leaflets. Sales, I assumed, imagining they would let me pass by unmolested, as no one really cares to sell to the baboon's-arse-face demographic.

However, somewhat to my surprise, they positioned themselves in my way and gave me dazzling smiles. They were very fetching girls indeed and a wistful little sigh-fart escaped my baboon's-arse mouth.

'Would you like to join us in eternal bliss?' asked one.

'Yes please,' I said.

She thrust a handbill on me. 'Then come and join the Church of Purification by Agonizing Pain.'

'OK,' I said happily. 'Oh, wait – agonizing pain?'

'Agonizing pain that leads to a new life of happiness,' she explained ecstatically.

'OK,' I said.

'After the initiation, we have group sex and mind-altering drugs, and later on Bingo and a tombola.'

'I like Bingo,' I said.

'Then we will see you there?'

'Please say yes,' smiled the other pretty lady.

'Yes,' I said obligingly.

'Wear something that won't show the blood.'

'OK,' I said.

Looking back, I suppose I was somewhat naive, but it all sounded very innocent. The way I looked at it, I was free in the evenings anyway, and it was that or take an origami class. The handbill was vague but intriguing, speaking of earning redemption through hideous torment – naturally appealing to one who had suffered as much as me. I noted the address and diligently earmarked the date in my diary as 'Bingo and group sex'.

The Temple of the Church of Purification By Agonizing Pain proved to be a converted Methodist chapel in a quiet side street. In the vestibule the same two pretty girls confronted me with clipboards and disarming smiles.

'The service starts in five minutes. You just need to sign the release form,' said the first pretty lady handing me a legal contract.

'Please say yes,' said the other pretty lady.

'Yes,' I said. I glanced perfunctorily at the document,

standard boring jargon studded with abstruse legal phrases like 'all my worldly wealth', 'never to tell the press or legal authorities anything I may witness hereafter', 'indentured servitude for the rest of my natural life' and 'not responsible in case of death' and obligingly signed my name.

I took a seat in the little wooden hall. The congregation numbered perhaps thirty, almost all of them men and rather shabby looking. Presently the doors at the back of the room were bolted, there was an expectant hush and a pinched-looking little man from the North walked out to the lectern.

'Ey up. Dearly beloved brethren, new friends, we are gathered 'ere tonight to hear t'good news of Purification by Agonizing Pain, as revealed in t'Book of Sid and the holy words of the Reverend Jim, and th'imminent cleansing of all th'Earth by apocalyptic fire and torrents of blood and rains of ferrets and that. And later on group sex and t'tombola. And while I think on there's a prize still not claimed from last week, lovely bottle of sherry kindly donated by Rita. I'd just like for t'remind those of you who haven't signed up for t'paintballing team, there's still time left, although as the cleansing of th'Earth by blood and fire is tentatively scheduled for the next few months, not much, so get a move on. Nah then.'

He walked off. I had to admit to feeling somewhat disappointed at that point. However then the two girls walked on, dressed from head to toe in skintight leather and carrying coiled whips which they tapped against their hands menacingly. They took up positions on either side of the pulpit and scowled at the congregation. Then a grey-haired woman sitting at a Bontempi organ at the side of the hall struck up a chord, and the Reverend Jim strode in.

He was instantly much more entrancing than the previous speaker. He had a mane of wild blond hair, cunningly back-lit to give a halo effect, and wore a flowing white garment. He carried a long flail-like weapon, something like a scourge or cat-o'-nine-tails. His voice was loud and thrilling and I quickly perceived he must have come from one of the southern states of the US originally. With intense, rolling eyes and dramatic gestures he started to preach.

'Brothers in payyyyyn!' he cried. 'We are gathered here today to celebrate the sayyc-red and Awful mysteries of Purification by A-gon-izing Pain! The mysteries revealed to us by our Lord Sid Croakey as handed down to him by Gawwwd his own bad saylf!'

'Amen!' cried the congregation.

'The flesh is sinful! The body must be flayyyled!' He lashed out at the front row of the congregation with his scourge. 'Only by embracing excru-see-ating agony, suffering and degra-*dayy*-tion at every opportunity can we hope to be saved!'

'Hallelujah!'

'When the Lord smites you with pain, you must eat it up, and when he forgets you must seek it out!' He flailed about frenziedly, evoking cries of 'Thank you!' and 'Ouch'. 'Can I get me some pain? Gimme me some pain, sisters.' The two leather-clad girls started to whip him as he quivered and rolled his eyes. 'Oh, that's the *goood* pain.'

'Testify!'

'A day is gonna come, sinners, and it's a-gonna come soon, when The Lawwwwd is gonna come down and chas-*tise* you with a belt with a big buckle. He is gonna shove a leather winklepicker boot up your ass, and then He is gonna sodomize you with the studded rubber truncheon of right-eous-ness!'

'Praise be!'

'And you know what he is gonna do then, my brethren?'

'Tell! Tell!'

'He is gonna piss on your face from a grayyyt big height. Grayyt big height. Hundred foot or more. Niagara *Fawls* of piss! And you know what that piss is gonna taste like?'

'Manna!'

'Nectar!'

'Champagne!'

He flailed them angrily.

'It is gonna taste like *naypalm* and he is gonna piss right in your eye. And then He is gonna twissst your nipple, and he is gonna grab you by the scrotum and clamp your balls in a vice and he is gonna call you *nayyyms*. He is gonna call you bitch-boy and punk-ass and toe-*rayg* and he is gonna call you Maurice. And you gonna say, why you call me Mau-reece? My name is not Maurice? And De Lawd will grab you by the ear and say your name is what I say it is, bitch, and I say your name is Maurice Q. Pink-Knickers, boy. Now what's your name? And you gonna say, 'Mau-reece, Lord, Maurice Q. Pink-Knickers is mah nayme, mm, mm, yes sir.'

'Amen!'

'Now who been blessed with pain this week? Who found the *real* pain, brethren? Lay it on me now.'

They started to stand and testify.

'I dropped a hammer on my toe.'

'Praaaaise de Lawd!'

'I had root canal without anaesthetic.'

'If I did not already follow Sid Croakey I would surely follow *you*!'

'I fell downstairs on purpose.'

'You are numbered among the righteous.'

'I self-published a book, and then I accepted a commission to write another with a three-month deadline,' whined a very handsome and brilliant-looking man at the back of the room.

'You are de Lawd's own masochist!'

'I support the England football team and British tennis players at Wimbledon.'

'You can take righteousness *too* far.'

'I bought a stereo and then found it cheaper elsewhere the next day.'

'That's the *subtle* pain, mm-hmm.'

'I trod on a rake and it hit me in the nose.'

'Your sins have been washed clean in the river of slapstick.'

And so forth. Next snakes were passed among them, which they handled and encouraged to bite them. However these were quite sluggish, despite being flicked and shaken, and when someone had finally been nipped on the thumb they sent up a cry of 'Hallelujah!' and went on to the next thing.

'We will now make the Sign of Pain to our neighbours.'

At that, everyone in the hall turned to the people next to them and punched them brutally in the face, murmuring, 'Pain be with you.' There were empty chairs on either side of me but I felt a tap on my shoulder. I turned to see the little old woman who worked the organ, who slapped my left face-buttock quite stingingly. When in Rome, I thought, shrugging, and gave her a reciprocal punch in the mouth, sending her flying.

'Now I see here among us,' said Reverend Jim looking out across the jaw-nursing, nose-bleeding, false-teeth-retrieving crowd, 'a new, and if I may say so, somewhat distinctive face.' I looked around curiously then realized he was referring to me. 'You have the face, sir, of a man who has known affliction. You are blessed of the Lawd. Are you ready to embrace more suffering?'

'Well—'

'He is ready! Praise God!'

'Praise God!'

Somewhat to my discomfiture I was slapped encouragingly on the back and thrust to the front of the hall.

'Are you willing?' the preacher asked me. 'Are you willing to be Purified by Agonizing Pain?'

'The thing is—' I began.

'He is willing! Hallelujah!'

'Praise Him.'

'Bring out the Jellyfish Jockstrap!'

'Hallelujah!'

'The what? Look, I've just remembered—'

I was held by the arms as the Jellyfish Jockstrap was brought out and attached to me.

My screams reverberated around the hall. For some moments I believe I was actually insane with agony. When I came to myself I was hunched up on the floor and the thing was gone.

'He did speak in tongues! Did you get it all, Rita?'

The elderly woman read back from a notebook: 'Shit, fuck, fucking hellfire, for the love of God, guhhhhhh, wuh, buh, my nads.'

'That is surely a message from on *high*! Unless I miss my guess that is ancient Mesopo-*tay*-mian for "It is now time for the group sex and tom*bola*!"' I had to hand it to him, he knew how to work the room.

My mouth was hanging open with the aftershock of the pain. But worse was to come. It was explained that as a neophyte I would have the honour of leading off the sacred orgy. What this meant in layman's terms was that everyone raped me, with strap-ons where necessary – Rita was particularly rough. So the group sex was something of a disappointment. On the plus side, I won second prize on the tombola.

After the bingo (which involved being slapped on the head whenever one of your numbers came up, and flicked on the nose by everyone if you won) we sat around in a circle and had the mind-altering drugs, some infusion that Rita brewed up in a chipped tea-pot and served up to us in a motley collection of chalices, skulls, mugs, and polystyrene cups. Either due to senile cackhandedness or to get her own back for my punching her false teeth out, she at first missed the cracked mug I was holding out to her and poured the scalding liquid straight on to my lap.

'Owww!' I shrieked.

'Praise Him!' said the preacher.

Perhaps because I was preoccupied with the blisters on my bollocks (already much abused by the Jellyfish Jockstrap) I didn't get much out of the experience. Everyone sat around swaying with eyes closed while the preacher put on a tape in the background: it seemed to consist of trance-like rhythms and his voice intoning and whispering some sort of mystical mantra. I concentrated and eventually thought I could make out words here and there:

'Ohhh, oh oh oh ohhh . . . *Obeyyyy meeee* . . . Ayyiyiiyiyiiii . . . *Submiiiit your willllll* . . . Laa, lalalalaa . . . *Giiiiiive meee your moneyyyyy* . . . ish kabibble, vade retro Santana, magna cum laude, dolce et gabbana . . . *Iiiii'm the bossss* . . .'

With everyone nodding and half-asleep I thought this would be an excellent time to take my tombola prize (a quite nice cheese) and tiptoe out in case the group sex started again. However, at the back of the hall I found the doors heavily bolted and barred.

'Going somewhere, brother?'

The Reverend Jim and his glassy-eyed flock had roused themselves as I eased out the bolts and bore down on me in unison.

'Yes, I thought I'd be off . . . it's been very interesting, thank you . . . I'll certainly think about . . .'

'But you should sign up for the full indoctrination course,' said one of the girls brightly.

'OK!' I said automatically. 'I mean, no, I really don't think . . . I have some minor theological objections.'

'Such as?'

'Well, you're all lunatics, aren't you?'

'Time for an intervention.' The Reverend Jim's nostrils flared with righteous exaltation. 'This soul shall not be lost to the Satan of physical ease. We must fill him with the grace of the Lawwwd.' He drew himself up majestically. 'Bring out the enraged wasps and the ice-cold ass-funnel.'

*

The intervention ritual was one of the most protracted and painful ordeals I have undergone in the course of my extremely painful life. My copper bowels protected me from the ravages of the wasps up the jacksy to a certain extent (I could hear their forlorn buzzing echoing through my intestines for hours – indeed I believe some of them are still there to this day) but there were also the Sacred Nipple-Clamps, the electrolysis of the nasal hair, and the hamster cage over the head – the way the rodent constantly ran around on its wheel right next to my ear almost brought me to the brink of insanity. When the Jellyfish Jockstrap was produced again I broke down and agreed to undergo the full indoctrination course and become a member of the cult, at which there was much rejoicing and an instant switching-on of warmth and good-fellowship, which manifested itself in a rain of friendly blows in the face to welcome me to the fold, and The Reverend Jim extracting my subscription fees, which proved to be the entire contents of my wallet and several huge IOUs.

I was taken immediately to the Chapter House, a large old Victorian house in the same street, and installed in an attic room there. It quickly became apparent that I was not allowed to leave. I was locked in at night, and once when I managed to manipulate the key from my side and sneak out I made it as far as the front hall before Rita felled me with a pickaxe handle.

There followed the brainwashing. To soften me up I was made to undergo a cruel regime of sense deprivation – I was completely cut off from all outward stimuli apart from the Entertainment Channel. Once released I was desperate for any intellectual stimulus no matter how spurious and would be bombarded with propaganda.

One or other of the acolytes, most usually Reg, the pinched little Northerner who had introduced the Reverend Jim at the first service, would read to me from their holy book, the Book of Dour, for hours on end.

I soon came to see that their philosophy entailed not simply physical mortification, but embraced a mental and spiritual greyness, joylessness and self-flagellation.

'Ye shall turn from beauty and dwell on that which is ugly.' Thus the book. 'Seek out that which turns your stomach and offends your eye. Revel in the degradation of man, for man is contemptible and no better than the beasts . . .

'You are not here to enjoy yourselves. Ye shall be joyless even in your revels. If you drink, do it until you puke. If you fuck, do it quickly and brutishly and with contempt for your partner. Ye shall denigrate your women, and call them bitch or ballbreaker or unclean ... Ye shall not raise them up above you but hold them cheap and commonplace ...

'May your meals be hurried and joyless and your operas filled with gritty social concern. Take no joy in your clothing – it should not be a thing of beauty – neither shall ye take any sinful pride in it – it should look like you dressed in a hurry and you should dress like everyone else.

'Your science-fiction TV series, aye, even your very spy shows, shalt contain dreary soap-opera elements, for no man can escape even for an hour from the tyranny of the kitchen sink, nor the nagging mother-in-law, nor the office politics, aye, even though he be possessed of a fuck-off big spaceship or an interesting job killing people. For these things are eternal; banality is eternal; and we shall celebrate these our dreary lives and no man shall dream of worlds elsewhere.

'If ye hear any man laugh, seeketh him out and make sure he is not laughing at anything improper. Ye shall say unto him, "What are ye laughing at?" And if it strike ye improper, ye shalt say, "Well, I don't think that's a laughing matter, actually" and take the huff. For you are not here to enjoy yourselves.

'Ye shall not read poetry, at least not any that rhymes or hath music or beauty. Rather shall ye seek out those that shall pretend to be gangsters that they may bluster and swear at thee. They may rhyme; ye shall say, "How clever, he rhymed motherfucker with cocksucker, that to me is poetry."

'Your art shall be relevant ...

'Your statues shall be rhomboid and not depict the human form in any recognizable way; yea, even the boobies on them shall be rhomboid. Ye shalt especially not make statues of any great man or hero, for man is a sinful wretch, the one as bad as the other, and you are not here to exalt yourselves.

'Likewise ye shall not take pride in your country, for pride is improper and sinful. When ye think of your country you shall flagellate yourself . . .

'Ye shall take joy in no thing without thou shalt feel remorseful and make thyself pay for it . . .

'If you drive a fast car or take a holiday, you must feel guilty and do penance and pay for your sin.

'It were better you did not do these things. But it were better that you do these things than that the heathen brutes who have heard not the word do these things; for they will feel no guilt and pay no penance, and feel the sinful joy that is denied thee; and you are better than they and charged to spread the word, so that there is some excuse for thee. Therefore thou wilt prohibit the heathens from doing these things.

'Thou shalt flail thyself, but flail the unrighteous harder. None shall know enjoyment and you suffer it to pass, for this is a vale of tears . . . Ye shall prohibit their pleasures in the name of righteousness . . .

'If a man shall draw on a cigarette, ye shall say, do you mind? You are killing me and my unborn children. Ye shall chase them out of buildings; ye shall chase them from the streets; then ye shall pursue them into their own homes.

'The bottom line is the bottom line. What profiteth a man if he make no profit? That which doth rake in the shekels is the good, though it displease thee. Beware the sin of pride in thy dealings. Ye shall not make moral stands. The market was put above thee by God and ye are but a humble unit therein.

'Ye shall concrete over your countryside . . . Ye shall tear down beautiful buildings and put up abominations . . .'

Before too long I was completely indoctrinated. Every day I would take part in the ritual mass confessions where we would sit around and flagellate ourselves for our failings: 'I had a cream cake', 'I drank a glass of wine', 'I drove to the seaside', 'I savoured the sound of my thighs rubbing together in corduroy.'

Punishments were inflicted, on top of the regular daily doses of pain we gave each other, and we were encouraged to denounce anyone suspected of enjoying themselves or failing to follow the rules.

For the richer members of the congregation, however, there was a system whereby for a cash consideration your sins would be remitted and someone on the other side of the world would be paid to take your regular doses of pain on your behalf. You would make your payment to the Reverend Jim, not forgetting his commission, and eventually get back a picture of a grinning Asian with a five-pound note in his hand and his nuts in a vice.

There were other hypocrisies that annoyed me even in my brainwashed state: for example, the elite inner circle were allowed to smoke in the house because it was considered they had enough pain already with the burden of regulating the behaviour of the rest of us.

The prophet they worshipped and whose word they followed was a man named Sid Croakey. I never really understood what was so special about him, why they had chosen to follow him or why God had chosen to speak to him rather than anyone else. They showed me pictures of a rather unprepossessing fellow, scowling and beetle-browed and with a bushy black beard and a battered black hat jammed down over his head. He had apparently suffered many afflictions and tribulations and been shunned and neglected by his fellow men. One day when he was standing glowering out of the window of his dingy bedsit, brooding over all the things he would never be able to enjoy, God came to him and told him that his sufferings made him righteous and that he must go forth and stop everyone else from enjoying themselves too. Inspired, he had started to preach, and dictated his great work of wisdom, the Book of Dour, which his devoted landlady had jotted down for him while he lay on his bed clipping his verrucas. I gathered that Croakey had followers all over the country, although not all were members of the Church of Agonizing Pain; those who were not were denounced as backsliding heretics by Jim and Reg.

I cannot say I was happy once I had accepted the word of Sid Croakey and the Reverend Jim, but I consoled myself that I was not meant to be and that the travails I underwent at the hands of the cult must be part of God's plan. My meagre savings were quickly taken from me in the form of tithes, contributions and fines. Still under escort at this point, I was taken back to my old lodgings and encouraged to destroy all of my books and anything that reeked of sinful luxury. Collecting only my shoddiest clothes I moved into the Chapter House permanently.

My sufferings began in earnest, but I learned not to grumble or question my lot. Apart from the ritual flailings, ordeals and mortifications of the flesh, I was used as a domestic drudge by the privileged inner circle and worked until I dropped. It always seemed to be my turn to do the washing up and clean the toilets, which I had to do without a brush, a sinful invention. It was always me who made the tea and toast while the rest of them sat around in a narcotic daze watching *Countdown*, not even lifting their feet up when

I hoovered. Just because the Reverend Jim was a charismatic cult leader who would one day lead us in a holy war to abolish the current Dispensation of Sin in an ocean of blood, I didn't see why he couldn't go to the twenty-four-hour garage to buy his own fucking Rizlas once in a while. And they never put their flails away tidily, they would have all got tangled up if it wasn't for me, and it was always Muggins who had to wash the blood off, and just when I'd got everything spick and span and was preparing to take my pinny off they'd inevitably start on an orgy. Group sex might sound like fun but someone has to clean the carpets afterwards. I found it's quite dispiriting to be called a nag by members of a fanatical pain-cult.

Whenever anyone dared challenge the Reverend Jim's edicts he would dramatically show them the scars on his back and tell them to have a bit of faith. Timidly, even after my conversion I once or twice ventured – not criticisms, but questions, and would be vehemently slapped down. To explain things fully to me I would be wired into the electrical mains for a while and made to sleep in a kennel in the yard for a week.

Once they were assured of my unquestioning devotion, and when my money had run dry, I was ordered to go forth and engage in fund-raising activities for the church. Specifically, I was instructed to sell myself sexually and bring back the proceeds. Once again it was time to don my trusty pink satin hot pants and head to the nearest Little Chef. (The worst part of being a trucker-whore isn't having to fellate lorry drivers. It is having to hang out in chain eateries and eat service station food.)

I was also instructed to make converts. However, I was no good at proselytizing and could somehow never sell the lorry drivers on the exciting benefits of a life of Agonizing

Pain no matter how much I fluttered my eyelashes or how expertly I masturbated them.

Then one day everything changed. A new and more sinister phase began.

After the regular weekly service the tombola was rolled out as usual, the two pretty girls draping themselves over it smilingly encouraging everyone to throw in for a ticket.

'You will take part, won't you?'

'It's a great prize this week.'

'In-deeeed!' cried the Reverend Jim. 'The prize this week, my brothers in righteous an-he-*donia*, is nothing *mawww* and nothing *layyys* than a Trip to Paradise!'

As the girls smiled and winked at me I eagerly paid my money and watched them put my name in the tumbler. I dared not hope to be the one to win. A trip to Paradise! In the course of my miserable life I had rarely had a holiday. Perhaps it would be a weekend in Skegness, maybe even Bognor.

Round and round the tumbler went. The Reverend Jim put his hand in and drew out a paper.

'Arthur Stubbins! Come forward, my brother, for you have been fingered by de Lawwwd!' There was a polite round of applause. However Reverend Jim held up his hand. 'There are more to follow!' He drew out half a dozen names. The last one was mine.

As hands clapped me on the back I stepped forward in a daze.

'Rita! Bring out the fan-*ta*-bulous once-in-a-lifetime prizes!'

Rita shuffled on, huffing and puffing, from the wings, weighed down by half a dozen dynamite belts which she hung around the winners' necks like garlands or wreaths. I stared in shock and confusion.

'Brothers in Payyyyyn! The time has come for the next glorious phase of our mission on this *fawwwl*len and sin-besmirched world! We must not keep the blessings of pain to ourselves any longer. Does it not say in the Book of Dour, "Thou shalt flail thyself, but flail the unrighteous harder"? The hour has come, my brethren, when our vengeance shall fall upon them like the signet-ringed bitch-slapping hayyynd of the Awmighty. They will not yield to our righteous demands! They will not cede to our heaven-sent authority! They disport themselves in wicked ease and sinful friv-*ol*-ity, they mock at the Path of Pain and corrupt our young with aspirin and cawwwn-plasters, they laugh and dance and tickle one another and fear not the word of de Lawd! They will be humbled!

'To this end, the holy martyrs you see before you will tomorrow go forth among them and turn themselves into human Bawwwwmbs of Goawwwd in such a way as to cause maximum payyyyn and bloodshed.

'Praise be!'

*

In preparation for my sacrifice I spent that evening and the next morning in prayer and farting.

We gathered in the kitchen for our final instructions.

'Warriors of Payyn! Rita will now demonstrate the correct use of the dynamite belt.'

Rita buckled an explosive belt around her midriff, pointing out where all the cinches went, and showed us how to prime and disarm the device. Then she shuffled out into the middle of the back yard and turned to face us.

'Death to the infidels!' she yelled.

She yanked the ripcord and there was an explosion. I saw her false teeth crash through the greenhouse of a garden three houses along. Her smoking zip-up furry ankle-boots were all that was left of her.

When we had all put our belts on bits of ironmongery and packets of nails were attached to them to make the carnage worse. The nails were rusty and I cut myself on one fitting them on. It would be just my luck to get tetanus. We put our jackets on and faced the Reverend Jim standing to attention.

'Now go fawwth, ye valiant, and make me proud!'

We started to march out.

'Hold up,' said Reg, 'who's not thrown in for t'tea fund this week?'

Grumbling, everyone put their hands in their pockets and paid up.

Then we trudged out to die for the pain cult.

In the back streets behind the Chapter House we mumbled farewells to our fellow martyrs and split up. To my dismay it was raining heavily and I had forgotten my umbrella.

'Fuck off,' said Reg when I went back for it, slamming the door in my face.

I skulked under a bus shelter until the weather cleared up, then headed for the centre of town.

When you are being lectured on the glories of suicide bombing and how lucky you are to be chosen no one ever tells you how weighty and uncomfortable the devices are or how much the straps cut into you and hurt. I am sure I slipped a disc toting the thing around and I have never been able to claim compensation.

However, the biggest problem with my divine mission was my terrible agoraphobia and fear of crowds. This has been a sore trial to me throughout my life but never more so than now when I wanted to blow up a lot of people. Obviously I wanted to cause maximum pain and execution to the infidels, but every time I tried to walk through the middle of a crowded street I started sweating and panicking. Instead I found myself skulking off down unfrequented side streets and back alleys as was my wont. I made my way to the park and sat down on a bench to get my nerve back, taking deep breaths and reciting calming mantras of hate and sadism.

Presently an old man came and sat down at the other end of the bench. I could at least take him with me. How far was the range of the bomb? I budged up a bit towards him but didn't want to invade his personal space too much. However he took my movement as a signal that I wanted to chat and smiled pleasantly and started to make remarks about the ducks and the weather. I thought it would be rude to interrupt him so didn't blow myself up. After a while he stopped, and my hand crept to the arming mechanism and primed the device. But then he started on a long but very interesting story of his experiences in the war, and I wanted to hear the end of it, so I disarmed the bomb again. When he had finished some ducks had waddled up from the pond to eat bits from his sandwiches. I thought it would be a shame to blow them up too as I wasn't sure whether ducks could benefit from the blessings of pain. Then the man left. One of the ducks, who hated me, hissed and pecked me on the shin, and I thought of blowing us both up just to spite it, but decided that would be a pretty feeble score, so blessed it for the gift of pain and kicked it in the arse. I considering following the old man but decided that would be feeble too.

I considered my options. If I had any friends I could invite them round for a party, then play a game of sardines and blow myself up when we were all really close. But the sad fact was I didn't know enough people to host a proper massacre.

So then I thought I would get on a bus and blow that up. The queue at the bus stop was long and the waiting was boring and interminable, so I thought I might as well do it then and there. However I was suddenly struck with guilt. Blowing up a bus stop or a bus itself might make people frightened to use them, and discouraging people from using public transport would be harmful for the environment. I tutted and sighed and trudged off.

Then I hit on the idea of a restaurant. However I have always been tragically unable to get good tables in restaurants. I was seated in a really crappy spot by myself in a corner, right next to the toilets and with a big pillar between me and the rest of the diners. I sighed. I would probably kill no one but the men's room attendant from here.

'Excuse me,' I said shyly to the waiter, 'I hate to be trouble, but would it be possible, at all, to change tables? Could I perhaps have something more central, that one over there next to that children's party perhaps?'

'I'm sorry, sir, most of our tables are reserved, and as you're dining alone . . .'

'Yes yes,' I said hastily, 'of course, I quite understand.' I hated both myself and him. If I had been more handsome and commanding he would have given me a good table surrounded by juicy targets. I decided to blow myself up when he came back to take my order and serve him right.

However the menu looked very tempting and I decided the really cunning thing would be to eat a vast meal and then blow myself up before the bill came. In fact, I ordered everything on the menu, and an expensive bottle of wine, the waiter not understanding why I was chuckling to myself.

After all, I hadn't eaten properly before coming out and it was best not to die on an empty stomach. The food was delicious. I sampled everything unstintingly and asked for more of my favourites. Guiltily I remembered I was not supposed to enjoy anything and stuck toothpicks under my fingernails. Then I remembered that martyrdom would wash away my sins and took them out and ordered more wine.

When the dessert trolley came the sweets looked really tempting and I went a bit overboard on them. I was rather bloated by this time and the dynamite belt was cutting into my distended belly. I took it off and put it over a chair, sighing with relief and patting my tummy fondly.

When the cigars and brandy arrived I sat and looked around me with benevolent repletion. Craning my head to one side I was able to see round the pillar. At the good table I had wanted I was surprised to see my fellow suicide bomber Arthur. I went over.

'What are you doing here?'

'What do you think?' he said gruffly, pointing significantly to his midriff.

'No, you can't, I am!'

'Piss off. I'm blowing up here.'

'I was here first!'

'I outrank you.'

'Awww! Not fair.'

'Go on, get out of it.'

I trudged off dejectedly. It would appear there was little sense of esprit de corps among suicide bombers. Arthur was enjoying a slap-up meal himself and the restaurant was already emptying. By the time he finished and blew himself up there would be no bugger there. I hoped God would kick his head in for it when he got to heaven.

I started to slink out of the restaurant. The waiter intercepted me smoothly. 'Your bill, sir.'

'I'm afraid I find I can't pay.'

'I quite understand. Please step this way, sir.'

In the kitchen a huge chef beat the shit out of me and I was put to work washing dishes, as if I hadn't had enough of that the past few months. I have been forced to work in restaurant kitchens several times in my extremely painful life and every time I do I decide anew that it is the most horrible thing that has ever happened to me. What made it worse was watching a succession of gourmet delights being efficiently ferried out to fatguts Arthur. He finished by ordering a Bombe Surprise. He had no taste, that man. Anyway, in the confusion and general dismay when the doors blew in and the waiter's severed head embedded itself in the far wall I took the opportunity to make my escape out the back.

I made my way back round to the high street to find chaos and screaming and the restaurant windows scattered across the road. (It was very traumatic. I was probably the seventeenth or eighteenth on the scene. My editor tells me I could probably write a book about that alone if I didn't have so many other things to write about.) Almost simultaneously another of my comrades detonated somewhere a couple of streets away. I felt left out. Even as a suicide bomber I was a failure.

Before too long the emergency services were on the scene. The police moved the braver gawpers back behind a barrier. I found myself trapped in the middle of a small crowd in the next street. It was now or never. I decided to seize my chance. I stood on the steps of the town War Memorial, flung open my jacket and yelled: 'Death to all enemies of God!'

Everyone turned and gaped.

'Are you – are you one of them?' asked a woman.

'I am a warrior of pain! Now we will all die!'

'You murdering pig!' screamed another woman.

'Quiet!' barked a man. 'You could be hurting his feelings. Low self-esteem is probably what brought him to this desperate pass.' He stepped forward. 'Sir, I am a qualified Conflict Manager, and trained in Grievance Counselling. You have my full attention and instinctive sympathy. How can we resolve this situation? What can we do to meet your needs?'

'You can die!' I yelled.

He nodded. 'I hear you saying you want us to die. But what are you really trying to tell us?'

'I am wired to explode! We are all going to die!'

'You poor man. You must be in terrible pain. Would you like to talk about it?'

'No! I'm not in pain! I mean I am. I like pain!'

'Why are you doing this?' someone asked. 'Is it because of the government?'

'No! I hate everyone! You must all submit to the will of Our Lord Sid Croakey and live in pain, or die in pain.'

'See, it *is* because of the government.' People nodded sagely.

'It isn't! It's the will of God! You are sinful heathens and I fucking hate you all!'

'Well that's just plain rude,' someone said.

'Can we open a dialogue?'

'I'm going to bury all of you godless bastards!'

'We feel your pain.'

'Stop saying that!'

'We're here for you. We're all here for you.'

'Right! Watch this,' I cried in irritation.

Exasperated, I went to yank the cord, and gave myself a painful pinch on the tummy. It was then I noticed the dynamite belt was no longer there. Frowning, I ripped open my shirt to be sure.

Shit. I had left the bloody thing back in the restaurant.

'Are you all right, love?'

'Stay there!' I yelled, pointing at them. 'Don't move! Stay right where you are. I'll be back in two minutes.'

'All right.'

I dashed off. Of course, the restaurant was cordoned off now. I gave it up and ran back to the Chapter House.

Jim and Reg were somewhat surprised to see me but very understanding of my little mistake, and after having some muscular acolytes rough me up in a number of inventive ways decided to say no more about it.

'After all,' said Jim indulgently, reclining on the couch canoodling with the Pain Girls and looking unusually mellow, 'suicide bombing is a learning experience, like everything else.'

From the TV we learned that two of the other human bombs had failed to detonate. Still the results had been satisfactory and we were famous. As I looked at the footage of the aftermath of the carnage I suddenly shuddered and decided that perhaps my painful life wasn't so bad.

The morning after next I was washing a big pile of dishes and wishing I had martyred myself after all when I saw a strange man in the back yard with his finger to an earpiece and carrying a walkie-talkie. As his jacket flapped I glimpsed a shoulder holster. I ran to a front window. There were an unusual number of cars in the street and similar men on the pavement. The game was up!

I spread the alarm. There was confusion and panic. There was a pounding on the door.

Five minutes later I was bringing tea and biscuits to two men who were sitting in the front room talking to Jim and Reg. One of them was a government minister. They took their tea with lumps of catshit in it after our fashion and did their best to smile politely after sipping.

'I understand,' said the minister to Jim, 'that you are revered as one of the foremost scholars of the teachings of Croakeyism.'

'I have that honour.'

'We would like to open a dialogue with you. We want to avoid any repetition of the recent regrettable occurrences. We would like you to become an official adviser to the government. Help us understand what we're doing wrong, how we can avoid offending the followers of the blessed Croakey in future.'

The Reverend Jim frowned and pursed his lips thoughtfully. 'That may be possible.'

By the time I was called back for a refill he was storming up and down thunderously expostulating at them as they took notes. 'Aspirin! Our people are not to sell aspirin or be sold aspirin ... No painkillers are to be sold within two hundred yards of our churches ... Dentistry! Ye shall dismantle the dental service for it is an abomination in our eyes ...'

'I'm not sure about that,' protested the minister.

'We've pretty much done it already,' muttered his aide.

'Good point ... Anything else?'

When I returned to collect the cups after they left Jim was sitting back on the couch sighing. 'Like I said,' he murmured with a dreamy smile, 'a learning experience.'

But as for me I had done my own learning. My experiences on the day of the bombings had been cathartic and disillusioning. I could see through their brainwashing now and saw the church as the exploitative cult it was. At my first opportunity I slipped away and never looked back.

While I did not abandon religion entirely and at various periods of my life would seek its solace, I was cured of my indoctrination in their beliefs, although not, it turned out, of the tetanus I had indeed picked up from the rusty nail, which very nearly killed me.

The fact is I do not believe God would wish us to inflict pain on one another. That would be encroaching on his department.

13

I have a pet dog. Briefly.

I would not have you think that my whole life has been misery, pain, and dull prolonged suffering. I believe in looking on the bright side, and can honestly say that only 99.99 per cent of it has consisted of that. And while most of the rest has been disappointment, resignation, and gloom, there have also been fleeting periods of, if not quite happiness or contentment, then something which might pass for them in the dark, buried like diamonds in a big pile of manure.

It is to just such a brief season of cheer that I must turn my pen now. While it lasted I was reconciled to existence and envied no man – for no one can be unhappy who is awakened in the morning by being enthusiastically licked and panted over by a devoted friend. During this all-too-short time I was, if not actually glad to be alive, at least not resentful about the fact. Alas, I was to pay a heavy price for it, for when it ended, it did so in the most heartbreaking manner imaginable.

If you have tears, prepare to shed them now.

I first saw Skip from my seat in the front row of the circus, to which I had treated myself to celebrate my recovery from a brief tussle with galloping mange of the armpits, successfully cured by my shoulder-joints being amputated and replaced with steel ratchets. (To this day, I make an untoward clanking sound when raising my arms, and it hurts me to do aeroplane impressions.) I was entertained enough by the clowns and tumblers, but it was when my dear Skipper appeared that I really sat up and took notice.

He came on riding a bicycle: a black-and-white mongrel dog with one ear missing and his tongue hanging out with enthusiasm. Instantly my heart went out to the little scamp. He cycled busily about the ring and then dismounted nimbly and proceeded to take part in some energetic tumbling tricks aided by a clown. Next he was strapped to a target board and calmly watched as a knife-thrower outlined him with blades. Then a helmet was placed on him and he was shot out of a cannon and caught in a net to wild applause. Finally he got back on his bicycle at the bottom of a ramp facing a hoop of fire with a tank of water on the other side. This was where it went horribly wrong. He misjudged the jump badly and crashed straight into the burning ring, and went flying off with his poor fur aflame. He raced round and round maddened and yowling until men with fire extinguishers appeared and doused him. The audience was horrified and screaming at this turn of events until we were diverted by the hasty appearance of the dancing elephants.

As I left the circus ground at the end of the show I missed my way in the dark and found myself among the performers' caravans. To my horror I saw an unshaven and seedy man in a dirty neckerchief beating poor Skip with a stout stick and pelting him with rocks, shouting, 'Go away!' At every blow Skip yelped and flattened himself but attempted to crawl forward to lick the man's hand.

'Get out of here, you ungrateful cur!' the man yelled. 'You're finished in this business! I have no use for a dog who can't perform a simple burning hoop jump! If you're still around come morning I'll sell you to the knacker's yard!'

With that he stamped into his caravan and slammed the door.

Skip, a quivering heap, whined inconsolably and then slunk off into the night, his one ear drooping sadly.

I hesitated only briefly. We were two outcasts and pariahs with no place in the world. I overtook him and, by feeding him the remnants of my popcorn and stroking him soothingly, endeavoured to win his trust and affection. Within minutes he was barking happily and wagging his tail and hanging his tongue out with joy. When I left the fairground calling him after me he immediately followed.

Back home we examined each other more carefully. Apart from his singed fur poor Skip was somewhat malnourished and bore the marks of his beating. On his side, Skip cocked his head in enquiry as he contemplated my baboon's-arse face in a proper light and sniffed at it experimentally. But then he wagged his approval and licked it and presently we were rolling round on the floor together tickling and nuzzling.

This was not the ideal time in my life to take on the care of a pet. For one thing I lived in a modest third-storey flat and animals were strictly forbidden. Fortunately my landlady was somewhat short-sighted and, by dressing Skip in infant clothes and a baby bonnet and making him walk on his hind legs (a trick he had learned in the circus) I was able to pass him off as my child when she was around. Perhaps because I had a baboon's arse for a face, she accepted his unusual appearance and occasional bark without much surprise or comment.

Moreover I was moving from one short-term job to

the next and at times was barely able to make ends meet for myself. Nevertheless I spent my savings on treatment for Skip's injuries, and steak to build him up. His food was my first priority whenever I had a pay cheque and some weeks he ate better than I did. But it was worth it to have someone to come home to every night and his delighted yelping as I put the key in the door was worth every penny. Before too long he was restored to health, still a mauled and battered mongrel like myself, but with his coat sleek and glossy and a bounce in his step.

Then began the happiest time of my life. I bought a little convertible car, and every weekend that summer I would take Skip out to the country and the two of us would romp together on the moors. He would retrieve the sticks I threw or enthusiastically chase after rabbits for hours on end until a happy exhaustion overtook him. We would frolic and play games and on the ride back sing and bark merry songs together. Once I took him to a funfair and I had a tattoo of Skip done on my arm and a fake photo of us flying a biplane taken. Though I did not realize it until too late, else I would have shown more caution, I was feeling something I had never thought I would dare to feel again – love. He was the one joy in my life.

Then, one day, I made the mistake of taking him for a walk near the Military Testing Range.

We had scrambled through many hedges and under and over several fences in Skip's exuberant pursuit of a rabbit. We were in unfamiliar terrain and from the occasional dull boom I heard I assumed there was some quarrying going on nearby. The first sign of our peril should have been the various skull-and-crossbones signs I encountered here and there, but I speculated that some local village had mounted a dry-land re-enactment of a pirate battle thereabouts. I felt somewhat more unease when I came across a sign which, as I thought, some illiterate farmer jealous of his property had put up, reading,

MINE
FIELD

Obviously the ungrammatical fellow would prefer us not to trespass and we should think about taking ourselves off. Still it was a lovely day and I had never seen Skip happier and more frolicsome. I shrugged and threw a stick for Skip to fetch and watched as he went bounding after it.

To my surprise, the stick blew up with a huge explosion when it landed.

My blood ran cold. It hit me. Minefield.

'Skip!' I cried. 'Stop, Skip, stop! Jesus God, no!'

It was too late. Skip was racing through the middle of the minefield, tongue hanging out with enthusiasm.

I couldn't bear to watch and yet I couldn't look away. To my horror I saw him reach the spot where the stick had landed and yelp with puzzlement and then start sniffing around for it. I had a vivid close-up of his doggy eyes looking at me reproachfully. What cruel trick was this I had played?

Suddenly there was an explosion of fur out of the long grass and the elusive rabbit burst out of hiding and went tearing across the field. Barking, Skip raced heedlessly after him through the danger zone.

'No, Skip! Stay! Stay, Skip!'

I had never been able to train him well. There was a reverberating BOOM! and I watched as clods of earth and a small furry body rained from the air.

I closed my eyes and swallowed. When I opened them Skip was lying at my feet, tail wagging proudly, a smoking, incinerated rabbit clutched in his jaws.

'Good doggy,' I said weakly.

Trembling, I bent and patted him, chiding half-heartedly with tears of relief coursing down my face.

Foolishly, I thought he was safe at that point.

I looked around frantically and fruitlessly for some indication of where the military range ended, but could not even determine the way we had come, and it was at random that I started to flee across hills and fields with Skip bounding happily at my side. Oblivious to our danger, he resisted all efforts to put him on a leash or bring him to heel and gambolled where he would. From time to time a shell whistled overhead; we crossed tank tracks and once a tree was blown to smithereens not ten feet away from us.

Suddenly, roving ahead of me on the crest of a rise, Skip spied something on the other side and went tearing towards it out of my view, barking joyfully. Another rabbit? Despairingly trying to call him back I hurried after.

When I got to the top I saw what he had spotted. Over on the next hillock was mounted a huge large-bore field cannon, some sort of monster howitzer pointing towards the horizon. Skip went dashing towards it excitedly.

As I watched, he reached the muzzle of the cannon and leaped head-first into it, disappearing down the shaft.

'Skip! No, Skip!'

I caught up as soon as I could and pounded on the side of the monstrous artillery piece. 'Come out, boy!' I could hear his excited woof echoing from within.

I was alarmed, fearing he would be trapped inside, the aperture not being much bigger than him, but not actually frightened until I saw that at the back of the giant weapon where you would expect an artilleryman to stand there was a computer device wired to it and a read-out ticking off some sort of countdown.

My heart pounding, I looked more closely. The display read:

AUTOMATIC TEST-FIRING SEQUENCE ENGAGED

ORDNANCE LOADED

ABORT SEQUENCE DISENGAGED

PAYLOAD: 1 x 5-TON HIGH-EXPLOSIVE NUCLEAR-TIPPED SHELL

TARGET RANGE: 3 MILES

TIME REMAINING UNTIL FIRING:

MIN SEC
00 : 59

. . . 58 . . . 57 . . . 56 . . .

The thing was about to be fired.

'Skip! SKIP!' I pounded on the side of the cannon again. 'Come out of there, boy!'

There was a happy woof and Skip's head emerged from the muzzle of the gun, but he came no further. Tongue lolling, panting with excitement, he gazed eagerly towards the far horizon.

My bowels turned to ice as a horrid memory came to me. Of course. Skip's circus training was coming out. He was looking forward to being shot out of the cannon.

'Skip! NO! Get out of there! Jesus God, Skip!'

I reached up to grab him but could barely touch my fingers to the lip of the weapon. I jumped up and down frantically, pleading with him to come out, but he merely barked with glee.

Tearing my hair, I looked along the line of the cannon's trajectory. I could barely make out the tiny white cross of a target on a distant horizon.

'SKIP! Please!'

In a panic I ran back to the triggering device, now showing 35, 34, 33 seconds to firing, and started to press buttons indiscriminately and then to pound at it with my fists. The mechanism started to spark and flash and strange symbols flickered across the read-out. With a whine of hydraulics, the cannon rotated around on its platform by about fifteen degrees, and then elevated its barrel to almost forty-five degrees into the air. I could hear Skip barking his little head off in a frenzy of excitement.

'SKIIIIIIIP!'

I had to save him. There was only one thing for it. My heart in my mouth, I clambered on top of the gun so I was straddling the monster barrel and started to shimmy up it towards the mouth. As I got further along and higher up vertigo started to kick in but I had to keep going. Ahead of me I could see Skip's muzzle protruding from the weapon's, and his one ear pricked up in anticipation as he waited obediently for what he thought would be a short and pleasant flight through the air ending in the familiar embrace of a safety net, little realizing that he would be riding five tons of red-hot high-explosive nuclear-tipped death three miles across the countryside straight to doggy Hades. When I was halfway along there was a bang from behind me as the guidance system completely blew, the motors kicked in again and the barrel started to swivel seemingly at random from side to side and up and down, threatening to dislodging me from my precarious perch atop it. Somehow I held on and kept going. I was almost in reach of him now. A few more metres and I could get him . . .

'Skip . . . please, Skip . . .'

Suddenly a tannoy sounded from a copse in the middle distance: 'Ten seconds to autogun firing . . . nine . . . eight . . .'

Almost there. I shimmied desperately to the end of the gargantuan cannon as the seconds ticked away. The barrel gave a final sickening lurch and then stopped. Clinging on for dear life, I reached out to grab the scruff of his neck just as the countdown reached zero.

The detonation was deafening, and indeed left my hearing permanently impaired. To this day, I have a ringing in my ears that sounds like techno music. (When other people hear techno on the radio, I imagine, they think, 'Oh God, not this crap.' I don't notice anything at all and think the DJ is just taking a really long pause.)

But none of that mattered then. All that mattered was safe in my arms. The recoil had flung us from the gun and we had dropped bruisingly to earth many yards below, but there was my Skipper safe and sound, licking at my face but whining his reproach for denying him his fun.

I looked up and saw a church steeple on the horizon evaporate in a small mushroom cloud. I swallowed queasily. That could easily have been Skip.

But he was safe now. I had saved him.

Or so I thought.

In fact, I had only saved him for something far worse, and it was a cruel fate for both of us that I had not allowed him to be fired across the countryside on a high-explosive shell.

But I get ahead of myself.

Anyway, on the way back from the firing range I stopped off at a Korean restaurant.

Naturally I left Skip tied to a lamp post outside. A Korean chef in a bloody apron, who was loitering in a nearby alley enjoying a crafty cigarette, smiled at him.

'Doggy . . . you?' he said.

'Yes, doggy me,' I agreed cheerfully, tickling Skip under the chin.

'Doggy nice, mmmm. But he a bit skinny.'

'A bit,' I agreed as Skip licked my hand affectionately, 'but he is very tender.'

'Mmmm.'

Skip started to whine as I made to go. 'I won't be long, Skipper,' I told him. 'You are safe now, no harm can come to you here.'

'I take care of doggy,' grinned the Korean chef.

'You see, Skip? This nice man will look after you.'

I went in and sat down with not a care in the world. The choice of dishes on the menu all had Korean names that were incomprehensible to me so I decided to take pot luck and asked for the speciality of the house.

As I waited I slowly managed to relax after the tensions of the day. I even started to feel a bit proud of myself. I had managed to save Skip against all the odds. I vowed that nothing would ever part us.

When the meal arrived it proved to be some sort of unidentifiable meat on a bed of rice, covered in a heavy and fragrant sauce. I asked the young man who served it what it was but he replied only with a Korean word I didn't understand, so I shrugged and tucked in. The meat was somewhat chewy but of a mouth-watering flavour. I was ravenous.

'Mmm, that was yummy,' I said when I had finished. 'My compliments to the chef. I don't believe I have ever tasted anything so delicious. Please bring me another portion.'

However, I didn't manage to finish the second helping so I asked for a doggy bag.

'Bag for doggy,' nodded the boy eagerly, and fetched one.

Dear Skip, I remember thinking, patting my stomach with repletion, how empty I would have felt without him.

Paying the bill, I was surprised to notice a charge marked for 'corkage'. I assumed this was because I had brought a bottle of lemonade in with me left over from our picnic. I thought it a bit mean of them but decided to say nothing about it.

I thanked the grinning Koreans and left.

When I got outside, Skip was gone.

Gone.

My beloved dog had gone.

The lead was still tied to the lamp post, but Skip was no longer in it.

I looked around in alarm. What could possibly have happened to him?

The same Korean chef in the bloody apron was standing nearby, talking to a small Korean child who was wailing and sobbing.

'Excuse me,' I said, 'do you know what became of my dog?'

The chef said something in Korean and then shrugged and added, 'Doggy go bye-bye.' The child launched into a fresh deluge of tears.

I had an ominous feeling. There was a heavy weight in the pit of my stomach. Suddenly I wanted to throw up the delicious meal I had just eaten.

Seeing our tableau the smiling waiter came out and shot an interrogative at the chef. At his reply he looked stunned and disbelieving, then when the chef nodded burst into a cackling laugh.

'Funny thing is happen,' he said to me. 'Is big comedy with dog, ha ha!'

'What?' I yelled, suddenly sobbing like the child and grabbing him by the lapels and shaking him. 'What has happened to him? What have you done with my dog, you bastards?'

Holding his sides with mirth the waiter said, 'You get big kick out of this, I know. By mistake this child is untie doggy to play with. But he say doggy is steal his bicycle and ride off down street!'

'You expect me to believe that?!' I yelled, shaking him dementedly. 'What have you done with him? What have you done with Skip, damn you?'

Just then there was the ting-ting of a bicycle bell and Skip sped past us on the child's bicycle, tongue lolling and peddling furiously.

'Jesus God, Skip!' I cried. 'Be careful!'

There was a blaring of horns and a squeal of brakes as to my horror Skip shot out into the busy main road at the end of the street and blithely cycled off around the corner, sounding his bell merrily.

'NOOOO! No, Skip! Come back!'

Quickly I got into my car and set off in pursuit. Around the corner I found a car had mounted the pavement and there were several bodies lying around but thankfully Skip was not among them. I could see him in the distance, peddling like mad, tail wagging with the fun – and on the wrong side of the road.

'Skip!' I yelled. 'Stop, boy! Heel! Dismount! Remember the highway code!'

But Skip was oblivious, careering through the traffic with a mad abandon, heedless of the horns and swerving vehicles all around. He was going at a remarkable clip and, frustratingly caught in the traffic and unable to weave through it as he did, I couldn't catch him.

I waved frantically at the oncoming drivers in case any of them couldn't see him. 'Clear the road! Please! Beware of the dog! Skip! Please! Oh God in heaven, spare my little dog! Stop, Skip, stop!'

Far from stopping, Skip started to show off. He began to pull wheelies, ride standing up with his paws off the handle-bars, and then, astonishingly, and I was forced to admit very skilfully, jumping up off the bike and spinning round in the air and landing back on the bike upside down, doing a handstand or at least a front-paw-stand on the pedals and continuing to cycle like that.

'Skip! NO! This isn't the circus!'

I was starting to have an ominous feeling about this.

That was when Skip fell off the bike.

Looming up behind him was a huge petrol tanker.

My heart caught in my throat. Time seemed to slow to a crawl.

Have you ever had an inexplicable feeling of horrible premonition, as though something terribly awful was about to happen, you weren't sure how? I have had that feeling almost constantly in my life and it has almost always come true. To balance that, however, quite often awful things have happened without my expecting them, so I suppose no paranormal significance can be read into it. Anyway, I had that feeling now.

With a preternatural clarity I took in every detail of the scene. Skip, sprawled dazed in the middle of the road, his bicycle clattering down nearby. On one side of the road, the huge fuel lorry bearing down towards him.

Some distance behind the lorry on the same side of the road was a steamroller.

Just ahead of me on my side of the road was a flatbed builder's lorry laden down with planks, sand, and a huge pile of bricks that I dimly noted appeared to be insecurely roped down.

Pulling out of a side street ahead of us, meanwhile, was a van bearing on its side a sign reading '"ACME" AXE-SHARPENING LTD, Making axes really sharp and delivering them to your doorstep since 1973.'

This homely axe-sharpener's van, a traditional sight of merry England, normally so unremarkable, even reassuring in its very ordinariness, for some reason filled me with a strange foreboding.

It seemed to happen in slow motion and it all had a terrible inevitability about it.

At the last second the tanker driver spotted Skip, putting on his brakes and swerving towards the side street to avoid him. The axe-grinder's van smashed into it. The builder's lorry smashed into the van and I rammed into the back of the builder's lorry. The bricks on the flatbed burst their moorings and came tumbling down on top of me, burying my little open-topped car almost completely until only my head was visible sticking out of a big pile of bricks, a couple of stray ones bouncing off it.

There was a moment of stillness. The vehicles were all crumpled together, the axe van in the middle wedged into a gashed hole in the side of the tanker, with fuel splashing all over it. I knew a nanosecond of relief as I saw Skip was still lying in the middle of the road, dazed but uninjured. All would have been well if the axe-sharpener's van, with its deadly cargo of freshly sharpened axes, had not exploded.

As it blew up I saw them all burst out of the roof and go flying high in the air and seem to hang there. For a second the sky appeared to be dark with hovering axes.

Then they fell to earth again in a fatal, widespread shower.

To my horror, I saw many of them were falling towards Skip. Skip was lying spreadeagled on his back, dazed, looking up at them.

With terror-heightened senses I seemed to see Skip's doggy eyes widen as the rain of axes descended from on high.

Time was slowed for me and I could see it all happen blow by blow. One by one they plummeted down on him.

The first whistled down and bit into the tarmac not an inch from his left ear. I saw his widened eye swivel to look at it in alarm. The axe stayed upright, the shaft quivering, so deeply was the blade buried in the road. Skip stood no chance. The second I saw actually trim some of the fur from his left leg. The third landed between his legs, scant inches from his little doggy bollocks. Then I saw him roll his eyes as the fourth hit an inch above his head. Not once did he move a muscle. A fifth fell, a sixth . . . Then time seemed to speed up again and the other seventeen showered down on him in an indistinguishable mass.

'NOOOOOOOO!'

If ever I believed in a doggy god, I believed in him then, for by a miracle every one of the axes missed Skip by inches. His poor little body was outlined with axes, when he got up he would leave a dog-shaped pattern in the road, but he himself had not been scratched.

He barked roguishly and looked very pleased with himself.

I sighed. 'Jesus, God, Skip,' I said weakly.

It was only then that I noticed the wooden handle above my forehead and felt the sharp pain in my head and realized a stray axe had embedded itself in my cranium. To this day, I have a slot in my skull you could post a letter in, and my brain feels the draught in winter.

But I scarcely felt it then. All that mattered was that Skip was safe.

Or . . . was he?

For I had forgotten about the steamroller.

But there it was, relentlessly chugging along the road at a speed in excess of 10 m.p.h., heading straight towards Skip.

'Skipper!' I called, not even particularly nervous at this point. 'Get out of the road!'

Skip merely woofed happily and stayed lying on his back where he was, wagging his tail as much as he could with axes an inch to either side of it.

'Come on, boy, get up.' As the steamroller continued to bear towards him I tried to shrug off the bricks that were pinioning my shoulders but was unable to shift them. 'Come on, Skip, stop messing.'

I frowned. Was he actually pinned there by the axes? No, only a couple had even grazed his fur. Then something about his position twitched a nerve of memory and my blood ran cold.

Of course. The circus knife-throwing act. That was why he hadn't moved a muscle when the axes fell. He had been trained to remain absolutely still when blades were hurled at him. He was staring straight above now, woofing his defiance of danger, waiting imperturbably for more axes to fall.

No more axes were coming. But slowly but surely the steamroller was.

'No, Skip! Move! It's over! Get out of the road!'

Frantically I wriggled myself trying to get free of the bricks. Surely this could not happen. Surely it would be too cruel. Surely I would not be forced to watch, trapped and helpless, as a steamroller slowly ran over my dog.

Except it wasn't a steamroller. It was eight of them, huge antique models, one behind the other, I saw now. On the front of the first was a banner saying something about an annual steamroller rally.

There was no way Skip could survive eight steamrollers running over him one after the other.

'Skip! Jesus God! Please! Get out of the road!'

I looked around desperately for help. The other drivers were dead or thereabouts, the shopkeepers who had emerged after the crash had been driven back inside when the fuel tanker exploded shortly after the axe van, demolishing half of the street. There were a couple of passers-by staggering around with axes embedded in them; they could be no use to Skip.

The steamroller drivers had naturally started to slow down as soon as they saw the crash, but there was no way they could stop their unwieldy vehicles in time. The lead driver was frantically waving at Skip to get out of the road.

'Skiiiip! Move!'

Sobbing, I frenziedly started trying to butt and bite the topmost of the restraining bricks aside so I could escape to rescue him, bruising my head and breaking my teeth, but they shifted grudgingly and by inches and I would never make it in time.

Chuff chuff chuff chuff, on the remorseless vehicles came as Skip lay there calmly. Twenty yards, ten yards, five yards . . .

Then there was a stroke of luck. The burning fuel tanker ignited a gas main. Several buildings collapsed and a huge wall of flame erupted right across the street itself, leaving a jagged boiling chasm across the road. Unable to stop themselves, the steamrollers drove into it and plunged down into the sewers one after the other.

I breathed a sigh of relief.

'You're a lucky dog, Skippy McSkippington,' I told him

shakily. By ceaseless painful jerking I at last managed to wriggle one shoulder and then an arm free and started to pick the bricks off me. There was still a certain urgency as the lorry in front was now ablaze and my car would be next. 'I shall have words to say to you when we get home, you disobedient boy.'

But when I looked round, Skip was no longer there. I could hear his excited barks and as drifting smoke clouds parted I located him. He was back on his bicycle, riding round and round in circles and yipping with glee.

Then he stopped on the other side of the street, the bike pointing nearly towards me. He put one paw on the ground and backed up across the pavement as far as he could go. His gaze was intent on something and there was a look of solemn concentration on his muzzle. What was on his mind?

Then I saw it, what he was aiming at, the thing he had spotted that had suddenly struck him as more fun even than an axe-throwing act.

A plank had fallen over the side of the burning builder's lorry and lay propped there at an angle. To a circus-dog's-eye view, it must have looked like a ramp. But that wasn't all. On the other side of the lorry was one of the few buildings still standing intact, a pet shop with a big plate-glass display window.

And in pride of place in the middle of the window was a huge fish tank. The plank leaning on the side of the burning lorry pointed straight towards it.

In a flash I could see exactly how it looked to Skip. Just like his death-defying bike-through-flames-to-land-in-a-tank-of-water act. He was going to recreate his greatest moment.

Or die trying.

Because for one thing, there was the plate-glass window.

And for another, on that plate-glass window, next to the fish tank, was a brightly coloured poster, which Skip couldn't read, saying:

LOOK – PIRANHAS!
FRESH IN TODAY
DEADLY! DEADLY!

'Noooooooooo!' I cried. 'No, Skip! Don't! Not that, oh Jesus God, please not that!'

Frantically I started to lever my way out of the bricks.

Skip was still paused solemnly straddling the bike with one paw on the ground, studying his target, estimating the necessary velocity, focusing on the moment, summoning all his reserves of courage like a warrior about to ride into battle. I saw his nostrils flare as he sniffed the wind, presumably to gauge the resistance.

I staggered out of the car just as he barked twice joyously, put his head down and started to peddle, tongue hanging out and tail wagging with glee.

'No, Skip, no!' I waved my arms. 'Stop, please, I beg you to stop!'

It was futile. Skip was just a carny-man at heart, I could never have tamed him.

He hit the ramp at a hell of a speed for such a small dog on such a small bike. Still I don't think he would have made it all the way across if the lorry hadn't exploded just at his moment of take-off. For an instant I saw him outlined against the flames. The force of the blast propelled him and the bike straight through the plate-glass window and he landed right in the fish tank with a neatly executed somersault, and then the piranhas started to gobble him.

'NOOOOOOO!'

I was already racing around the wreckage of my car to

get to him. Lacerated by falling shards of glass, I clambered through the remains of the window. All I could see in the fish tank was a red turbulence. I plunged my arms in to grab it and then screamed as the piranhas started to strip my flesh to the bone.

I lost three fingers and large chunks of flesh out of my arms and chest. Skip had been quite badly nipped here and there, and was somewhat singed by the flames and cut by the glass, but was essentially unharmed, having fought the piranhas gamely and given as good as he got, emerging from the tank with three of them clamped triumphantly between his teeth.

I collapsed on the floor with relief and joy and blood-loss, Skip in my arms woofing and licking my face.

Looking back, it would have been better if we had both been eaten by piranhas. But we were not to know that then. Conquering heroes, we merrily made our way home yelping and singing. Afterwards we referred to it as The Day Skipper Caught Some Piranhas, although the evening newspaper placards we passed all talked of DOOMSDAY FOR SMALL TOWN.

*

Far from chastising him for his rash behaviour, to celebrate his escape from the shadow of death I spent the last of my savings on steaks, sausages, and, what the hell, several big jars of caviar, which the dear creature sniffed at suspiciously at first but quickly developed quite a taste for.

Although it had all ended happily I had nevertheless had a terrible fright. From that point on I was reluctant ever to let Skipper out of my sight in case some harm should befall him. I took him everywhere with me, even to work, determined to keep him safe.

I worked, as it chanced, on a demolition site at that time. We used carefully placed dynamite to bring down old buildings. I knew the foreman would object to Skip's presence so I secretly tied him up in a condemned building I understood wasn't to be demolished for at least a week.

What harm, I thought, could possibly come to him there?

However, the foreman found him and said, 'No, are you out of your mind, bringing a dog to an unsafe place like this? Take him home again at once.'

So I took him home again and nothing happened to him.

He had seemed to have recovered well from his mishaps that day (far better than I, who, apart from losing fingers and some hearing, had developed a nervous twitch about one eye, which manifested itself as one of my face-buttocks clenching and unclenching reflexively) and his minor cuts and abrasions I treated myself. The night of our return he had been as full as vim and vigour as ever.

But a couple of days later I found him sprawling sluggish and whining on the floor. I tried to gee him out of it but he seemed in quite some distress. Delayed shock, I decided, and doubled his rations to build him up. But the symptoms persisted, grew worse. They eventually wore off but would recur at intervals. Sometimes he would be his old bouncy self for hours at a stretch, but as time went by I could no longer deny that he was often in great discomfort. As soon as I could afford it, I took him to the vet for a check-up.

We would be in and out in a few minutes, I thought, and he'd be right as rain in a week. Skipper was indestructible.

How wrong I was.

I can still remember every detail of the hateful little veterinary surgery where Skip received his sentence of death, but forgive me if I do not put them down. (Oh God! Did I have to use those words?)

The diagnosis was not good. It was the worst one possible.

'Prepare yourself for a shock,' said the vet solemnly.

Nervously I tried to laugh it off, not liking his tone. 'The bill?'

He did not smile. 'No. Your dog is dying.'

He said my dog is dying.

My own smile faltered. 'I don't understand. It isn't possible.'

My Dog.

Is Dying.

'Does Skip engage in unprotected sex, or share needles?'

'You mean . . . ?'

'Yes. Skip has doggy AIDS. There is no cure, I am afraid.'

Skip.

No Cure.

'There must be some mistake.'

'There can be no mistake.'

No Mistake.

'He's fine, look.' I went over to Skip, sprawled lethargically on a table. I tickled his tummy. He howled in pain.

My Dog is In Pain.

'There is no chance of recovery. He is in tremendous pain already and it will only get worse. He must be put out of his misery at once. If you have the money, I strongly recommend you let me do it immediately.'

No Chance.

Immediately.

Ashen and silent, I look at Skip. 'Of course, Doctor. I would be much obliged.'

It hits me:
My dog is dying.
My Dog.
Is Dying.
Going To Doggy Heaven.
And I Hold Him.
And Cry.
And Cry.
I Cry.
Like.
A.
Six-Year-Old.
Girl.
Who's Dropped Her Ice Cream.
I really, really Cry.
A lot.
As I cradle him Skip growls in pain.
And I Cry some more.
And then Skip bites a chunk out of my ear and I scream.

I recoil into the vet, who has the lethal injection ready in his hand and inadvertently shoots into it my arse.

I scream again.

My arse has turned purple and is swelling to the size of a beach ball.

I am Dying.

I pass out.

I come to on the floor to find Skip wagging his tail and licking me on the face, and the vet presenting me with the bill for the lethal injection and the antidote he has just administered.

★

After that, I could not afford to pay to have Skip put down by the vet. Nevertheless, Skip, the only creature that had ever loved me, had to die.

There was only one thing for it. I would have to kill him myself. Perhaps it was better that way.

Fortunately I still had the gun from my suicide attempt.

Heartbreakingly, all the way home he was in as high spirits as he had ever been, bouncing all over the seats and licking me as I wept.

Back in my seedy flat, I poured myself a stiff drink, fed him the last of the steak and a bowl of his favourite doggy-bits, and loaded the weapon.

Skip cocked an ear and whined enquiringly.

I turned, gun in hand, tears pouring down my cheeks. I could not face him as I did it.

'Look out of the window, Skipper,' I said, voice breaking. I pointed behind him. 'Rabbits! Rabbits! Soon you will be able to chase them all you want . . . in doggy heaven . . .'

With a joyful bark of excitement, Skip turned and hurled himself through the open window.

'SKIP!'

I rushed to the window. Three storeys below, Skip lay spread-eagled in the street.

He still seemed to be alive, barely.

As I watched, a car ran over him.

I staggered brokenly down to the street and cradled him in my arms, weeping unashamedly into his bloody fur.

'Skip . . . Skip . . . goodbye, sweet Skip . . . we will meet again one day, my friend . . .'

As I howled, Skip's tail started to wag and he licked me on the face.

Astonishingly, he was still alive, if in great pain. As I watched in disbelief he hauled himself up on unsteady legs and gave a defiant woof. One leg was injured and several ribs seemed to be broken, but he was still fighting.

I picked him up and carried him back to my flat. I made haste to close the window as he started to hobble eagerly towards it again as soon as I placed him down.

I drained my drink.

I took out the gun again and drew a bead between his big doggy eyes. 'Forgive me, Skip,' I said. 'Happy hunting, old chum.'

I remember his tail was wagging.

I still couldn't face him. Heart breaking, I turned my head away and pulled the trigger.

There was the roar of the gunshot, and then a tiny thump.

I looked back. Skip was lying on his back with all four paws neatly in the air. Keening, I threw myself across him and sobbed my heart out.

After a few moments, I heard a soft swishing noise. Then I saw. His tail was wagging upside down.

Some automatic reflex, I thought, unable to bear it. I got up. 'Skip?'

Skip rolled over and got to his feet. A bullet dropped from his mouth.

Quickly I aimed and fired again. Skip flipped over in the air and landed on his back, paws neatly in the air as before.

I bent over him and looked closely. There was a bullet clenched between his teeth.

Of course. Skip was a circus dog. He must have taken part in a dog-shooting act and been trained to catch bullets in his mouth and feign death.

It was too cruel. It seemed our agony would never end.

I wandered casually to the other side of the room, whistling to affect nonchalance, then whirled like lightning and fired three times in quick succession. Skip yelped and spun and crashed heavily to the floor.

I sighed.

Skip spat out three bullets one after the other and got to his feet looking proud.

'Good dog,' I said bleakly.

I was to be spared nothing. I held him in my arms and put my gun right against his head. I would have to blow his brains out from point-blank range.

This, reader, was the saddest moment in my dreadful life. Skip's big doggy eyes looked at me quizzically as I cocked the gun and shoved it into his one good ear. I stroked him sadly, half-blinded by tears, and softly bade him farewell.

'Goodbye, old fellow.'

I pulled the trigger and the gun went off. Blinded by grief, I had misjudged the shot. I managed to blow Skip's one remaining ear off, but the bullet merely grazed his skull and went speeding across the room to shatter a pot which had been made for me by Sally-Ann, my one true love, and which was all I had to remember her by. (Later on I stood on one of the shards in my bare feet and cut one of my toes off.)

Skip whimpered in pain for a moment and then licked my face and wagged his tail.

In a rage, I reversed the gun and started to pound on his head with the butt.

'Die, damn it, die!' I screamed.

Unfortunately there was still a bullet in the gun, which went off and shot me in the wrist.

(To this day, my hand is really floppy and it often looks like I am making a derisory limp-wristed-homosexual gesture, and I have been beaten up and arrested several times because of it. When other people see a Gay Pride rally, I suppose, they think 'Ooh, how nice, look at all the exotic costumes.' I think 'I hope they don't lynch me.')

The pain was unbelievable but I barely noticed it at the time. My one priority was to put my beloved Skip out of his pain as quickly as possible. I hurried to my tool cupboard and came back with a sledge hammer.

Perhaps fortunately, before I could get in more than a couple of glancing blows that made him shake his head dizzily, the neighbours started to pound on the door, alarmed by the sound of gunshots.

I came to my senses. I got rid of them with an excuse about the television and thought furiously.

There was only one thing for it. I would have to blow Skip up with dynamite.

'Let's ... let's go for a drive, Skip ... a trip to the country ...'

He looked blank. Remembering he was completely deaf now, I listlessly mimed rabbits, trees, a car, and he started to leap and yip excitedly in a hearing-impaired off-key way and followed me eagerly out.

'I just need to stop off at work for something,' I said casually in the car, again forgetting he was now without ears. 'Something to make our day out', my voice quavered, 'end with a bang.'

Forgive me if I do not describe that last dreary drive.

At length I found a sunny meadow, full of butterflies and rabbit holes. A good place, I thought, for a little doggy to spend eternity. I pulled up.

'Come on, Skip.'

He romped and frolicked as merrily as ever. I watched with tears pouring, unable to bear it. When I could take no more I sat with my back to a shady tree in the far corner and beckoned him.

He lay down by me panting. Stealthily, when he was quite relaxed, I attached the leash to his collar.

The leash I had already attached to a rope I had tied round the tree.

It was a long fuse I lit. If by some mischance he knew what was coming he would have time to make peace with his doggy God.

He stared curiously, tongue lolling with the fun, as I laid the hissing stick of dynamite between his front paws and patted him for the last time. He took it between his teeth and gnawed it, tail wagging, as I got up and left him.

His bark was eager as I walked off, strangulated as he tried to follow, agitated and reproachful as he realized he was tied there. I would not look back to meet his eyes.

I could hear his barking and only his barking all the way back to the car. It was only when I sat inside with tears streaming down my face that I realized my phone was also ringing.

It was the vet.

'Mr McCreary? You'll be relieved to know I made a mistake. I got the test results mixed up. Skip probably just had a tummy ache. Did some arsehole feed him a big jar of caviar? It often presents the same as doggy AIDS. Anyway, he will get well soon and probably live forever. Bye.'

'NOOOOOOOOOOOOOOOO!!!!'

Rushing, rushing, rushing across the field, screaming his name, I was too late, I must be too late, the fuse should have burned down already, Skip, Skip—

As I saw him rushing too.

He had slipped his collar. Probably he had taken part in an escapology act at the circus. He was bounding across the field towards me.

'Skip, oh Skip!' I sobbed in relief, flinging my arms out

towards him, continuing to run, no longer for the sake of a futile rescue attempt but towards a joyous reunion and—

His tail was wagging, but he wasn't barking.

He had something in his mouth, something long, thick and red, and fizzing with sparks at one end.

The stick of dynamite.

'No, Skip, no! Drop it!'

We met in the middle of the field.

When he was two yards away he leapt joyfully towards my arms, bringing me the last stick he would ever fetch me, and exploded in mid-air. I was blown backwards and showered with his body parts.

'SKIIIIIIIIIIIIIIIIIP!'

I sank to my knees in agony, his brains dripping all over my face, his charred fur welded to the second-degree burns on my arms.

His tail, caught on barbed wire a hundred yards away, tossing to and fro in the wind, looked like it was still wagging.

He will always be with me, because most of his jaw is lodged somewhere behind my seventh rib.

14

I become addicted to necrophilia

Even in an age utterly free from taboo, necrophilia is the social problem we would all prefer not to talk about. Probably only turtle-molesting is more hushed up. In popular culture it still hasn't really made the jump from arthouse films to daytime talk shows, although perhaps I should be patient in this regard.

So I am pleased now to be able to do my bit to raise awareness of this disease. You may think that you do not wish to know about other people's struggles to stop having sexual intercourse with the dead, but thankfully we live in times where nothing is swept under the carpet, and you really should not bury your head in the sand. The government may choose to avoid their responsibility to warn people of the dangers, but I will not.

In talking frankly about my battle to overcome this problem, I hope in particular to alert the parents of teenage children to the perils. Anyone who thinks their own family could never be at risk from this scourge is being dangerously smug and complacent. Ask yourself the following questions:

- Does your child ever casually say 'Just popping out for a minute' while carrying a spade?
- Do their bedrooms smell of formaldehyde?

- Do they become unnaturally alert when green women appear on *Star Trek* or other SF shows?
- Or when someone crosses their arms over their chest?
- Do you ever catch them smelling mouldy pork chops and smiling mysteriously?
- Do they get really excited during trips to the Egyptian Mummy Room in the British Museum?

If you answered 'yes' to any of these questions, then your child may have necrophiliac tendencies. It is important that you show them love rather than judging them. Get them to talk about it openly if you can. Try to take an interest and make them feel it's something they can share with the family; perhaps go on day trips to funeral parlours or cemeteries together.

For the worst part about an addiction to necrophilia is the terrible loneliness. There are almost no support groups for the problem, as it is very hard to get funding for them, even from the Lottery.

My own descent into the hell of necrophilia began, as it normally does, in a small and innocent way, with a severed hand. Specifically, the hand of Sally-Ann Larouche my first love, which I had kept in a box after it had dropped off one day, and which I had retrieved the last time I visited my parents' shack. I had kept it faithfully by me ever since, occasionally kissing it and shedding a tear. And one lonely night . . . well, you can imagine. Probably that innocuous, even romantic experiment would not have led to anything stronger if it were not for the unfortunate fact that I happened to work the night shift in a mortuary at the time.

Several times I was nearly caught. Once I remember I was sneaking a really choice young corpse back to my bedsit, when my over-inquisitive landlady caught me on the landing and I was forced to reluctantly introduce her to my new girlfriend.

'She's very quiet,' said my landlady after a while.

'Oh, she's foreign,' I explained. I had my arm lovingly draped round her shoulder so I subtly moved her jaw. *'Javol,'* I ventriloquized.

To my horror her jaw started to come away in my hand and I had to hold it in place.

'Does she have . . . a tyre-print on her face?' my landlady asked squinting puzzledly.

'Her mascara ran. Must be off.'

I resolved to be more careful. I knew the outcry I would face if I was caught. Society would not understand. I would be judged harshly and no longer invited to any funerals. But necrophilia is probably a medical condition. It might be that there is a genetic predisposition that has been inherited and may be passed on, although admittedly most necrophiliacs find it difficult to procreate in the normal way unless their spouses lie very still, and wear tags on their toes.

I vowed to give it up. But how could I? They looked so cute, so pale and serene. And they were so convenient, stashed in their metal drawers. And so lonely looking and neglected. Who would love them if I did not?

Then the thing that every necrophiliac fears happened to me: I got careless and was trapped in a body when rigor mortis set in.

I had known she was probably too fresh but she had been too lovely to resist. Now her soft yielding flesh had turned to marble. Worse, no sooner did I realize I was stuck than I heard voices in the mortuary corridor. The pathologist – or someone coming to identify the body. This would be highly embarrassing to say the least. In a panic I got down off the mortuary slab taking her with me, still firmly attached to the most intimate part of my body. Like leading a clumsy dance partner, I shuffled her off to a side door and escaped seconds before the other door opened.

I dragged her desperately through the back corridors and to an exit. En route I grabbed a white lab coat from a hanger and draped it over her nudity. If I could just make it to a bus stop. I had hooked one of her legs around me and now it was frozen like that. I smooched her as I dragged her along with me through the streets, hoping we would pass for a courting couple. Suddenly I had a brainwave. There was a late-opening department store nearby. If I could sneak in before closing we could hide in the window and pretend to be mannequins until the petrification wore off. In preparation, I took a pen from my pocket, grabbed the toe-tag dangling from the foot hooked around my waist, scribbled out her name and time of death and wrote SALE, £29. I dragged her down the high street in stages, pausing to pretend to snog her under every lamp post and then scurrying for the next when I thought it was safe, and made it to the shop, attracting quite a few stares for our apparent state of erotic abandon but not actually causing any screams. We shuffled into the shop arm in arm when the guard wasn't looking. I made for a remote corner, stood on a display stand already occupied by a couple of real mannequins, and gave a sigh of relief. It was only temporary.

'Ooh, look at those mannequins, very naughty,' a girl's voice giggled close behind. I froze into immobility.

'Ooh, look at that, though, that lovely white coat, only thirty quid, I might fancy that,' said another one. To my horror she took the coat from my paramour's rigid shoulders. 'They're terribly lifelike, aren't they?'

'Why's she got gunshot wounds in her back?' So she did, now I came to think of it, I'd forgotten about that.

'That's disgusting! I'm going to complain to someone.'

I tiptoed off as soon as their voices receded. But one of them looked back and screamed. I fled. There were many other screams. They were a narrow-minded bunch. It was hard to see where I was going with a naked dead woman solidified around my cock. I collided heavily with a guard and the three of us went crashing through a crockery display.

I hoped to keep things quiet but it somehow got in all the papers. BABOON-ARSE-FACED-MAN CAUGHT IN DEPARTMENT STORE IN DEAD WOMAN. It must have been a slow news day, I suppose.

I was arrested and sent to rehab for my necrophilia addiction. The agony of withdrawal was intense; they had to use a crowbar.

15

Onanism rehab; and a tragic accident

As I said there is little funding for necrophilia rehabilitation, and it is not yet recognized as a unique mental health problem with its own specific set of challenges. Therefore when I was sent to rehab I was committed to an institution dedicated to the relief of those with Masturbation Addiction. At first I rebelled against this and demanded to be put with my own kind, or at the very least with ordinary sex addicts, but a couple of preliminary sessions with a counsellor eventually made me realize that necrophilia was in fact a very elaborate form of onanism rather than anything that could be classed as making love, that really my cherished partners had been nothing more than a series of slightly mouldy sex dolls, no matter how good I had become at enhancing the experience by means of ventriloquism and the manipulation of marionette-strings.

★

'My name is Pullman, and I am a masturbation addict.'

It was the first group therapy session.

'I suppose I first knew I had a problem when I had to re-paint the ceiling twice in one month.' A couple of the others nodded or smirked in recognition. 'It got so I was doing it at work, which, as I was working in a sandwich factory at the time, wasn't quite the thing. I remember there was a certain kind of ham roll with mayonnaise which . . . well . . .'

'Oh, I know the ones,' said someone eagerly. The facilitator looked appalled.

'Yes. Well. Then I started doing it on the way to work. After a while no one would car-pool with me. I cut holes in all my trouser pockets for easy access. I kept forgetting and losing my change. Mind you after a while I got to like the feel of nice cold coins sliding down my genitals. You ever try that?' A couple nodded excitedly. 'It wouldn't have mattered except I'd lost my job in the factory and was working as a fruit machine engineer. I would stick it in the cash outlet and make it pay off.'

'I've been there, bro,' said a voice. 'I used to use the reject-coin dispenser in payphones.'

'Well. I lost that job too. I still couldn't stop. It got so I had to cook, drive, do everything one-handed. My habit was costing me a fortune in Kleenex. At my height I suppose I was getting through something like five boxes a day.'

'Five!' came a derisive voice. 'Is that all? I want to be on a different ward to these sophomores.'

'Be quiet, Wanger, you'll get your turn.'

Wanger was a laid-back, drawling American trust-fund kid, forever challenging the authorities and needling the facilitator.

'So my old man sent me here to make me fit into his corporate whore world,' he explained when it was his turn to speak. 'Couldn't stand me beating off in the boardroom in front of his uptight friends. Whatever. So I'm supposed to dry up now and, who knows, start having sex with some woman the way the amateurs do. Not this boy. When you prise it from my cold, dead hand.'

The facilitator noticed me shifting in my chair. 'Perhaps

you could choose your words better in front of Sunny,' he said.

'Oh, sorry, man. But, you know, so what? So he likes to fuck corpses. Why bug the guy? This is propaganda for the machine, training us to fit into industrial society. Keep it zipped, keep your head down, pick up the paycheck Friday. You'll never feel as *alive* as we do.'

I felt sorry for the therapist after a while. Sometimes everything he said would turn into a trigger phrase for Wanger and Pullman and the others.

'I've warned you about your attitude, Wanger. You're here to reform. I'm not going to treat you with kid gloves.'

'Kid gloves!' Wanger groaned lasciviously. 'Who remembers kid gloves?'

Obviously not a few of the others did. Several hands were raised urgently. 'Doctor, can I go to the bathroom a minute?' 'Me too. I have to go now.'

'No!' he snapped. 'Sit down!'

'Rubber gloves,' moaned Pullman. 'The fingers of rubber gloves.'

'Rubber!' tutted Wanger. 'You mutant. Am I the only one of the old school left? What about mink, for Christ's sake? You ever try the mink glove, doc?'

'Shut up, the pair of you. Now today I want to talk about tapering off.'

Hardwick sat up alertly. 'What's that? I never tried it with a taper. I fucked a molten candle once.'

'He's talking about the test-tube method, moron,' said Pullman. 'You stick it in a wide-bore test-tube and then insert a lighted taper to burn out the oxygen. The suction from the vacuum—'

Wanger drawled, 'Not a taper, man, a *tapir*. Furry thing with a squat snuffly nose. You put some insects on your cock and let it snuffle you off. Trust me, you'll never look back.'

Ah, my poor doomed brothers in onanism, how I miss our camaraderie. As we laughed Wanger and Pullman gave each other a high-five. Their hands stuck together and it took them a few moments to peel them apart, with a schlurping rasp.

(It pains me to record that all my friends from masturbation rehab are dead now. Pullman hung himself while practising autoerotic asphyxiation; Swifthands died of a heart-attack while doing the Balinese hand-tremble – it took them three hours to close the coffin; Hardwick crashed his car when a Wonderbra billboard and a stuck zipper distracted him; Phil did himself a mischief with a foot-pump; Wanger was shot by a nervous liquor-store cashier who thought it was a gun he was fumbling with in his pocket.)

I was surprised that quite a large number of what I might describe as white-collar wankers passed through our circle in my time there. I must name no names but there were judges, top businessmen, academics, an Archbishop of Canterbury, a noted Mayor of London and a prominent former prime minister among them. I remember the therapist saying he could always spot a masturbation addict by the use of evasive language, double-talk and jargon.

Not a few of the inmates were addicted to esoteric forms of porn.

Don had spent a fortune on internet websites dedicated to pictures of women in pantomime horse costumes.

He showed me one he'd smuggled in with him.

'Two ladies completely nude,' he said nudging me.

'I only see a horse.'

He nodded, wide-eyed and slobbering. 'They are inside a *pantomime horrrrrse costume*,' he whispered ecstatically.

The panto horse was vaguely feminine and had big fluttery eyelashes, which it was winking.

Matt's thing was gadget porn. After lights out he would sit in bed reading electronics catalogues with a flashlight. 'Ohhhh . . . a multi-compatible hand-held sandwich-grill with broadband and twin-track recording . . . a hands-free electric razor with wifi SMS capacity and seven-day programmable memory . . . a multi-head musical toothbrush that doubles as a 28 gig pen drive, built-in colonoscopy attachment . . .' He actually had a girlfriend but had made her dress as a giant MP3 player before he'd download into her.

At night we had the humiliation of being made to wear boxing gloves before going to bed. As this proved no obstacle to a couple of the better-hung inmates, and as some of the others just used to punch themselves in the groin until they felt something, often doing considerable damage, eventually this was discontinued. In its place was put a practice I thought far more inhumane, where electronic sensors were attached to the hands and groin; bringing the former too close to the latter caused an electric shock to be sent through the genitals. As a couple of the boys got to like this, this was soon replaced by the activation of an alarm bell that would bring a couple of guards running with coshes and buckets of icy water. 'Beatdown! Hands where we can see them!'

Unable to touch themselves (degradingly we were escorted to the toilets, watched vigilantly by the guards who tapped saps menacingly and growled 'Three shakes maximum') they resorted to other expedients. A long pigeon feather that could be gripped between the teeth was rented out around the ward for a few pounds a time (I shuddered and passed) until it was confiscated; a drill that was briefly smuggled in put the guards to the necessity of checking pillows, mattresses, doors, partitions, walls and tables for convenient holes; when that failed they resorted to taking it in turns to stand in front of the draught from the electric fan. Hardwick once rigged up an ingenious device of ropes and pulleys suspended from the ceiling, with one end knotted around his manhood and the other dangling in mid-air as a bellpull-type affair, enabling him to tug himself by remote control without bringing his hand to the alarm zone.

'Oh yeah . . . I should have thought of this years ago,' he murmured appreciatively, rolling his eyes, as the others begged to be given a turn next. 'The pulleys give a multiplication of force. It saves wear on the arm, the gentlest tug on the pull rope does it . . . and I mean *really* does it . . .'

'The guards! Quick!' someone cried. It was a random inspection. We turned out the lights and everyone dived into bed and made snoring noises. There was no time to hide the contraption. A guard's flashlight caught the hanging pull rope. Frowning, he tried to yank it down and Hardwick was dragged up to the ceiling screaming, hoisted by his own tool.

They would lay awake at night tormenting themselves with memories. 'Did I ever tell you I once worked on a farm with a milking machine?'

'You ever put it through a mangle?'

'Trust me. Three words: jokeshop chattering teeth. Never. Look. Back.'

To tell the truth they started to repulse me. I didn't want to end up like that. I started to work earnestly at rehabilitating myself and was eventually released.

We had a support network system in place. If you ever felt the urge to succumb to temptation you could ring your designated partner and they would try to talk you down.

'Sunny? It's Mike. I need help. The word "nipple" was in the crossword.'

'Those thoughtless bastards. Don't they know better than to tempt people like that? All right, Mike, just hold on.'

'I am holding on . . . and it's a *good* holding on . . .'

'No, no, let go.'

'I'm not . . . quite ready.'

'Come on, Mike, pull yourself together, you can beat this thing.'

'Uhhhhh . . .'

'Think of . . . think of innocent things . . . raindrops on roses, whiskers on kittens . . .'

'Sex kittens . . . raindrops on nipples . . .'

'Um. Think of, think of stern, forbidding . . . Queen Victoria, Mike. She's frowning at you disapprovingly, she's averting her eyes with disgust . . .'

'Queen Victoria! Averting her eyes from my engorged tool but deep down she wants it . . . slowly she unbuttons her sensual bombazine dress to reveal a whalebone corset cut wickedly deep to reveal the tops of her nipples . . . We do it on the map of the empire, a quarter of the globe coloured red like her nipples . . . she is a naughty ruler . . .'

'Think of your grandmother.'

'*Granny's nipples . . .*'

'Icy water, Mike. You're splashing in icy water. You're in the Arctic, sub-zero. Ice all around, you fall through a fishing hole. The Arctic Ocean! Brrr! It's cold, Mike.'

'I am fished out by an Eskimo princess in a seal-skin bikini, her nipples like arrowheads with the cold . . . My cock is a solid block of ice; her eyes widen with delight at the sight . . .'

'No, Mike . . .'

'Let me thaw it out . . . We rub noses . . . Her igloo, a polar-bear-skin rug . . . the nights last for six months . . .'

'Mike . . .'

'She takes me on a fur-covered sleigh to the North Pole and we have an orgy with Santa's elves . . . elf nipples, all magic and sparkly . . .'

'Industrial accidents, Mike. A horrendous boiler explosion in a sweatshop, awful injuries.'

'Yes, yes! I am a roving inspector for the Health and Safety . . . the voluptuous young sweatshop owner will do anything, anything to stop me closing them down . . . Forgive me not being fully dressed, sir, gets so hot down here . . . steam, steam everywhere . . . the girls work naked, sultry, pouting . . . I am surrounded by nipples . . .'

'No, no, industrial accidents, I tell you . . . dead bodies everywhere . . . uhhh . . . fresh dead . . . *bodies* . . . hurrr . . .'

'I, uh, have to go, Sunny.'

'Me too.'

That's the way it works: when you're trying to clean up your act, the world seems to go out of its way to throw temptations in your path. Once my landlady dropped dead of a heart attack right in front of me, the shameless harlot; once I was first on the scene of a terrible gas-main explosion that took out a busload of swimsuit models. I was completely unable to resist the opportunity, and had to pretend to be giving one of them CPR when other people arrived and caught me on top of her. Thinking I could at least carry off a leg or so, I stole a street-sweeper's cart and pretended to be tidying up the debris, casually grabbing whatever body parts I fancied here and there. I had enough for about five brides of Frankenstein before I was caught.

I was sent back to the institution, for a mandatory six months this time, back with the rest of the gang locked in the dingy ward with the cream-painted walls.

But then something happened which meant I would never have to worry about my rogue libido ever again.

'What you got there?' Whispers on the ward, after lights out, someone had a torch, someone else clutching a shoebox.

'A bat! I caught a bat!'

'Urgh. Get rid of the filthy thing.'

'Are you crazy? You never tried a bat in a shoebox? This is the ne plus ultra of sexual degeneracy. Dying Persian emperors used to choose to go out like this and expire in ecstasy. This is the reason Howard Hughes never left the house for thirty years. You ever wonder why bats are protected? The elite, man, they know all about the bats. Every meeting of the Illuminati, they round off the festivities with the head of the oil companies clapping the bat-box on the President's dick. That's how they keep him in line, he'd kill his own mother for it now.'

'A bat? You're disgusting.'

'The wings, man! Listen to it! They *flutter!*' Wanger was poking a hole in the side of the box. 'Oh, baby, you little rafter-grabbing bundle of delight . . . Shit.' He stopped. 'I can't do this, I got my competency hearing tomorrow, I start chasing the bat I'm going to stagger in drooling and grinning. Pullman, my friend, I make you a gift.'

'You must be joking.'

'Oh, what a waste. Pete? No, Sunny! It's Sunny's birthday tomorrow! Sunny, wake up, I got you a present.'

I stared at it dubiously.

'It's going to be a long hard six months, man. Trust me, you'll never look back.'

Impulsively, I took the bat in a shoebox from him and put it under the bedclothes.

I located the hole.

I felt a fluttering. It couldn't quite compare to a nice ripe corpse but I had to admit it was pleasant.

I had forgotten the instinctive antipathy most animals

felt towards me. I screamed as the bat sank its fangs into my tool and hung on for dear life. I ran around the ward yelling in agony as it chomped.

The guards had to sap, taser and stamp on it repeatedly to make it let go, redoubling my screams. By that time it had chewed my penis to rags. I passed out.

I came round the next day to find the doctor standing over me.

'There's good news and bad news, Sunny. The good news is you can go home tomorrow. You are cured of your sex addiction.'

'And . . . the bad news?'

He handed me what at first glance appeared to be some pallid gherkin floating in a pickle jar. 'You can carry your penis in your hand luggage.'

They had had to amputate.

16

The members of my onanism rehab group buried my tackle in the grounds of the institute with full honours. As I left the doctor gave me a reorientation pamphlet, *Living Without a Penis*, which strove to keep an upbeat and consolatory tone:

> As you no longer have to worry about ever having sex again, you are set free to explore things you have hitherto been unable to. For example, there is now nothing preventing you from taking up morris dancing or working as a claims adjuster. You can start to experiment with brightly coloured socks, and ties with cartoon characters on them.
>
> Your life goals will now be very different. Men with no penises often gravitate towards middle-management positions, where they can compensate by ordering people around and sublimate by making exciting bar charts . . .'

It gave the addresses of Penis Loss support groups. I attended one for a time, but the grief-stricken confidences of other afflicted men became too heart-rending after a while:

'I miss him most in the evenings and nights. And the mornings. The afternoons are pretty bad too.'

'I miss the way he used to wake up before me in the morning and be there to greet me.'

'Two large-breasted joggers ran past me and I thought, I wish he could have been here to see this.'

'It's like I lost my best friend and guide. There's no one to give me advice any more.'

The pamphlet suggested I use up the spare time I suddenly had on my hands by finding some nice hobby. This seemed like a good idea and I took up heavy drinking.

*

My years as a drunk could make up a book by themselves, were it not for the fact that much of that period is a blur to me now. I do have a couple of drink diaries I was given during my sporadic attempts to cut down. They do not make for very edifying reading, e.g.:

MONDAY

AMOUNT:
1 x 6 pack Special Brew
½ bottle sherry

LOCATION:
Queueing up to sign on, dole office

BENEFITS:
Felt damn good actually

DRAWBACKS:
Kissed dole officer then vomited on him

THOUGHTS:
Civil servants have no sense of humour

TUESDAY

AMOUNT:
2 bottles vodka
8 cans Special Brew

3 x bottles red wine
½ gallon cider
½ bowl punch (Tizer, Cinzano, paint stripper)

LOCATION:
Home

BENEFITS:
Felt like a god even while watching Countdown

DRAWBACKS:
Fell asleep with takeaway in oven burning down kitchen
Wet pants
Went temporarily blind

THOUGHTS:
Lay off the Cinzano

WEDNESDAY

AMOUNT:
2 btls vodka
lighter fuel chaser

LOCATION:
New job on building site

BENEFITS:
Gave me self-confidence while meeting
new workmates

DRAWBACKS:
Found self singing and tap-dancing
on scaffold pipe above sixty foot drop
while carrying hod of bricks

THOUGHTS:
Maybe should work in cabaret?

I was prone to spectacular blackouts. Once I passed out in a small pub in Truro and woke up, nude but covered in feathers, on the Machu Picchu railway in Peru with no memory of how I came to be there. Another time I popped into a hotel in central London and came to three years later to find I had been elected to the Scottish parliament. Worse, I appeared to be in the middle of a speech. I vomited violently, to rousing cheers, and fled.

I was a complete mess. Some days I didn't bother getting dressed and it reached a point where I would simply leave bottles of gin wedged between the buttocks of my baboon's-arse face all day long, tilting my head back when I wanted a drink. When I did go out it was to stagger to the off-licence or hit some seedy bar.

I was never, thank God, a violent drunk, but many times in the kinds of dives I was frequenting I would have violence thrust upon me. There's no sense in bragging about it, but I like to think I knew how to handle myself.

I pray you never end up in the kind of violent and dangerous underworld I was inhabiting at that time. But if you do, the following rules may give you some clue as to how to survive.

The first thing to know about barfights is that *it is always kill or be killed*. There are no codes of honour, no Marquis of Queensberry rules, in the lower depths. He who doesn't leave on his feet leaves on a stretcher, and your primary aim is to make sure it isn't you. No hesitation, no mercy, no weakness. Do it fast, and do it first.

Take this example. I was enjoying a quiet drink in my tavern of choice when I became aware of a *presence* at my elbow. Someone entering my personal space. The sophomore mistake to make in that situation is to turn round and look at them. Fatal, fatal error. In doing so you expose your face; you could turn round right into a fist, chain, or sledgehammer. I wasn't falling for that. I played it cool. Acting casual, I reached along the bar and picked up an empty beer bottle. I had hold of it just in time to feel the tap on my shoulder from whoever it was behind me. Quick as lightning, I slammed my elbow backwards into their face, feeling a satisfying crunch of bone, and then turned and let them have it over the head with the bottle.

Then and only then did I properly evaluate the menace: a little old woman in a black uniform, one hand clutching a collecting tin, the other holding her face, a Salvation Army cap askew on her bleeding head. She was whimpering and crumpling to her knees.

I was horrified by the sight. The alert reader with any combat experience whatsoever has already perceived the danger I was now in. Let that heavy coin-filled collecting tin connect with my temple just once and it was all over. Moreover, down on her knees she was at a level where she could have butted my bollocks or gone for my ankles. The adrenaline was pumping with the terror but I managed to keep my cool. Thinking fast, I dived sideways to put some space between me and the tin, rolled, and came up grabbing hold of a bar stool, with which I proceeded to club her across the head.

She was now sprawling full length on the floor, the deadly collecting tin fallen from her grasp. I could afford to ease off now. Right?

Wrong. You just earned two months in traction. There's nothing more dangerous than a floored opponent. I kicked her in the stomach twice, grabbed the tin, and smashed her over the ear with it. It may sound cruel, but at least I'm here to tell the tale.

Now I could pause for breath and take stock of the situation. There seemed no imminent danger from that quarter. It was time to scan the immediate environment for further threats.

And guess what? Not ten feet away there were a pair of grey-haired but whippet-lithe men in the same sinister uniform and also brandishing collecting tins, staring at me in outrage. The Salvation Army code would probably mean they would feel obliged to avenge their fallen comrade.

Two of them. Against one of me.

Unless I moved fast I was done for.

As I saw it, my options were as follows: I could die like a cornered animal.

Or I could take a running jump through the plate-glass window and make a break for it.

Yelling my defiance, I chose the second. I escaped with superficial cuts and lacerations and didn't stop running until I got home and barricaded myself in.

Two nights later, leaving another pub, I staggered incautiously into the road and was run over by a car that didn't stop, and was in hospital for a fortnight afterwards.

Of course, I cannot prove it was one of *them* that did it – and if I could, I wouldn't dare. Nevertheless I recommend this as the most important rule of bar fights: never tangle with the Salvation Army.

This was actually my low point and after that I decided I had to clean up my act. That took months, however, and I was in and out of various rehab facilities and tried numerous treatments. Eventually I was cured by a rather cruel and controversial form of aversion therapy in which a stern-faced sponsor would follow me around carrying a sack of kittens and kill one every time I had a drink. If I just had a shandy or a spritzer, he would merely break their legs. He would make me bury the dead ones in my garden and by the time there were 165 little reproachful crosses in my flower bed I decided enough was enough and successfully dried out.

*

Not much worth mentioning happened to me for the next couple of years. I had a series of relatively good jobs by my standards, and I had very few accidents and hardly got maimed at all. On the whole, looking back, it has to be chalked up as a brief period of merciful respite from my ordeals.

True, I suffered from several diseases about this time, but for the most part they were low-key, only moderately painful ones, resulting in nothing more than the loss of half a lung, a bit of my liver, and the heel of one foot between them. Perhaps the worst was my bout with Yo-Yo Bollock Disease, about which do not enquire. Suffice it to say it is extremely painful and I was unable to wear shorts for several months and used to startle the hell out of people in changing rooms.

I also endured a higher than usual incidence of animal attacks during this period. On a forest camping trip abroad I was bitten, scratched and bullied by every creature imaginable, and then beavers built a dam to divert the course of a river and swept my tent away while I slept. Driving away from there at top speed that night, I was almost lured over a cliff-edge by a team of wild cats who had stationed themselves in the road ahead of me, crouched down low one behind the other, so that their eyes reflected my headlamps in such a way as to impersonate road-surface Catseyes and give the illusion that the lane veered sharply to the right.

Worse, I was driving through a safari park one day when my car broke down and went on fire. I was forced to get out and take my chances, and almost immediately a motley variety of maddened animals came charging from every point of the compass to attack me. Fortunately, they were all so enraged with bloodlust that they started to fight each other to determine which of them should be the one to tear me apart. Lions tussled with rhinos, giraffes butted hippopotami, baboons fought leopards and a rabbit clung grimly on to the ear of an elephant. By the time the park wardens got there with rifles, all the creatures were already dead or dying in a bloody circle all around me; then the wardens started to shoot at me, and I was forced to flee into the bushes.

I think the most scary incident, however, was the time I was followed home from a zoo by a mob of penguins. At their first sight of me they proceeded to escape from their enclosure with a chilling efficiency and started to trail after me as I fled. They were eerily silent but clearly up to no good. I still wake up screaming at the memory of them slapping sinisterly down a dark alley after me. Waddle, waddle, waddle, on they relentlessly came. I took refuge in a cinema thinking they wouldn't be able to follow. However when the lights went up at the end of the adverts I saw to my horror that there were small beaked figures occupying every other seat in my row. As I watched frozen in terror the one on my left turned slowly to look at me, a world of menace in its beady eyes. Obviously my number was up. I was saved only by the merest lucky chance, namely that the film happened to be a revival of *Ice Station Zebra*. As soon as the ice floes appeared they all leaned forward intently and started to clap and make excited noises. They became completely absorbed in the film and I was able to sneak out and escape while they were intent on a fight scene between Rock Hudson and Patrick McGoohan.

Another noteworthy thing that happened to me about this time was that I was victimized by midgets. I found a whole house full of them living next door to me, and from the time I moved in they made my life hell. No one has ever taken this seriously when I have told them, but anyone who has ever been picked on by midgets will know it is nothing to jeer at.

They would peer in at my windows and then hide when I went out to remonstrate. They would lurk in my bushes and sing midget songs all night, and blow raspberries when I threw water on them. Whenever I ventured into the street they would attack me. They would stand on each other's shoulders so they had the height advantage and whack me with sticks, then quickly get down and start whistling casually whenever someone came. They look so angelic and innocent when they aren't being vicious, no one will believe anything bad of them, and if you pick them up or hit them everyone yells at you. They would climb down my chimney and run around the house getting up to mischief. They got into the cavity space and made noises in the night, and played irresponsible pranks such as switching my toothpaste with cheese spread or putting jelly in my pockets. I eventually got a ferret in to chase them out, but in retaliation they tried to run me over in a pedal-car. I had to sell the house at a loss.

On the positive side, I was almost entirely free from addictions in those years. Well, there was that strange compulsion I developed where I kept putting clothes-pegs on the end of my tongue, but that was nothing physiological, I just really, really liked it, I could have stopped at any time, it was really more of a hobby. I don't know what it was, it just made me feel good to have my tongue hanging out and a clothes-peg snugly clamped to it. Once I managed to have five clothes-pegs stuck to my tongue at once. That was ace.

It was unfortunate that I was working in a customer call centre at the time and started doing it at work.

'My washing machine is broken,' people would say.

'Thh-thh thh-thh thh-thh?' I would reply. 'Thh-thh-thh-thh, thh, thh thh thh-thh-thh thh thh-thh-thh?'

My manager remonstrated with me and eventually gave me two official verbal warnings and was consulting with his lawyers about a written one, so I thought I had better go to the doctor about it. I asked if there was a support group or free medication available for this problem, but he couldn't understand what I was saying.

'Why don't you take that clothes-peg off your tongue?' he asked.

'THHHHHHHHH!' I shrieked.

I eventually grew out of it (although I still occasionally indulge in the odd one at the end of a stressful day) but before I did I started an internet group for people who like to put clothes-pegs on their tongues, but I had no takers apart from a man who liked to put them on his ears, the freak.

Which brings me to the one arguable addiction I think I did have at that time, the internet.

My particular vice was spending hours at a time reading online diaries full of people's political opinions. But I still don't think I can be blamed for this as they were mandatory reading for anyone who wanted to engage.

'The government is shit. They are a bunch of inept tyrants who are taking our liberties away and undermining the foundations of society.'

I would nod eagerly and say, 'Thank God, tell it like it is', and then click on the links to other sites where they were saying the same. Then I would read the comments:

'Yes, I agree. We must do something about it and soon or this country is doomed.'

'Yes, we really must.'

Then I would click on the site archives and start reading them from three years ago.

'I hate the government.'

'Me too.'

'I hate them as well.'

'Something must be done quickly or we are in trouble.'

'Yes, something must be done at once.'

I felt that revolution was in the air. It was very exciting. It was like watching a powderkeg being set under the established order with a very, very, very long, slow fuse. Any year now, I thought, the people would rise up and take back control of their lives. The suspense was awful.

And then I joined networking sites. I would ask people if I could be their friend and they would say, 'Yes, you can be my friend.' I had lots of friends and a more widespread network than Blofeld off James Bond. But sometimes I wondered if they were really my friends or just a bunch of work-shy tossers killing time.

And there were articles about it in the papers. Lengthy articles, every fucking day. There were profiles explaining to us how the likes of Gandhi and Garibaldi had been reincarnated in the form of farseeing Silicon Valley businessmen who would lead us all to a new epoch of liberation. It was an exciting time to be alive. One felt part of a vast, far-reaching evolutionary upheaval – *a rewriting of the paradigms of human hardwiring*, if you will – that allowed people to say 'Hello' to other people without getting dressed or leaving the house. Bliss was it in that dawn to be alive.

And you could listen to music without putting things into other things. Because that used to wear me out, putting discs into slots.

And people got really excited about destroying copyright.

You could take all the music you wanted for free without having to pay the greedy musicians, and soon you would be able to download all the books you wanted for free without paying the grasping author or setting foot in a smelly old bookshop. Record shops were going out of business, and maybe soon bookshops and publishers and newspapers would as well, and everything would be free for everyone where they wanted it and when they wanted it and would just appear by magic.

And in the meantime the newspapers were better, because you could read columnists, but instead of them not being able to hear you swearing, you could leave a message saying, 'No, you are wrong, you are a fascist and I hate you', and hope they would read it and feel sad. It was empowering and made us all feel valued and important.

In time I somehow got bored with the internet and instead went back to putting clothes-pegs on my tongue of a night. But at one stage I had positively decided to live entirely on the internet. I took all my savings and spent them on a castle in a virtual reality world. It was a nice jolly Japanese anime land, full of pink unicorns and talking hedgehogs and friendly squirrels and elves and pixies. My avatar was a handsome wizard. But my first day after moving in all the animals attacked me and chewed my ears off, and the pixies burned down my castle and stole all my mushrooms and sold me to work in a goblin mine. I was in counselling about it for a long time.

17

I am married against my will and become a battered husband

Loneliness is a terrible thing. Deep down I knew that Sally-Ann, forever lost in hibernation, was the only woman for me. But it was hard to trudge my weary road alone. On one level I had resigned myself to it always being that way; on another there was always a stubborn spark of hope.

But as I was to discover, there are far worse things than loneliness.

It was hard to meet women, harder to approach them with a baboon's arse for a face. I had hit on a few people in various support groups and psychiatric hospitals I had been in but had only ever managed to steal a few kisses from catatonics and women who were so depressed they didn't have the strength to fend me off, and had got into trouble for that.

One day in the office where I was working my colleagues were teasingly asking me whether I had a girlfriend. Over the years I had found that the best way to deflect this sort of thing was with a noncommittal 'Shut up or I will stab you all to death', but this time they were persistent in their ragging. I had learned the hard way that faking pictures of me holding hands with supermodels could backfire in the long run so I kept my head down and endured it. Before they left off, however, one of them had suggested that if such a good catch as I was really still single I should consider a lonely hearts ad.

That night this struck me as worth a try, actually, and I placed an advert in several newspapers running as follows:

> I am a depressive office drudge, no sense of humour, slight history of necrophilia, etc. Fear of doors, pigeons, midgets, etc. I have a baboon's arse for a face, vestigial tail, several body parts missing sadly including penis. I am obsessed with the severed head of my first love but the only real joy I have known is with a dog. You: caring, sophisticated, huge knockers. Strictly non-smoking please.

I placed similar with dating agencies and settled back to sift through the applicants. However, to my surprise and disappointment there were only 117 responses, all young women forwarded by Northumberland Brides agencies, all desperate to escape from their terrible lives of degradation. I thought it would probably be wrong of me to take advantage of their plight, and besides anyone from that background would obviously be far too damaged ever to fit into normal human society. I glanced through their photographs but the harrowed looks on their faces made me shudder.

But eighteen months later, when I had quite given up hope, Bertha entered my life.

> *Can it be true? The man of my dreams? Please tell me you are still available* (she wrote). *I fear it must be a clerical error that a paragon such as yourself should still be left on the shelf after so long. Or you are some mythical perfect man invented by the agency to draw in the foolishly romantic such as I. Your picture, at least, must have been photoshopped, assembled lovingly by a connossieur of male beauty as a challenge to Michelangelo's David or a concrete answer to the question 'What Do Women Want?' If this is not the case, if this is not a waking dream, please please please let me meet you, once at least, if only to convince myself that miracles* can happen.

Her letter made it hard not to blush and harder not to smirk. I ran to a mirror, patting my face-arse-cheeks and preening complacently. I still had it. Although I had better trim the hair from my crack before we met. Her own photo showed her to be comely as well as perceptive and discerning, and she had a sweet shy smile and busters that could smother a yak. I arranged a meeting with all haste.

I was not disappointed. She came running across the cafe where we met to hug me in welcome and appeared dazzled by me. We sat and ordered and hit it off immediately: Bertha appeared inordinately fascinated by my stumbling and rusty attempts at small talk, and as for her she was charm itself. When I had relaxed somewhat we discovered we had a certain amount in common. I had lost my beloved dog, she had just buried a cat and was still grieving; we had both worked in Buenos Aires; we were both afraid of midgets. We had both spent time in therapy – I for various reasons you know of, she to overcome a slight narcissism disorder. She still occasionally attended a narcissists' support group, but, she said, found it unhelpful – she would finish bravely and lengthily baring her soul to the entire room only to find the rest of the group glancing up from their hand mirrors and innocently asking, 'Did someone say something then?'

'But I think you may be the best treatment for that,' she suddenly said. 'Now I am with you I forget how pretty I am. What an attractive brute you are,' she sighed.

'I am relieved you find me so,' I confessed. 'You . . . do not mind my . . . defects?'

She blinked in puzzlement. 'Defects?'

'For example, the fact that I have a baboon's arse for a face?'

She made a great show of taking a lorgnette from her handbag and peering through it at me. She appeared mildly surprised. 'Why, so you have. I would not have noticed if you had not reminded me. Your personality blinds one.'

'I currently have armpit fungus too,' I told her. 'You must watch out for the exploding spores if I ever raise my arms.'

A brief look of revulsion passed across her face to be replaced by a determined smile. 'I . . . I like a man who takes an interest in horticulture!' she jested gamely. 'You plainly have green fingers.'

'Oh, you noticed.' I had thought I had succeeded in keeping my hands hidden. 'My doctors tell me that will clear up when the skin sheds.'

'I . . . see.'

'Or the flesh rots off.'

Her smile stayed in place but her eyes appeared to glaze for just a second. 'Even the Taj Mahal has a single flaw, to ward off the jealousy of the gods. I myself am far from perfect and hardly worthy of a man like yourself. My busters, for example: you do not find them too intrusively big?'

'I will overlook it, as long as you do not smoke.'

'Oh no.'

'And . . .' I hesitated. 'I hate to ask . . . a very delicate question . . . the healthy bloom of your cheeks alone assures me . . . but in this day and age, it is best to be certain . . .'

'No, I do not come from Northumberland.'

'Thank God.'

'Yes.'

We both grew solemn for a moment, unconsciously linking hands for comfort, looking at the latte machine we took for granted and thinking of those less fortunate than ourselves.

Eventually Bertha roused herself and smiled brightly again.

'Well,' she said, 'shall we get married, then?'

I was flattered but somewhat taken aback. Besides now that I had found I was attractive I didn't want to be tied down and limit my playing field too soon.

'Perhaps we should ... take things slowly ... get to know each other a bit better first?' I suggested.

Disappointment, even pique, seemed to show momentarily in her face.

'Of course ... I understand ...' She turned away and lowered her eyes, muttering, 'A spinster of twenty-two, I will be left on the shelf', and burst into tears.

Alarmed, I rounded the table and put an arm round her. 'There now, dry your eyes. I would like it at least if we met each other again.'

'Oh thank you, thank you, you are so kind and generous to a poor love-crazed wretch.'

In truth, I had been bewitched by her. We made arrangements to meet again. Then as we were leaving the cafe something happened that in retrospect should possibly have been a warning sign. A waiter bumped into her, spilling a small drop of tea on her sleeve. Snarling 'Damn your hide, why don't you watch where you're going, you clumsy oaf?', she grabbed him by the neck, slammed his head repeatedly against a table, then pulled out a dog-whip from her coat and lashed his ears until they bled, cackling wildly. Then she glanced at me and pulled herself together.

'I ... have a fearful temper sometimes,' she said, biting her lip and smiling winsomely.

'I think it charmingly girlish,' I reassured her.

We dated several times. In the early stages of our courtship she was very gentle and ladylike with me. She would courteously open doors for me and show me there was nothing nasty lurking behind, and chase off pigeons that came too close. Occasionally she would threaten waiters or grab them by the testicles if she felt they weren't obsequious enough or the service wasn't up to scratch, but as someone who had always felt intimidated by serving staff this quite impressed me, and I felt obscurely flattered that she was doing it on my behalf. Or she would laugh at beggars or throw them our after-dinner mints, but I put this down to puckish high spirits. Once in a long while she would ring me in the night to say she was bored and did I want to come and help her petrol-bomb a synagogue, but I told myself that women are strange moody creatures and it was probably that time of the month.

Nevertheless after a while alarm bells started to ring. Sometimes she drank too much, which as a former addict myself made me think that perhaps we were not a good match. On such occasions she would become most unlady-like in her language and maim any waiters that came within range. A couple of times I caught her rolling her eyes or openly yawning while I was telling her about my day, although I supposed that anecdotes of photocopying mishaps or blow-by-blow accounts of the progress of rare skin diseases weren't everyone's cup of tea.

Then there was the strange incident of my present. At our first meeting she had told me how distraught she had been at the death of her cat and how cats were the things she loved best in the world. There came a day when I thought our relationship had progressed to such a point where it would not be presumptuous of me to offer her some material token of my affection. I bought an adorable little grey kitten, being careful in the pet shop to choose one that didn't hate me and wouldn't plot my death in any way, and tied a little ribbon around its neck and put it in a gift-wrapped box for her (carefully punctured with air holes, of course, something I had learned the hard way with the vole I had caught for Sally-Ann which had lain under her Christmas tree for three days). That night over dinner I humbly presented it to her.

'You shouldn't have!' she protested, but I could tell she was pleased.

'I hope you will like it. It is what you said you loved most in the world.'

She gasped. 'Tickets to a Chinese public execution?'

'No, what you love even better than that.'

Her eyes lit up. 'Diamonds!'

Eagerly she tore the wrapping off, opened the box, yanked the kitten out and impatiently tossed it aside, upended the box, shook it angrily when nothing came out, then held it up and peered into it frowningly.

'Bertha—'

She grabbed me by the lapels and shook me. 'Diamonds!'

I fished the kitten out of the won-ton soup tureen, prodded it in the chest until it spat out the liquid and started to breathe again, dried it off a bit and handed it over to her. 'This is my gift, Bertha.'

Frowning, she held it to her ear and shook it, then opened its mouth and peered down its throat. 'Diamonds?'

'The cat is the present, Bertha.'

'Oh. What a lovely thought! I shall call it . . . Diamonds.' She popped it in her handbag and smiled.

I frowned thoughtfully. 'Perhaps you should be with a man who *can* buy you diamonds.'

She took my hand and squeezed it tenderly, although not forgetting to gingerly avoid the infected green bits. 'Trust me, darling, your love will make me richer than I could ever hope to be.'

Two nights later Bertha asked permission to walk me

home. On a moonlit bridge she suddenly stopped and went down on one knee. She produced a box and flipped it open. It contained a ring, glinting effulgently in the night.

'Sunny,' she said, 'I can wait no longer. I must make you mine. Will you consent to be my husband?'

My heart fluttered like a pinioned dove as the ring winked at me. I had expected this crisis for a long time, and half longed for and half dreaded it.

And instantly, instinctively, I knew what my answer must be.

'I am sorry, Bertha, but no,' I said.

'Whaaat?' She got to her feet with a face like thunder. 'You dare spurn me?'

Faintly but resolutely I said: 'I do not love you. For all your winning ways your heart is not good. You abuse waiters and set fire to rabbis and, worse, I sometimes smell cigarette smoke on your breath in spite of what I specified in my ad. I will try to remember the kindnesses you have shown me and pray God for your redemption, but we must go our separate ways. In short, you are dumped.'

Snarling, she flung the jewellery box at me and shook her fist in my face.

'Bah! I'll humble your pride yet, my haughty stallion. Remember, you had your chance!'

With that she stormed off into the night, tapping her dog-whip against her leg.

I thought never to see her again.

However, one week afterwards I was set upon by two footpads outside my lodgings. I struggled and cried but a sap connected with my head and I fell into unconsciousness.

I came to in the back of a taxi with all the windows blacked out. We were speeding along at a furious rate, jolting over a rough road. Bertha was beside me, swigging from a hipflask and scowling. To my alarm, I saw she was attired in wedding dress and bridal veil.

'What are you doing with me? Where are we going?'

Bertha smiled nastily. 'We are going to a wedding, my dear – yours!' She tapped her flask against a groom's hat on the seat between us. I suddenly perceived I was dressed in a formal wedding suit.

'No! No, you can't!'

'I can and I am!'

Desperately I yanked at the door, but it was locked. I started to pull down the window but with a rough curse and cry of 'You damned little fool!' Bertha dragged me away and slapped me brutally across the face twice. I swooned.

I was revived by some foul liquor being forced down my throat. 'Don't try anything like that again or you'll regret it,' she snarled. I cowered away from her whimpering.

Impatiently she rapped on the driver's partition with her dog-whip. 'Faster, damn your eyes, faster!'

'Please,' I implored, 'I beg you . . . do not do this.'

'You had your chance to do it the easy way. By God, I'm going to make you regret turning me down.'

Our destination proved to be a neglected little church on a barren moor outside a small village in the middle of nowhere. It was the dead of night and storm-clouds rumbled and lightning cleft the sky.

Bertha dragged me out of the car.

'Help, help! Somebody save me!' I cried. 'Oh, won't somebody please help me?'

But the only people around were Bertha's waiting confederates, a motley band of bent-nosed thugs and sinister cut-throats in bridesmaids' dresses. They dragged me kicking and screaming into the church and up the aisle to where a clearly drunken old priest with his vestments awry peered at us owlishly.

'This is the lucky man, is it?'

I went down on my knees beseechingly. 'Please help me, kind sir, a terrible injustice is being done!'

A leering Italian bridesmaid with a gold tooth and an evil monkey on his shoulder hissed and laid a stiletto to my throat.

The priest glanced at me uncertainly. 'They all say that, you'll find it isn't so bad . . . Still it's all very irregular, this hour of the night . . . You have the licence, at least?'

Bertha briefly flashed him a dog licence at which he squinted myopically, then her henchmen handed him a pouch of gold sovereigns and a six-pack of Special Brew, at which his eyes lit up.

'Seems to be in order . . . but ought to have posted the banns . . . I really don't . . .'

Bertha snarled, 'I told you, we are eloping. His father's men are after us. Now make it quick, curse you, or I will thrash the hide off your back!'

'If the groom doesn't object . . . ?'

The Italian bridesmaid pricked me with his blade while his monkey bit my ear. I was silent save for a single wracking sob.

I only dimly remember the grotesque farce of a union that followed. The church seemed to swim around me as the shambolic proceedings lurched to a climax. I determined that nothing on earth would compel me to make the vows, but to my horror I discovered that the Italian, as well as being a knife-man and, presumably, an organ-grinder, was an accomplished ventriloquist, and at the crucial moments as the priest looked at me expectantly, a sepulchral hiss of

'*Si, Signor*' appeared to come from my lips. The final indignity was that my ring was clearly a cheap and shoddy one that couldn't have cost Bertha more than half a week's wages.

'I now pronounce you man and wife.' I collapsed with a cry and was hauled from the church more dead than alive.

Outside the wind howled.

With a gloating laugh Bertha planted a rough kiss on my arse-cheek.

'Now, my pretty, you are mine!'

*

My honeymoon night, about which I had once had so many innocent youthful fantasies, was spent in a dingy lodging house in the village. I spent the night fearfully waiting in bed with the coverlet pulled up to my nose, but my new wife preferred to spend it down in the parlour, drinking, gambling and roaring with her villainous cronies. Towards dawn I slept.

The next day I was conveyed to my new home, a run-down dwelling in Limehouse, surrounded by sinister Chinese opium dens and TV production companies. There a new life of torment began.

I was not permitted to go out to work, Bertha declaring the *Church Times* offices where I was temping were doubtless filled with whores, and was virtually a prisoner in the house. Every evening Bertha would come home and expect to find her meal on the table and the house immaculate and would shake me and box my ears if they were not.

All traces of the fine manners and ladylike behaviour with which she had wooed me had vanished. She would wander around the house in her underwear, and leave make-up and fashion magazines lying around everywhere. Despite the fact that I hated the smell and had been born with a ticklish lung she smoked openly now, not just cigarettes but cigars and occasionally pipes, and would blow the smoke at me if I complained. She would drain a bottle of beer in several chugs and then take great delight in belching in my face. The only time she ever held a door open for me now, she slammed my head in it when I was halfway through and laughed.

She was given to a morbid jealousy. Once when the Queen Mother, in her final declining years at that time, was scheduled to open a local youth centre, and desiring a change of scene I tamely suggested we go and wave at her, Bertha called me a trollop and beat me senseless for wanting to flirt with other women, and after a great deal of brooding about it later paid a visit to Clarence House and threw a brick through the window wrapped with a note warning its occupant to keep her hands off married men.

She warned me that if ever I tried to leave her she would kill me. I was severely lectured about dressing like a slut when I went to buy the groceries, and was not permitted to leave the house except in a long drab raincoat that hid my shape. She forbade me to talk to Mr Hutchinson, the househusband next door, because he looked like a fallen man and would lead me into bad ways. Several times a week she would beat me viciously, or thrash me with a dog-whip or her belt, for burning the cooking or skimping on the housework or just for seeming to look at her defiantly. I learned not to provoke her and to be humble and submissive but nothing I did ever seemed to be right. I tried to start normal conversations but she would mostly be slumped in front of the TV watching her soap operas, grunting briefly or telling me to shut my damned yap. If I ever left the toilet seat up she would drag me back to it by my ears and flush my head in the bowl. And she made me sell all my comics my head in the bowl. And she made me sell all my comics and spent the money on pointless fluffy things made out of lavender and stuff. She would put my CDs back in the wrong place on the shelf or even put the discs in the wrong cases. When I remonstrated, she set fire to my hair.

Her belongings always took priority over mine. Her most prized possession, apart from her bronze knuckledusters, was a strange silver ornament which had pride of place on the mantelpiece, a figurine of a cat with its eyes crossed and its tongue sticking out oddly.

One day I timidly asked, 'Is that a memorial to your beloved late cat?'

She roared with coarse laughter and gazed at the thing fondly. 'That', she said almost amiably, standing with one foot on the fender and tapping her pipe-ashes out on my head, 'is the apple of my eye, the only thing my old mum ever gave me and the greatest thing she could have. It is her Cat-Strangling trophy.'

'C-cat strangling?' Our own cat Diamonds pricked its ears up and hid behind my legs.

'Yers. Near two hundred of the buggers she despatched in an hour at the Bermondsey meet – and one-handed, too. See that you clean it every day and mind you don't mark it, for it is more valuable than your life.' She gave me a negligent backhand to drive the point home and strode off about her business.

Despite my attempts to stay on her good side the beatings grew more and more frequent. I realized it was nothing that I did that provoked her, rather that she enjoyed it. An unholy glint came into her eye as she put on her brass knuckles or boxing gloves or polished her favourite cosh and she would be breathing heavily and plainly aroused as she beat me bloody. I do not have the stomach to describe the attacks in lingering detail or list all the injuries I received, including many broken bones, contusions, and haemorrhages, but my editor assures me the public has a right to know, so I will send my medical reports to any reader who cares to write to me, and perhaps a copy of the honeymoon video she made showing her slamming my head against a wall until I was comatose.

She would thrash me with her dog-whip, belts and curtain rods and once fractured my arm with an iron bar. She kept various of her favourite weapons prominently on display in glass cases I was forced to clean, and a monstrous strap-on hung permanently over the fireplace as warning of the ultimate sanction in case of disobedience, and also as a conversation-piece to break the ice if the neighbours came round.

On more than one occasion she would pin me down and bludgeon me about the face with her naked breasts, which I can assure you is no fun at all. Perhaps slightly preferable to being beaten with iron bars and so on, so I would cunningly say 'Oh, no, not the breasts, anything but that' but still no laughing matter.

As time went on her drinking became progressively worse. She would stagger home drunk later and later, sometimes bringing crowds of raucous ne'er-do-wells with her, whom I would be expected to feed and wait on hand and foot, while they dirtied my clean kitchen with cock-fighting and dancing monkeys.

Knowing my aversion to them, several times she threatened to bring midgets into the house and eventually did so. As I had foreseen they completely messed up the place with their antics, climbing on the furniture, juggling and tumbling, getting into the jam and leaving sticky handprints everywhere.

I started taking care to be in bed when she returned, huddling under the covers with dread as the sounds reached me of Bertha and her friends carousing and breaking up the place. Then, when the last of them had passed out or staggered home, there came the hated sound of her unsteady footfall lurching up the stairs, the crash of the door being flung open, her weight collapsing on to the bed, her stertorous breathing in my ear and beery breath assailing my nostrils as she pawed at my flinching shoulder and thickly mumbled:

'Husband . . . not a bad little husband after all . . . not sho bad to you, really, am I? . . . Why don't you put on your . . . hic! . . . pink shatin hot pantsh and dance for me?'

So I would, but five minutes later she would be snoring brutishly.

All her money went on booze now and when I asked for some for housekeeping she would cuff me. I was reduced to the humiliating expedient of going through her pockets while she slept. But more often than not that would yield only a few stray coppers. We were behind with the rent, utilities and hire purchase and more than once I had to hide from various sets of bailiffs. I had no recourse but to pawn our belongings. However when Bertha caught me at this she would batter me furiously, saying I had brought shame on us and we would soon have all the money we needed. But when I pressed her to say how, she would angrily strike me and growl, 'Do not question me! Fetch down my strap-on!'

I suspected her scheme for betterment related to a strange visitor we sometimes had, a cadaverous lawyer whom I believed I had seen on the night of our wedding. He would turn up unexpectedly, his mordant smile sending a cold shudder through me, unerringly choosing moments when Bertha was alone and relatively sober. Even Bertha

seemed intimidated by him, and would hit the bottle hard
after he left. They shut me out of their conferences, but
once when I was fetching them refreshments I walked in as
Bertha growled, 'In my own time! In my own time, damn
it!' and then seemed to glance at me almost fearfully.

One morning when I was going through her coat pockets
I stumbled on a strange legal document, headed 'In the
matter of the legacy of Goneril Beaumont'. I wondered if
this had anything to do with the money she expected.
However, before I could peruse it she unexpectedly staggered from the bedroom and commenced to puke over the
banister, so I hastily thrust it back and fled.

There came a day when the electricity was to be cut off
for non-payment. By this point most of our belongings had
been repossessed and the house was almost completely bare
down to the stripped-pine floorboards, which were themselves taken not long after and a mangy carpet put in their
place. As I paced agitatedly about the gutted house wringing
my hands, a fearful expedient came to me. There remained
Bertha's prized silver Cat-Strangling trophy which she had
had from her mother, gleaming in lonely pride of place on
the mantelpiece just beneath the strap-on. I almost did not
dare but our need was extreme. Before I could have second
thoughts I bundled it in newspaper.

I wrapped my shawl around my head and scurried
furtively through back streets to the pawnbroker.

I got just enough for the trophy to meet our immediate
needs and buy a few groceries. How I would redeem the
pledge or what we would do next week I did not know.

I hesitated and told the man: 'I also have a fine leather
strap-on, not much used.'

'No thank you.'

The first thing now was to hide the evidence of my

crime before Bertha got home. There was only one thing for it. I sought out our cat Diamonds, tickled and stroked him to a state of untroubled ecstasy, and then hit him on the head with a mallet. Quickly I wrapped him in tinfoil and then placed him on the mantel with his limbs arranged in a fair approximation of the statuette, taking care to pull his tongue out. I could only hope that Bertha would be too inebriated to notice the substitution until I somehow had a chance to redeem the pledge.

I had barely finished when the front door banged open. I leapt away from the mantelpiece guiltily. She shouldn't even have finished work yet.

She was surly and clutching a bottle of rum but seemed relatively sober. She came in and glowered at me.

'You're home early,' I said.

She waved her bottle and growled, 'Fight at work, lost m'job, don't want to hear any complaints about it, see?'

'No, of course,' I said.

She squinted suspiciously. 'What's the matter with you? You seem . . . odd.'

'I am just delighted to have you home early for a change.' Desperately I tried to manoeuvre so that Bertha would be facing away from the mantelpiece. 'Perhaps we should make the most of it. Shall I put on my satin hot pants?'

Bertha cocked her head and made a noise in her throat. 'Why are you so deuced friendly all of a sudden?'

To my horror I suddenly saw Diamonds's silver-wrapped ear twitch. Damn it, I couldn't have hit hard enough. I grabbed Bertha by the hand and smiling falsely said, 'Come, why don't you fling me around the room the way you used to? Or try to stuff my head through the letterbox, we haven't done that since we were first married.'

'What's going on here?'

Behind her back a shudder ran through the fake silver statuette. Its limbs slid apart and then the cat fell off the mantelpiece with a yowl.

Bertha gave a start and turned. The silver cat had picked itself up and was walking unsteadily towards us.

'Mother! A sign!' Bertha's face went pale and she jumped into my arms.

However, soon the tinfoil started to unravel and the truth was evident. Bertha beat the truth out of me and then chased me round the house in a roaring rage pounding me with a mallet. I had never been so in fear of my life and really thought she would finish me this time.

'You'll pay,' she panted thickly at last. 'I'll do as he asks now.'

She stormed from the house.

I awaited her return in terror. I dreaded to think what she would be like when she finally staggered home from the pub.

However she was back within an hour and, although somewhat drunker than before, seemingly in a better mood. She carried a jug of ale from one of her villainous dives.

'Decided to forgive you,' she muttered. 'No sense in quarrelling. Man and wife got to stick together. Come, have a drink with me to show all's well.' She thrust the pitcher on me.

'I – I would rather not,' I stammered.

'Drink, damn you!' she roared, grabbing hold of me menacingly.

Hastily I opened my mouth and she poured it down my throat, not stopping until the jug was empty, cackling to herself.

'There, now, isn't that better?'

All of a sudden I felt dizzy and overcome. It was years since I had drunk and this stuff tasted vile.

'I – I am not used to the drink,' I said faintly. 'It has gone quite to my head.'

'Well, now, you go and have a nice long sleep, then, and you'll feel better in the morning.' Bertha chuckled unaccountably and rubbed her hands. 'Off you go, my poppet, I'll be up in a minute, I just have – a few things to take care of down here.'

As I mounted the stairs I heard her sniggering. It was strange, I felt very tired all of a sudden, no doubt the stresses of the day. I barely made it to the bed before collapsing.

I was wakened, I do not know how long after, by my faithful cat Diamonds licking at my face and mewing urgently. I sat bolt upright, immediately sensing something was wrong. After a second or two, I pinpointed what: the bed was on fire.

Shrieking and beating at the flames that were creeping up my legs, I leapt up and dashed for the door, only to find it barricaded by something on the other side. By shoulder-charging it I managed to jar it open a few inches only to see more flames on the other side. The whole house was ablaze.

I lurched towards the window only to collapse, overcome by the pain in my legs and the accumulating smoke.

Just as I was passing out the window was smashed and a burly firewoman stepped in from a ladder, flung me over her shoulder and carried me to safety.

*

Although during the fire Bertha had been found standing on the doorstep imploring people to save her poor husband, when I turned up on the firewoman's shoulder she screamed. She had not been subtle in her arson and was quickly arrested. By the time I left hospital she had confessed and the whole fantastic story was set out before me.

It turned out that unbeknownst to me Bertha's motives in marrying me had been mercenary all along, or perhaps a mixture of opportunism and lust, for I am sure she must have fancied me a bit. Imagine my surprise to be told that, unknown to me, I had come into a fortune!

It seemed that my foppish lorry-driver friend Tarquin had been in line to inherit a large sum of money from a great aunt of his, who had lately passed away. As he had named me his heir it had thereby devolved on me and enquiries had been put in place for my current location. However, the evil old lawyer who was in charge of the estate had found me first and plotted for Bertha (his niece) to get her hands on the fortune by marrying me before I was aware of my good luck and then to make herself my widow.

The full majesty of the law was brought to bear on Bertha, and she fainted in the dock when she was sentenced to three months' community service. After a few sessions of marriage counselling I decided our differences were irreconcilable and we parted.

In a romantic twist, upon my divorce from Bertha I married the heroic firewoman who had saved my life. However, she beat me up as well, spent most of my money at the dog-track and then ran off with a midget.

18

I make a friend. We are trapped down a mineshaft together and I am forced to eat him.

Reader, perhaps the most painful aspect of my Painful Life has been the fact that I have not had many friends to lighten my sorry load. In fact, I could count the number of True Friends I have known in my life on the fingers of one hand – even after the incident with the piranhas.

My various afflictions make befriending people difficult for me. Even before I had a baboon's arse grafted on to my face, I have never had much social confidence, and before I overcame my incontinence problem there was always the fear that I might wet myself in the middle of talking to someone. I tried to get around this by striking up genial conversations with people while up to my waist in a pool at the swimming baths, but sooner or later a tell-tale tinge to the water would alert them that something was amiss and I would find my listeners wading off in alarm. Then too there is the problem of my Fear of Doors. It is hard to become intimate with someone who pukes on you when you invite him into your house, or who enters pubs and cafes with a grimly determined running jump with a forward roll at the end of it.

On several occasions I thought I had found a friend, but invariably they turned out to be false and stole my life savings, or a kidney, or my identity, although in this last case they very quickly gave it back again. Or they wanted to put me in a travelling freak show, or they would kidnap me and take me to Buenos Aires to dance the tango again, or they were grooming me to take the fall for an assassination attempt on a major statesman – I need not go on, anyone who has spent time in big cities knows exactly the kind of phonies I mean.

One day, however, I met Gerald. He was on the steps of the library of the city where I was then living, cringing in front of the door. He was a somewhat striking figure, rather dingy and downtrodden looking in aspect, wearing an overlarge grey mackintosh that billowed about him when he moved and a large top hat. There was something slightly wrong with his nose, I saw: it only had one nostril.

'Excuse me,' he said in the morose and dolorous voice of one who has endured great suffering in his time, 'could you help a poor wretch who has known nothing but grief in his life?'

'I will if I can.'

'You are kind, sir, unlike the majority of mankind in my sorry experience.' He fetched a great sigh. 'Could you open that door for me? I . . . am afraid to.'

'Alas,' I sighed in my turn, 'I do not dare, for as a child my stepfather would place traps behind our door, javelins and crossbows and mantraps, and occasionally anvils balanced on top. But are you, too, afflicted by a Fear of Doors?'

'Among my many other afflictions, I am,' he intoned funereally.

In his youth he had worked in a Door Factory, and one day his co-workers had played a cruel trick on him, placing a great stack of doors on end in front of the toilet door when he was inside there. When he opened the door to leave, he found his way barred by another door in front of it, and when he opened that there was another one beyond it, and so on almost infinitely, until he thought he would go insane.

'What is more,' he said in his dolorous voice, 'by the time I finally escaped them, I found I needed to go back to the toilet once more, due to my premature incontinence, so I was forced to negotiate the whole regressive nightmare again.'

I gasped. 'I, too, suffer from premature incontinence!'

'So I perceive,' he said dryly, glancing significantly at some telltale stains on my trouser leg and shoes and a small puddle on the floor between us.

'Oh, forgive me,' I said, delicately shaking my leg. I thought for a moment about what he had told me. 'But to return to your ordeal: surely the doors placed in front of the toilet were not attached to walls? Why did you not simply step around them?'

He sneered. 'You make it sound so easy. The tragic fact is, I have no peripheral vision, and a rare syndrome which means it hurts to move my eyeballs. When I want to see what is to the right or the left of me, I must turn my head dramatically to look at it. It is a sore trial,' he intoned. 'Very often, as in the case of the doors, I forget and just keep going forward. I miss out on a lot of side streets.'

'You poor devil.'

'I am not looking for pity,' he sniffed. 'Not that anyone would give me any if I was,' he added gloomily.

Moved by fellow feeling, I patted him consolingly on the shoulder.

'Ouch,' he said in the same gloomy monotone. 'I have abnormally feeble bones. I believe you have just dislocated my shoulder.'

Indeed, it appeared to be hanging awry. Blushing, I helped jerk it back into place.

'Thank you,' he said, 'the agony was minimal.'

'Listen,' I said to make amends, 'I can show you a way out of your predicament with the door. Follow me.'

I led him down a back alley at the side of the library to my private entrance, a ventilation shaft whose cover I had partially unscrewed some time before. I crouched down and cupped my hands for Gerald to step on so as to boost him up into it.

'Ouch,' he said morosely as I thrust his leg upwards, 'I believe you have dislocated my trick kneecap. I will be searching for it all day now. No matter.'

I climbed up after him and we crawled along the metal tunnel into the library.

'It is the next turning on the right we want,' I called ahead to him.

But I had forgotten Gerald could only see straight ahead. He turned his head dramatically to the right to look for the exit. The metal shaft reverberated loudly as he banged his head forcefully on it.

'Ouch,' he said.

Eventually I was able to steer him on the right course.

'There will be a grille in the floor at the end of the shaft,' I told him. 'I will have to pass you my screwdriver to unscrew it.'

'There we have a problem,' intoned Gerald dismally. 'I have a terrible fear of screwdrivers. As a child my father used me as a toolbox and stowed all his implements up my arse. I was almost an adult before I discovered it was possible to sit down without feeling a dreadful stabbing pain in the fundament. I also have a Fear of Chairs.'

Fortunately, or unfortunately, depending on how you look at it, I had neglected to screw the ceiling grille up properly after leaving the library last time, and as soon as

Gerald crawled on to it it gave way beneath him, precipitating him down into the room below with a crash. There were hysterical screams from below.

I lowered myself down to find Gerald had landed on his head on a table in the middle of the library room. He gave no sign of toppling but remained there upside down with his arms by his sides, apparently balanced perfectly on his hat.

'I am not hurt,' he said, upside down.

The screams proved to come from several small children: we were in the junior room of the library. Their cries redoubled at my appearance and they pointed at my face, which, you will remember, had a baboon's arse grafted on to it.

'Hello there,' I said reassuringly, attempting to clench the buttocks into a smile. 'Do not be alarmed.'

'Are those children?' asked Gerald interestedly. 'I have a pronounced Fear of Children.'

I helped put him the right way round, dislocating his arm again in the process, but he was disinclined to come down off the table, insisting that the children would bite him.

'Make them stand in the corner,' he droned.

As soon as I approached the children they backed away screaming into a corner.

'Satisfactory,' said Gerald. 'Now, if you would be so kind as to move all the chairs back, I will venture to descend.'

I hastened to oblige. However, my new friend suddenly gave an eerie ululating cry.

'There are *books* here!' he cried, pointing at the shelves.

'It is a library,' I pointed out.

'I have a Fear of Books,' he groaned. 'My grandmother used to smash me in the face with them as a child. Kindly turn their spines to face the wall so that I at least cannot see the titles.'

I started to do so. 'Why,' I asked, 'were you loitering outside the library if you have a Fear of Books?'

'I wished to avail myself of the toilet facilities,' he said. 'Alas, it is now too late.' A puddle was trickling off the table and on to the floor. The children, I noticed, had wet themselves as well.

'Now we have probably given these children a Fear of Books too,' said Gerald lugubriously. 'So the world turns.'

It was at this point that a pair of female librarians appeared, doubtless drawn by the screams.

'Thank God you came,' said Gerald, turning his head dramatically to look at them. 'Please remove these books at once.'

'What are you doing?' shrieked a librarian.

To my surprise and alarm I saw that Gerald had his fly open and was groping deep in his trousers.

'I am searching for my kneecap,' he informed her with lofty dignity. 'It has become dislodged.'

The other librarian was pointing at my face and gasping. I cowered away shielding myself with an arm. I had only ever visited this library at night before.

'The phantom! The arse-faced Phantom of the Library! The stories are true!'

'Will you both please leave at once!' yelled the other.

They started to roughly manhandle us out. The library was open plan, so we made no demur as we were shoved through the doorless doorway into the main reading room. However, once in there, Gerald started to keen and shriek.

'Books!' he screamed, pointing. 'Books! Did you ever see so many?' He turned his head dramatically. 'They are all around me! Take them away, take them away!'

He commenced to tear his hair and jump up and down and eventually curled up in a foetal ball. Two male librarians grabbed his arms – dislodging them from their sockets to his further screams – and dragged him towards the exit, while the female pair shoved me along.

When we reached the doors Gerald's screams reached a higher pitch of intensity and I started to join in too. We resisted all efforts to push us through them and dug our heels in crying, 'No, no, not the doors!' Gerald bit his escorts on the ankles and wet himself again. Then he started to keen in a high pitch and beat himself on the head. I was sobbing uncontrollably and pleading to be allowed to leave via a window.

Eventually, however, reinforcements appeared in the form of patrons of the library and ten of them acting in concert managed to shove us out and down the steps.

'Well that was a fucking disaster,' said Gerald in his monotone voice as the terrible Doors were slammed behind us. 'Last time I enter a library.'

I dusted myself off and regarded this unusual man interestedly.

'Would you like to come for a drink?' I asked him.

'Very well,' he said sepulchrally, 'but you must sit opposite me rather than next to me. I dislike people sitting next to me due to my tunnel vision. When people sit next to me I can never be sure if they are not pulling tongues at me or smearing nasty things on my clothing. I bet they are.'

'I know a pub,' I said, 'where it is possible to enter via French windows on the garden.'

'You are a man of great resource.'

'My name is Sunny.'

'Mine is Gerald.' We shook hands. 'You have dislocated all my fingers.'

At the pub I noticed that, although he lowered himself down towards it, due to his Fear of Chairs Gerald didn't actually sit on but merely hovered a few inches above his seat.

'Isn't it uncomfortable crouching like that?'

'Incredibly,' he said firmly in his dismal voice. 'However, I always find a certain amount of physical discomfort is to be welcomed as a means of distracting me from the terrible pain of my eternal loneliness.'

'But how can you be lonely just now? You are with me.'

'Alas,' said Gerald, 'even in the midst of a crowd I would be lonely. There is that about me which sets me apart from all mankind.'

'You mean your nose? It really isn't that bad.'

'What is wrong with my nose?' said Gerald in alarm, trying to see his reflection in a glass. 'What are you talking about? My nose is lovely.'

'Yes, it is, forget I spoke,' I said hastily. Privately I was starting to think him a hypochondriac; certainly he could not begin to know the pain, affliction and loneliness I did. 'I was just at a loss to know what sets you apart from everyone. Really, you strike me as a fairly average chap, and far better off than some I could mention.'

Gerald looked me in the eyes for a long time. Then with an air of coming to a big decision, he took off his hat.

There was a foot growing out of the top of his head.

There followed a pause in the conversation as I took this in.

'You are staring at my Foot,' he said sadly.

This was true. 'Were you born like that?'

'Alas.'

'Well,' I said at length, 'really, it is not so bad; hardly

noticeable except at close quarters. Perhaps if you were to arrange your hair a different way.'

'The finest barbers in the country have laboured in vain.'

'Well, look on the bright side: it enables you to do very good headstands.' Gerald stared at me gloomily. 'Really, you know, some people have it far worse than—'

'You do not grasp the half of it,' said Gerald quickly. 'Not only do I have a foot growing out of my head, it is a Club Foot, and therefore makes me very self-conscious.'

'That is unfortunate,' I was forced to admit.

'Moreover if you look closely you will perceive it is beset with verrucas. It causes me great pain.'

'I am sorry,' I said. 'You have my sympathy. You must have suffered a great deal.'

'I have,' he said, seeming somewhat mollified.

There was a pause.

'I cannot help noticing,' he said at length, 'that you have a baboon's arse where a human face would more normally be situated.'

There was a further pause.

'It suits you,' he said. 'I find the effect rather dashing.'

'You like it?'

'Why not?'

'It has certain drawbacks. I have to prise the buttocks apart in order to eat properly.'

'Well, count your blessings. At least you are able to eat properly.'

'As it happens I have had a long struggle with eating disorders. Moreover I am allergic to crisps.'

'I am allergic to all possible foodstuffs save Pot Noodles,' Gerald came back lugubriously. 'Raw Pot Noodles at that – adding water makes them poisonous to me. The fumes alone would kill me at thirty paces. Furthermore I have a Fear of Spoons.'

'I fear most cutlery, since you mention it. My home ec teacher, Sister Sweeney Todd, used to jab forks into my eyeballs and laugh. I was raised by nuns, you know.'

'A tough upbringing, although not as tough as the one you get on a pirate ship,' he countered. 'The threat of a keelhauling soon makes you learn your tables.'

'Of course in early childhood I was reared by pigeons.'

'Pigeons!' said Gerald disdainfully. 'Proper Little Lord Fauntleroy, aren't we? For the first five years of my life I was reared by dogs. You should see my unusual method of cleaning my genitals.'

'Alas, I have no genitals.'

'I *wish* I had no genitals,' said Gerald enviously. 'I have both pathological satyriasis and a syndrome that makes erections agonizingly painful for me. Moreover a psychiatrist has established that I could only be sexually satisfied by Ann Widdecombe sitting on my face and farting. She has yet to respond to my letters.'

'My one true love is now a severed head in a fridge somewhere.'

'I am regularly forced to see my one true love on *Question Time* and wish I could be her chair.'

'I am unable to watch television as my stepfather pounded nails into my head.'

'That would be ace, to be her chair. If it was not for my fear of them I would hide myself face up in an armchair and have myself delivered to her. But I suppose she is too much of a lady to . . . sorry, where were we? Oh, nails. That hardly compares to screwdrivers up the arse.'

'I was also forced to move my paralysed mother's limbs while she pulled tricks for lepers.'

'Don't talk to me about lepers, I was gang-raped by them. Then I was gang-raped by my Victims of Leper-Rape support group. Then my Victims of Support-Group-Gang-Rape support group pimped me out to a gang of lepers, thereby completing the circle.'

'My own parents pimped me out to truckers.'

'At least you saw the world. I was kept down a well between the ages of ten and fifteen. All I ever saw of the world was a distant circle of light a hundred feet above me. I believe it accounts for my tunnel vision and the terrible crick in my neck.'

'My neck was almost wrung on more than one occasion by my own wife,' I said. 'It is hard to think of a worse betrayal.'

Gerald looked dismissive. 'Don't talk to me about betrayal. I was sexually abused by my own Siamese twin. The man who is to publish my life story assures me that is the ultimate form of betrayal yet to be discovered. Moreover when it came time to divide us he moved the boundary line shamelessly after I was anaesthetized. He has more than half of my duodenum and I only get access to the pancreas every other weekend.'

'I', I said, 'was forced to live in Northumberland.'

Gerald was silent. He turned pale and shakily took a drink.

'Yes, well,' he mumbled, somewhat abashed, 'if you're going to be obscene, obviously I can't compete . . . utmost sympathies, of course . . . Christ, in this day and age . . . kinder to kill you afterwards . . .' He shuddered like a wet dog.

In truth, reader, though no one has had as painful a life as I have, in spite of his silly competitiveness I admit Gerald ran me a close second.

I waved a hand modestly after my coup, trying not to gloat. 'Really, it could have happened to anyone.'

'Don't say that!' Gerald shuddered again. 'I would have to start going around with a suicide pill sewn into my clothing if I believed that to be true.'

'Then let us not speak of it. But what is this about your life story being published?'

'It is true,' he droned. 'A poor misbegotten creature who is forced to make a living increasing the number of Books in the world – ' he shivered – 'has offered me a large sum of money for the story of my life. It will make many people very sad,' he said with satisfaction.

'Congratulations!'

'I am not to be congratulated. It is an onerous burden. Writing is very painful for me.'

'I believe it is for all writers, or so they let on.'

'Not as painful as for me. My premature arthritis makes it agony for me even to pick up a pen.'

'Perhaps you could use a keyboard?'

He looked at me pityingly. 'As a young man, my uncle trapped my penis in his typewriter and typed a limerick on it. I cannot bear to look at the things.' He took a drink, narrowing his eyes thoughtfully. 'You know,' he said with a flicker of something like animation in his dreary voice, 'I think my publisher would be quite interested in your life, too. I believe I will introduce you to him.'

He was as good as his word. It is thanks to Gerald that the book you hold in your hands exists. (Alas, poor Gerald was destined never to finish his own life story. It would not have been as painful as mine, but would probably have been miserable enough to while away a summer afternoon or so quite rewardingly.)

'I really can't see,' I protested as Gerald ushered me into

his dingy flat two nights later, 'why he should be interested in me.'

But of course I was wrong and Gerald was right. The publisher became increasingly effusive as the evening went on. Was it just a trick of the light, or did pound signs light up in his eyes? Towards the end of the night I caught him pinching me to make sure I was real.

'Nails ... nuns ... rehab ... arseface ... Northumberland! ...' he kept muttering.

'And don't forget the Cossack rape,' put in Gerald with a hint of envy.

'How could I? None of our competitors have got their hands on a Cossack rape yet.'

Before leaving he made me an astonishing offer for an advance, whipping out a contract there and then. I fobbed him off but promised to at least think about it. I wasn't sure I wanted to drag it all up again, and despite his assurances to the contrary was sure that the lack of any literary training had to be a drawback.

I should have been excited, I suppose, by the prospect of the money. But to tell the truth, I had found the man a distraction and was glad when he left. I was much more stimulated simply to be spending time with Gerald again. Gerald seemed pleased, in his dismal way, at having successfully launched a literary protégé; I would even go so far as to say he showed signs of a muted joy. We killed another bottle of wine and compared tragedies far into the night.

He was currently working as a disease-tester for a biological warfare research facility. I miss him ringing me up in the evening to drearily report on his latest symptoms:

'I have a new blight of the feet. A toe has withered away. I think it is a more painful form of leprosy.'

'Look on the bright side. Perhaps it will spread to the foot that grows out of your head and relieve you of that.'

'You are a constant ray of sunshine,' he said disapprovingly. 'You missed your true vocation as a presenter of children's TV programmes.'

At the weekends I volunteered to act as amanuensis for his book. He would trudge up and down his grotty flat and dictate to me:

'Episode 17, A New Hope, Quickly Squashed . . . Forced to choose between having a weasel sewn up in your arsehole or sucking off a warthog, any sane person would hesitate. Yet my sadistic mother, her gun thrust in my mouth, had only given me ten seconds to make that potentially life-changing decision. It was the most disastrous birthday party I had yet had, and I was missing the comforts of the well. One by one she had shot or otherwise disposed of all the little friends I had invited round for tea, and decorated her study wall with the brains of the clown. My father, as usual, was too far out of things to curb her excesses, being too busy trying to persuade my sister to lick jam off his bollocks by promising to plug her iron lung back in if she did so . . .'

A couple of nights a week we would meet up at the pub or attend support groups together: working as a team, we were easily the most miserable people at any one we went to, and would monopolize the talk all night and take a great joy in putting down any upstart pretenders who dared to threaten our crown.

One night as we bade each other goodbye it suddenly Hit Me.

This man is my friend.

My Friend.

My Soul-Brother.

My chum.

My compadre.

My droog.

Me old mucker.

He will.

Always.

Fucking.

Be There for me.

I Cry.

We Hug.

Like Men.

We are Not Queer or Anything.

Just Mates.

We hug some more.

He Cries.

I have dislocated his Weak Shoulders.

Oops.

I am happy to say that my feeling was not unrecipro-
cated, and that Gerald himself eventually came to admit this.

'Sunny,' he said mournfully one day, 'I have something
very puzzling, almost alarming to confess. Apart from when
you are dislocating my shoulders, I find your company
strangely unpainful.'

'I think we are – friends, Gerald.'

'No good can come of it,' he said in a tone of foreboding.

Alas, he was right.

One day, a day for which I will ever reproach myself, I
suggested we make a trip into the countryside for a picnic.
Gerald protested he was not over-fond of the countryside
but eventually allowed himself to be persuaded. He warned
me he was slightly allergic to sunlight, and also stung by
rain due to a chemical imbalance in his skin. So on the first
somewhat cloudy but not too overcast day we set out.

En route, I remember, we passed the Military Testing Range where I had so nearly lost Skip. I found myself relating the story of Skip's tragic death.

Gerald sniffed.

'I once had an armadillo I was very attached to,' he droned. 'It hurled itself off the balcony of the tower block I was living in and shattered in several pieces on the concrete below. I suspect it was suffering from depression.'

'At least that was a quick death,' I said. 'Not long and drawn out like Skip's.'

'Did I say it was a quick death? By the time I reached him – which was delayed somewhat by my terrible Fear of Lifts, and indeed Steps – I was in fact forced to abseil down the stairwell – he was just giving up the ghost, his little jointed tail fluttering feebly. I believe he had repented his suicidal urge. I got there just too late to comfort him or say goodbye.'

'I have never told anyone this before, but I once gave in to a suicidal urge. It was a very painful experience.'

'I succeeded once, but was rashly brought back. I was foolishly glad of my revival, however, for I had spent the intervening hours in Hell being skewered and spitted by devils with flames playing about all three of my feet. It was agony.'

'Come now, that must have been a hallucination.'

'You are very quick to minimize other people's pain. It was real enough to me and highly agonizing. Furthermore I saw my poor little armadillo being tortured for all eternity for his sins. He had died unshriven and with the stain of self-slaughter upon his soul.'

'You talk like one of the members of the pain cult who took me in. That was an awful time in my pitiable life. I remember—'

'Did I ever tell you about the time I was jumped by a gang of Amish?' he countered quickly. 'They were armed, of course, with woodworking tools. I was sanded down viciously and then given three coats of varnish.'

At last we reached a pleasant spot and got out of the car to picnic.

'This seems ideal,' I said, clambering over the fence into a lovely empty field.

Gerald seemed hesitant to follow.

'I have a Fear of Fields,' he admitted.

'Come now, Gerald! One is never safer than in a field.' There is some almost sadistic impulse that makes generally timid people want to make a show of our relative bravery in the company of those more fearful than we. I advanced across the field boldly, whistling and swinging my arms, although keeping a sharp eye out for bulls, minefields, runaway tractors, meteorites, etc. 'I will lay the blanket, you bring the picnic hamper.'

Reluctantly Gerald complied. I got one of the wine bottles and a couple of glasses out of the basket.

'To friendship,' I toasted.

'To living dangerously.'

We clinked our glasses. Suddenly there was a subterranean rumble and the ground started to subside beneath us.

'I knew this would happen,' said Gerald with gloomy resignation as the earth gave way and we tumbled down an abandoned mineshaft.

I seemed to fall forever but really I suppose it cannot have been more than a hundred feet. Fortunately the shaft was studded with projecting pit props, beams and metal rails, off which we caromed, breaking our fall. We plummeted the last thirty feet uninterrupted, followed by a cascade of dislodged rocks, which bounced off our heads. It was very very painful.

'Gerald!' I cried as the dust settled. 'Are you all right?'

'On the contrary, I am hideously injured,' he said with relish. 'My pelvis is shattered, I have a compound fracture of the left leg, and one of my lungs appears to be protruding from a hole in my ribcage. I believe it will develop silicosis from the coal dust.'

'Well, one of my legs is broken too, in three places actually, and I think it has gangrene, and I have a fractured skull as well. At least your mutant head-foot protected you from the falling rocks.'

'Hardly. The ankle is twisted and all six toes are broken. The agony is beyond belief. Am I succeeding in keeping a note of recrimination out of my voice with regard to your role in this entirely foreseeable catastrophe?'

'No.'

'Good.'

As our eyes became accustomed to the gloom we took stock of our situation. It was not good. Daylight reached us from a hundred feet above. The bottom of the shaft was perhaps fifteen or twenty feet square. We could not hope to climb back up. I felt a draught of dank air from a narrow tunnel off to one side, the entrance of which was partially blocked with soil and debris from the collapse. I scrabbled a way through this and crawled along the dark passage, in agony from my leg, but after only ten feet it ended at an impassable cave-in. I made my painful way back to Gerald. He had propped himself up and was staring fixedly at the distant sunlight high above.

'I am used to this kind of thing, from being raised down a well,' he said. 'After the first three years or so you start to adjust somewhat.'

'Someone will rescue us. We must shout for help.'

'Shouting hurts my preternaturally sensitive eardrums,' complained Gerald.

'Nevertheless, we must venture it this once. HELLLLLP!'

'Ouch,' said Gerald.

I redoubled my cries and Gerald reluctantly and feebly joined in, but I had to admit it was hopeless. With the echo the sound might reach to the top of the shaft, but what were the chances of someone being around to hear it?

'Someone will cross the field and see the cave-in eventually,' I said.

'It could be days, or even weeks; most likely months. No one in their right mind crosses fields for the fun of the thing. You see what comes of it.'

'My car will be noticed.'

'Some rural yokel will steal it and use it to keep hens in. Then if they see us they will bury us alive to cover their tracks, and most likely sodomize us first.'

'People will miss us. We will be searched for.'

'No one has ever missed me,' said Gerald dingily. 'If anyone even notices I am gone they will probably throw a party.'

Privately I thought he was right. I expected to die there, slowly and painfully. (With the benefit of hindsight, if only I had.) But I felt obliged to try to keep Gerald's spirits up.

'Come now, things aren't so bad. Why, look – the picnic hamper!' It was battered and half buried beneath rubble but essentially intact. 'We have food, Gerald! Look, look, sandwiches, a chicken, fruit, jam, I made us a feast! We will be able to hold out here for days if necessary.'

'I suppose that is something,' he conceded grudgingly. 'Maybe things will seem better once I have eaten. Pass me a Pot Noodle, then.'

'I – ' I hesitated. 'Perhaps we had better leave it till later. We have to make it last.'

'You didn't bring me any Pot Noodles, did you?'

'I'm sorry. I forgot about your Food allergy.'

'No matter,' he said tonelessly. He lay down in the dirt and turned his face to the wall.

The first night was the worst. Actually, now I come to think of it, days and nights both became exponentially worse and worse the longer the ordeal went on, but the first one was pretty bloody bad to start with. After the agony of splinting each other's legs, and gingerly poking Gerald's lung back in, we sent another barrage of feverish yells for help reverberating up the shaft, but abandoned it after half an hour when Gerald's ears started to bleed. Guiltily, I sneaked some morsels from the picnic basket and crawled off down the blocked side tunnel to nibble them where Gerald couldn't see me. (In the days to come, I would try to force tiny tidbits on him, but his allergies were unconquerable and the merest piece of cress caused his tongue to swell and turn blue and his whole body to spasm. Eventually he was able to gain a measure of relief from his hunger by chewing on the basket itself.) All too soon the sun abandoned the remote world above us and we were plunged into tarry darkness. The sense of claustrophobia was overwhelming. We spread the picnic blanket over us in an attempt to keep out the dank, bone-chilling cold but sleep was far away. There was an uncanny silence save for a faint echo of water dripping, ghosting out of the side tunnel from somewhere in the distant ramifications of the mine. To dispel the gloom we started to reminisce loudly about our past lives, but somehow this only depressed us further.

The food from the hamper lasted a week. Our bottles had not survived the descent but on the second day there was a rainfall we were able to catch for drinking water. Gerald had anyway started drinking his own urine to recycle the nutrients, as well as nibbling bits of moss from the walls, which he found quite palatable and which he intended to use to supplement his raw Pot Noodle diet if we ever got out of there; he became quite enthusiastic about it after a while and started talking about a plan to open a chain of moss restaurants. But by that time he had started raving; his wounds were inflamed and malnutrition was taking its toll. I was not in much better condition. From time to time we sent up feeble and futile cries for help. We measured our days out in hunger, pain, fever, and querulous arguments about who had the more grievous wounds.

By the tenth day Gerald was fading fast. He spent most of his time semi-comatose and drifting in and out of delirium. I had given up hope by now, if I had ever had any to begin with. The best I could do was to make him comfortable. Once I saw the blanket had ridden up over his mouth in his tossing and turning. '. . . On my face . . . right on my face . . .' he muttered feverishly. But as I drew it down I heard him mumble, 'That's right, Ann, please, Miss Widdecombe, oh I knew you would agree one day.' Tenderly, I leaned close and blew a long flatulent raspberry in his ear. 'Ahhh, thank you,' he breathed ecstatically, a gratified smile lighting up his harrowed features.

Two days later he suddenly revived somewhat and startled me by sitting up and gripping my arm. His eyes were intent and mesmeric and riveted on mine commandingly.

'Don't let my life have been in vain, Sunny,' he said sternly.

'Alas,' I said shedding a tear, 'I think we all live in vain, my friend.'

'If I should die, you must go on . . . no matter what.' He squeezed my arm meaningly, his eyes pierced mine. 'Do you understand? You *know* what you have to do.'

I evaded his gaze. 'I . . . do not think I can.'

'You can and you must. For me. I want you to. Promise me!'

'I promise.'

He subsided again and sank into unconsciousness. Darkness fell. Sometime in the night he gave a last scream of unutterable agony. Then he was still and I heard his breathing become shallower and shallower. At last I could hear it no more.

'Rest well, Gerald,' I murmured, giving his cold numb hand a farewell squeeze. 'Your long sorrow is finally over.'

When daylight came he looked perfectly at rest. My grief and sense of loss were unbearable, so too my gnawing feeling of responsibility for his death. Worst of all, however, were my hunger pangs.

Out of respect for the dead I put off what I knew I would have to do until lunchtime. I was tempted to have a quick nibble for elevenses but sternly resisted and made do with moss.

At last the time came. Could I really do it, after all? Could I eat the corpse of my best, my only friend? *No!* cried my outraged sensibilities. *Hell yes!* enthused my rumbling stomach.

I had no choice. I consoled myself that it was what he had wanted.

During my appetite-disorder therapy I had been taught that a lot of the appeal of food is in its presentation. So I washed his face with a dab of spit on a handkerchief, did his tie up properly, wiped the dust off his lapels and combed his hair.

I reached out for the picnic basket and dragged it towards me to get a fork and carving knife and I supposed a spoon for his brains. As I did so, I dislodged some of the fallen soil and rocks and a little yellow-green sphere that had lain there unnoticed for days came rolling towards my feet.

An apple.

Silently I blessed this unexpected, almost miraculous bounty.

I opened Gerald's mouth and stuck the apple in it. He looked quite appetizing now. Finally I found the little paper crowns that had been over the legs of the roast chicken and put them over his toes.

I got out the salt and pepper and half a jar of leftover mayonnaise. I tucked a clean napkin into my collar, sharpened my knife, and remembered to say grace.

Not being very partial to dark meat, I ignored his somewhat gangrenous broken leg for now and started on the sound one.

As I swallowed my first mouthful I was suddenly stricken with a terrible guilt. This would probably be a lot of calories and I couldn't even jog to run it off. I was visited by an urge to stick my fingers down my throat to bring him up, but decided this would be disrespectful to my dead friend who, when all was said and done, was rather tasty. I cut another slice of his calf and spread it with mayonnaise.

His thigh looked rather nice too, I decided as I munched, prodding it experimentally and finding it firm and lean. I had a slice of that next.

Suddenly it hit me.

I am eating my best friend.

Eating him.

Right.

The fuck.

Up.

Scarfing him.

Down.

Like A Bowl of Ice Cream.

With Cherries on Top.

I burp.

I had half eaten his leg and was looking speculatively at his arms when Gerald suddenly sat up.

He spat the apple out of his mouth and said, 'You promise?'

I quickly swallowed the toes that were protruding half-eaten from my mouth. The salt and pepper cellars had fallen from where I had stood them on his stomach when he sat up. However I could do little about the greasy napkin in my collar or the knife and fork poised ready in my hand.

I stared at him for several long seconds. He looked at me wildly. 'You really promise?' he repeated urgently. 'You will fulfil my dream of a chain of moss and dry Pot Noodle restaurants for people who are allergic to food?'

'Yes,' I said.

He gripped my arm. 'Thank you, my friend, thank you!'

Carefully I laid my knife and fork down and said, 'Is there . . . anything else you want me to promise to do . . . in the event of your demise?'

He waved a hand, 'Oh, just make sure I get a decent civilized burial. I am a convert to the Ancient Egyptian death-religion so be sure my body is buried intact or I will be dismembered in the afterlife. But why talk about dying? Actually, I feel great.'

Indeed, I had rarely seen him so animated. He suddenly sent lusty cries of 'Help, help, help!' up the shaft.

However after a few moments his newfound strength seemed to ebb a bit and he lay back down.

He took my hand. 'There is something I want you to know ... I have never trusted anyone before. But I trust you, Sunny. I know you will always look after me.'

I stared at him silently, unable to speak.

He suddenly looked down his body and blinked. 'What happened to my leg?' he asked interestedly.

'A mouse came.' I failed to stifle a belch.

He sneezed. 'Why is there pepper all over me?'

I shook my head slowly. He examined me and took in the greasy bib, the knife and fork, and my bloated stomach.

'You utter bastard,' said Gerald reproachfully, and died.

*

Two days later a stray sheep fell down the mineshaft. I had polished off Gerald not five minutes before and was too full to even nibble it before the shepherd came and found me and arranged for my rescue.

Not a day will go past when I do not think of the horror and my guilt. Yet I write this not to mourn Gerald but to celebrate him. He was a rare spirit, who embraced all his life experiences unflinchingly and had the stoicism to trudge drearily along his way without ever once succumbing to the temptations of optimism or positivity. Of course, mine is the harder part, for I must go on without him whereas he is happily dead. But I am proud to have called him my friend and grateful to have fleetingly had one.

He will always be with me, if only in the form of subcutaneous fat.

19

More therapy and support groups

I was wracked with guilt for a long time after the death of Gerald. Sessions with a psychiatrist didn't help much and my sole visit to the only Survivors of Cannibalism Support Group I was able to find did not prove satisfactory. As most of the other members appeared to have arms or legs missing or chunks bitten out of their heads, I came to suspect that I wasn't in quite the right place and that the group was for those who had survived the relatively easy role of being the eaten, rather than the infinitely more painful one of being the eater. This was confirmed when I was asked 'What did you find the hardest part to get through?' and replied 'The kidneys' and they tried to lynch me.

I do not propose to talk more now about my agony of shame and remorse for the fact that I had been found greasy-cheeked and lip-smacking over the picked-clean skeleton of my best friend. However, this seems as good a place as any to do a brief and incomplete tour of some of my other experiences of therapy and self-help which I have not yet found space to mention.

I have spent a lot of time in therapy of one kind or another. Some of it was productive, some of it less so. I remember one psychiatrist, apparently a reputable and accomplished one, whom I consulted for a depression I was suffering from. He asked me to describe my problems and life experiences and then listened patiently with brows furrowed for over an hour as I did so. I told him everything – the nails through the head, being pimped out by my parents, the abuse by pigeons, Sally-Ann, my years lost in the sewers, the long protracted death of my little dog Skip, the sad loss of my penis, my substance dependency, the burning out of my bowels, and the baboon's-arse face transplant (which he had probably already noticed anyway, as the room was quite well lit). As I rounded off with the breeze-block that had fallen on my head just a month before, resulting in severe concussion and a temporary brain damage that meant I could only walk backwards and for two weeks had to reverse everywhere looking into a hand-mirror pointing over my shoulder (ironically cured when I sustained a second blow to the head after falling down another manhole), I noticed a look of consternation on his face.

'Well, doctor?' I said. 'Can you do anything for me?'

He steepled his fingers in front of his face and mused for a long, long time. I could see his knitted brow flickering as he considered and rejected possibilities. Then after maybe half an hour of this, his face lit up. He suddenly sprang round the desk and started to tickle me.

'Is he ticklish? Is he ticklish?' he said as his fingers worked at my ribs, a fixed manic grin on his face. 'Ooh, he's ticklish! Come on, then, give us a smile!'

Alas, he was not to know that being tickled induces epilepsy in me, as I had omitted to mention this as the narrative was long enough already. At first he thought my thrashing around was due to his tickling succeeding beyond his wildest dreams, and it was only when he noticed I was not laughing but frothing and had put a leg through a glass coffee table that he called for an ambulance.

However, I had the last laugh, for the ambulance crashed

on the way to hospital, and while I merely suffered multiple cuts and a fractured pelvis as my stretcher was flung out and through the windscreen of the car behind, the psychiatrist, who was accompanying me, was so badly concussed he was in a coma for two years. When he eventually revived I attempted to resume the therapy, but he declined.

At a somewhat earlier period of my life I had attempted to seek treatment for my ghastly Fear of Doors. My case proving an intriguing and difficult one, the first doctors I consulted having great problems even in cajoling or man-handling me through their own doors, I was referred steadily upwards through the psychiatric ranks until I was consulting very eminent figures indeed. These gave up on me, and I was then passed back down the pecking order until I ended up in the hands of quacks, or at the very least unconventional scientific researchers of little recognized standing with everything to gain if they succeeded with me and little to lose if they failed.

One of these came up with a most ingenious scheme for curing my phobia by means of positive reinforcement. Inside one room of his laboratory he secreted a treasure trove of nice things – chocolates, sweets, a big pile of money, and three beautiful scantily clad women. He opened the door to show me them – the women waved and blew kisses and pointed at the money and sweets – and then closed it again and told me that I had only to open the door and walk boldly into the room to have everything in it. (At that time I still had my penis, but unfortunately also my baboon's-arse face, but he gave me to understand that the women were ladies of easy virtue and had been well paid in the interests of science.)

Furthermore, there was to be a system of negative reinforcement to discourage me from loitering on the threshold. He bade me take my shoes and socks off and pointed to a metal pressure-plate he had installed in front of the door. Once I stood on this, he told me, I would have only two seconds to open the door and step boldly through to the other side before a time mechanism in the device would give me an electric shock.

'No dithering, no shilly-shallying, no crouching down with your hands over your head in case crossbow bolts come out. You open the door and walk through like a man, understand?'

I nodded, swallowing drily. 'Perhaps you could go first and hold it open for me?'

'No!' he snapped. 'Come on, you can do this,' he coaxed. He opened the door again; the girls waved. 'Look, look, pretty ladies, sweeties, money, you know there are only nice things beyond this door, all you have to do is go through and take them.' He shut the door and clapped me on the shoulder. 'It's time to stop crawling about in the ventilation shafts of life.' He stepped back. 'In your own time. I believe in you.'

I took deep breaths and focused. A door, only a door. People all over the world stepped through them every day with very few mishaps. True, there was that woman in Rio who broke her nose on the entrance that had been bricked up without her knowing it, or the man in Rhyl whose front door fell on top of him because kids had nicked the hinges (I had masochistically made myself a master of the lore of door-related injuries in an attempt to justify my phobia) but those were rare occurrences. You *know* there are nothing but good things behind this door. This is not your stepfather's house and you are a grown man. You can do this.

I took a half-step forward then stopped, whimpering and sweating.

No. No. No. Never.

Yes! Yes, you can and you will! Are you going to lurk on the outside all your life?

For minutes I wavered back and forth, gnawing my lip and digging my nails into the palms of my hands as I tried to summon the courage.

Only good things, I told myself, yours for the taking. What's more, you will have conquered this stupid fear that has crippled you all your life. The world will be your oyster, every room, every cupboard, every wardrobe, every Advent calendar you will at last be able to explore without fear and to your heart's content. Be a man. The world is behind that door.

Suddenly, without hesitation, I stepped on to the plate, turned the handle, opened the door and stepped boldly, eagerly, joyfully through.

Well, you have probably already guessed the ending of the story. I had lingered so long on the threshold that the whores inside had got bored of waiting. One of them started idly playing with the laboratory gas-taps, another eventually lit a cigarette, and to cut a long story short I opened the door and stepped joyfully through just in time to catch the explosion. A sheet of flame set fire to my hair and a burning whore came flying out and knocked me over, pinning me to the electro-pad which gave me a prolonged agonizing shock.

Not only was my Fear of Doors worse than ever at the end of it, but I have been unable to look at sweets, whores, or big piles of money since. (To other people, I imagine, sweets are redolent of childhood and sugar-rush; to me they evoke panic-adrenaline and the stench of charred flesh.)

I went through many travails attempting to cure or come to terms with my unfortunate Premature Incontinence. The Premature Incontinence Support Group I attended was not very helpful – there was never really the togetherness and full attention necessary for successful group therapy, indeed it was hard to ever speak your piece without being interrupted, because the members of the circle would all be shifting agitatedly in their chairs and putting their hands up for permission to leave the room every two minutes. Still I hung around for a while and gained some measure of companionship. I attended the Premature Incontinents' Annual Dance at a swank hotel, which turned into something of a disaster as no one had warned us of the large illuminated fountains that suddenly gushed into action on the terrace outside the ballroom as night fell, provoking uncontrolled imitation in all of us present.

Hypnotherapy techniques eventually allowed me to gain some level of mastery over this embarrassing ailment, but for many years inventions of the hard sciences were the most useful in helping me to cope with it – blotting-paper pants, a penile tap, and, my favourite, a handy ice-making machine worn around the groin, which turned any untoward accidents into a solid block which could be tossed into a waste-paper basket or chucked out of a window at your earliest convenience.

I also underwent hypnotherapy several times in attempts to relieve feelings of insecurity, anxiety or dread. It was not successful in this, but during one such course the doctor made a startling discovery that astonished me: I was suffering from multiple personality disorder. While I was under on his couch I suddenly started talking in a deep, merry, carefree voice and discoursing with a confidence that was completely at odds with my normal manner. Intrigued, he had a private detective follow me and confirmed his suspicions. It seemed that once a month, completely unknown to my everyday self, I would don a cape and a domino mask and roam the streets helping people in distress and strangling pigeons. I never stayed to be thanked for my efforts, leaving amazed bystanders wondering 'Who was that arse-faced man?'

This was cured but I found my bout with mental illness frightening and humiliating. (Gerald's abuse by his own Siamese twin was nothing in comparison: to be betrayed by your own self must be the *ultimate ultimate* betrayal.) May I say here how much I resent how insensitive society is to those in similar cases, thoughtlessly bandying words like 'loony' and 'nutjob' as pejoratives? Moreover, as a former sufferer of split-personality I am horribly offended when I overhear people using expressions like 'She's so two-faced' or 'I'm in two minds about it'. I hope a day will come when no one anywhere will be able to open their big fat gobs to say anything without first taking a minute to consider whether their words will cause offence to someone somewhere.

Now I come to think of it (it is hard to keep track of all the ailments I have suffered, and I have unfortunately lost the prescription scrapbook I used to have) I was also at one time diagnosed with a schizoid disorder of a slightly different type. One of my psychiatrists had noticed that I seemed under a compulsion to constantly contradict myself, often within the space of a single sentence. Upon hearing that I was at that time working in the City of Westminster, he triumphantly cried 'Aha!' and informed me that I had contracted a syndrome by the name of Janus-Schrödinger Derangement, which usually only afflicts politicians. Colloquially known within the medical profession as Bi-Polling Disorder or Fence-Straddler's Split, it manifests itself as the desire to send out two completely different signals at the same time and a morbid fear of taking a position. He showed me some examples from his casebook of the typical speech patterns of those he had treated for the affliction:

'Change and continuity.'

'In Europe but not run by Europe.'

'We must show criminals care and love, and simultaneously hunt them down with dogs.'

'We must have open borders and the benefits of mass migration, and at the same time guarantee the jobs and wages of British workers.'

'Guaranteeing our liberties within a framework of knowing who your Daddy is, bitches.'

Sufferers will often preface such statements with words like 'My position is crystal clear' but in the final stages they will start appending 'Delete as applicable'.

I suppose this was the most embarrassing and undignified illness I had ever been afflicted with, but once he had demonstrated how utterly moronic I sounded I was able to curb the tendency. However, before I eventually quit my job and escaped what I realized was the mental plague-pit of Westminster, I briefly contracted another occupational hazard of the modern politician, Tourette's Syndrome by Proxy, the condition of causing uncontrollable swearing in other people whenever you speak.

Before I move on I must mention, I hope with all due modesty, that along with the three previously undiscovered physical illnesses now bearing my name, I have also had a neurotic condition named after me: Sunny's Foreboding, which is defined in the medical books as an entirely justified paranoia.

20

I adopt a child with Asperger's AND Tourette's Syndrome.
It is a pain in the arse.

After losing Gerald I was horribly lonely. Before meeting him I had been more or less used to this, but he had shown me that human companionship, even a guarded, suspicious warmth, was both possible and desirable.

So I decided to adopt a child. As a former rhino-porn star, drug-addict, known cannibal and recovering necrophiliac I expected there would be some obstacles in the way of this. However a quick flick through the Yellow Pages provided me with the advert of a Non-Judgemental Adoption Agency which promised a child in two minutes with no questions asked, although it warned that the Drive-Through window was closed at weekends.

In the event it proved to take somewhat longer than this. Every child I was presented to screamed or cried at the sight of my baboon's-arse face, even though I had my buttock cheeks clenched into my most winning and avuncular vertical smile.

'Perhaps I had better forget it,' I sighed.

The child dispatcher looked thoughtful. 'There is . . . one child we haven't tried. But . . .'

'Yes?'

'Frankly she is a very difficult case. Not only was she abused horribly at a very young age, she was born with a cruel cocktail of mental abnormalities. I don't know if . . .'

'Nothing in my life has been easy.'

She shrugged and unlocked a soundproofed door. In a small room beyond, an angelic-looking girl with pigtails and glasses was squatting on the floor scribbling on a small toy blackboard. She glanced briefly and uninterestedly at my face as we entered then went on with what she was doing. I peeked over her shoulder and saw a chalked mass of esoteric mathematical equations and the word COCKSHAFT.

'This is Euphemia,' said the guide. 'She has both high-function autism, *and* Tourette's Syndrome. She lives in a world of intellectual abstraction and scatological profanity. Euphemia, what is the square root of 598,638?'

'773.717, you fucking cunt,' piped the girl promptly.

'You see? This gentleman is considering taking you away to live with him, Euphemia. How do you feel about that?'

'I will only fly on Qantas, twatbag.'

The carer shook her head sadly and drew me away. 'A hopeless case. It is impossible to establish an emotional relationship with her. Not only will she call you a cunt, she will not even look you in the eye as she does so. Intellectu-ally she is prodigious in a wide number of disciplines including Maths, Physics and Latin, but she has no social skills whatsoever: she thinks it is acceptable to bore people by listing all the episodes of *Doctor Who*, and will boast that she can recite the statistics of every creature in the *Dungeons and Dragons Monster Manual*. She will do it, too, if you give her half a chance – and then say "buttfuck" at the end of it. Her combination of intellectual superiority, helpless self-absorption and compulsive obscenity can be highly frustrat-ing to deal with: it is annoying to be called a fuckhead in Sanskrit, for example; if only for the time it takes you to go and look it up. Several other attempts at fostering have ended in her new parents physically attacking her and, frankly, I find it hard to blame them.'

I studied the child, going on with her scribbling completely oblivious of us. I was torn between a feeling of pity and a feeling that she would not need or welcome it. Any creature that had ever shown me any love had been taken from me. Perhaps this child that was apparently incapable of it would last longer.

'Euphemia,' I said, 'what do you think of my face?'

She studied it briefly. 'It has approximately 235,672,345 molecules in it, fuckjob,' she said.

'Do you . . . like it? Or . . . dislike it?'

The girl glanced at the woman with alarm and suspicion. 'This is one of those trick questions that normal-brained people ask and then they throw a tantrum if you say the wrong thing, isn't it, you withered old wankstain?'

'Yes.'

'Then what's the right answer, you puling ratscrote?'

'The right answer is to say "Yes, I think you have a very pleasant face" and then smile.'

'Really?' said the girl in interest and mild surprise. 'It looks like a fucking baboon's arse to me, not that I could give a flying fuck.'

'I will take this child,' I said.

'Thank the nice man, Euphemia.'

'Wrinkly gonads, I'm sure,' said Euphemia, curtseying politely.

Euphemia collected her belongings while I went through some formalities and was told more about her case. At the carer's prompting Euphemia emotionlessly went round a few fellow inmates who had gathered to watch her leave, solemnly shaking hands and bidding them fuck off.

'I will miss you after a fashion, Euphemia,' said the carer at the door, as the child prepared to walk out without looking back at her.

'Indeed?' said Euphemia, pausing, with polite interest. 'That is probably some sublimated maternal instinct. Your biological clock stopped ticking 522,334 minutes ago, whoreface.'

'Get out of here, you ungrateful little shit,' screamed the woman.

'How rude,' blinked Euphemia, shocked. 'No spunking manners whatsoever.'

Despite several attempts to draw her out she was completely silent during the ride home in the car save to suddenly say:

'I can recite the stats of any buggering creature in the AD&D Monster Manual. Can you?'

'No.'

'Fucktard.'

When we reached the house and I showed her her new room, she glanced round it briefly, said, 'Acceptable. I will take it, my good man. Please notify me when my shagging meals are ready and have a powerful electron microscope sent up at once, you piss-swigging pox-cart. Goodbye,' and promptly slammed the door shut on me.

From the start Euphemia was a baffling and at times irritating child to look after. All normal people, I believe, have an instinctive revulsion for the Autistic, with their icy self-sufficiency and reluctance to hug. It is like having a little Clifton Webb or Gore Vidal in your house. Anyone who has ever cared for or inadvertently given birth to an Asperger's child will be familiar with feelings of hurt and rejection and an overpowering urge to shake them until their teeth rattle and yell, 'LOVE ME, you little bastard!' Beyond this there is the ever-present suspicion that the emotionless little creeps with their uncanny mental superpowers are some evil mutant race plotting to make humans redundant, who communicate with each other in the night by rattling their branches against their stems like Triffids. I cannot be the only Asperger's parent whose biggest challenge was fighting the compulsion to kill their child with a rake.

And yet at other times she could be a delight, and enabled me to see things afresh, like any child only more so. Due to her syndrome there was much of the untainted innocent about her. Indeed I believe Tourette's should be regarded not so much as an affliction as a new and original way of looking at the world. I remember one morning she came down looking thoughtful and said to me:

'The neighbour's dog didn't fucking bark in the night. It was probably sucking its own cock.'

Whenever she was forced to venture outside her comfort zone she had recourse to little private rituals to reassure herself, such as yelling 'Stiff throbbing grunt-levers' repeatedly like a mantra, something that was a little disconcerting the first time I took her to church with me.

Her autism complicated things further, contributing all manner of unpredictable quirks and foibles. She had an inexplicable aversion to the colour orange, something which came in handy when disciplining her. When she behaved badly I would roll oranges towards her while she stood there wide-eyed and paralysed with horror, or chase her round the house holding a paint catalogue opened to a page of various different shades of the colour until she collapsed screaming in hysteria. And she would only buy underwear from Aldi or Lidl, which was just bloody embarrassing in case she ever got run over.

Of course there were ways in which she made herself

useful. With an autistic savant child, one doesn't need to keep a phone book or calculator or diary or A to Z, or atlas or almanac or set of logarithmic tables or *Monster Manual* or episode guide for *Dr Who* or *Star Trek*; and she proved a dab-hand at picking out five-horse accumulators and playing the stock market. I was able to buy the house I had been renting and for the first time in my life became financially secure. I overreached myself, however, when, after we had cleaned up on all the pub quiz machines in the area, I got the idea of going on a national TV quiz show with a huge cash prize, with Euphemia nominated as the friend to be phoned for help in case of a difficult question. This backfired somewhat when, somehow reaching the quarter of a million pound mark unaided, I was stumped on a particularly tricky question of geometry; when the host called her and introduced himself, she snapped 'I happen to be busy, you utter cunt' and slammed the phone down.

Schooling was a problem. While Tourette's sufferers are not as feared and hated as they were in less enlightened times, and may be permitted to find employment as comedians, DJs, and Scottish writers, the condition is still too little understood and not very well catered for in some areas. The government policy of inclusion meant there was no special schooling available for Euphemia and she was put in a normal class with ordinary children, where she would sit saying 'Cunt' and 'Fuck' and reciting her favourite venereal diseases to her heart's content, with the teacher unable to stop her. Of course, many of the other children were doing pretty much the same anyway, and due to inclusion the class also contained a catatonic, a manic, a paranoid schizophrenic, a pathological masturbator, a heroin addict, a drug-gang enforcer and a convicted rapist. The teacher herself had gone mad some time ago and, having bribed a child with

Munchausen's syndrome to fill in the teaching plans and class-progress reports, sat quietly in a corner rocking back and forth and humming tonelessly.

As Euphemia had memorized the *Encyclopaedia Britannica* at the age of seven anyway, I decided to keep her away and home-school. We set up her little blackboard and a desk in the front room and she would spend every morning lecturing me. I finally started to make up some of the gaps in my education; although at times I learned a little more than I wanted to know. More than once I was rapped on the knuckles with a ruler for not being able to recite the list of actors having played companions in *Dr Who*; worse, she would then proceed to do so:

'. . . Billie Bastard Piper and Freema Frigging Agaya,' she would conclude smugly with a triumphant wiggle of her mortarboard. 'Now. I will give you a chance to redeem yourself, you ignorant fucker. Please point out all the known continuity errors in the *Doctor Who* backstory and suggest possible resolutions – for today we will limit ourselves to only treating the TV series as canon, as jejune as that may titting well be.'

'I haven't got a bollocks and nor could I give a fuck.' She was having a terrible effect on my own language.

'This is important, fuck it!' She threw chalk at my head. She sighed martyredly. 'Very well, obviously I will have to do it. 1963, series one . . .'

'For the love of God, stop!'

'1963, series shagging one . . .' she repeated more loudly.

'What about series seventeen? Where he is menaced by the colour orange?'

She put her hands over her ears and said, 'Aiiieeee!'

'Really, stop, this isn't acceptable, no one sane cares.'

'Fudge-sucker! You're just jealous because you don't know.'

'Tell me something that matters. History! Let's do the Second World War.'

'Very well, frig it. Um. How many people died in the Holocaust?'

'Six million.'

'Bastard well done that pupil! Now, name them.'

'Euphemia!'

'I can, alphabetically! Listen: Aaronovitch, Aaron Cunt-face. Aaronovitch, Abraham Dogbollocks . . .'

'No, no, no . . .'

When it came to maths and swearing she was sadly forced to conclude I was a sub-normal moron and beyond rehabilitation. She finally despaired of teaching me the first million prime numbers or all the conjugates of the word fuck. In the afternoons we would pursue our own studies. I was beginning to start work fumblingly on my memoirs at the behest of the publisher Gerald had introduced me to. I had bought Euphemia various pieces of scientific equipment she had asked for and she spent most of her days childishly attempting to create rifts in the space–time continuum. In her spare time she was also trying to design the most awful swearword ever, prototypes of which she would try out on me.

As time went on I thought our relationship improved; I grew fond of her and she sometimes remembered to walk round me instead of pushing me aside when I was in her way. Nevertheless she continued to be a trial and exasperation in many ways and at times I doubted could ever properly get through to her.

The most painful thing about Euphemia was the things

she simply didn't get. In particular, she didn't get the stories I would tell her about my awful life.

One day, in an effort to bring us closer and encourage her to open up about her own experiences, I told her about the time I was forced to eat Gerald.

If I did not quite get the reaction I expected, I at least succeeded in getting her attention.

'What did he taste like?' she asked interestedly. 'Cunt,' she added as an afterthought.

'That's not the point!'

'Then what, pray, is the point, my dear rimjob?'

'You're supposed to feel sad!'

'You are looking for sympathy, arsewipe?'

'I . . .' I frowned uncertainly. 'No . . . I just expected . . .'

'By all means take it, fuckpig. I hereby offer my heartiest condolences on the fact that you guzzled your best friend. Satisfied?' She went back to the miniature cyclotron she was assembling.

'That was not sincere, you heartless little cow!'

'You wish me to cry, you absolute nippleclamp?'

'I . . .'

'You want me to share your pain, you abysmal cock-splash? You want me to feel bad?'

'I want you to feel something!' I paced angrily. 'You can be very difficult to get along with at times, you know.'

'*Tu quoque*, you fucking shitsticker.'

'You really don't care? You really don't care that I ate my friend? It means nothing to you?'

'It is of some minor interest, admittedly, and I have stowed the information away in case it ever becomes useful: I will certainly never venture down a mine with you, dildo that you are. However, I cannot understand why you wish me to have an emotional reaction to it. I was not present: I did not know the man: your diet is none of my cuntlicking business.'

I was exasperated.

'If *I* died, would you even notice?'

'Certainly. It would be much quieter for one thing, you shit-sniffing grannybanger.'

'Would you feel sad? Would you miss me?'

She considered. 'I would miss the food,' she said judiciously. 'Nob-gob.'

'What would you do?'

'Put you in a bin-bag and go to the fucking chip shop, I imagine. Arsehole.'

'Euphemia!'

'I don't do affection. I do swearing and higher mathematics. If you wanted showy displays of affection, you utter shitterblister, you should have bought a pet.'

'I had a pet! I had a little dog that loved me! I gave it dynamite and it blew up in my face!'

'How fucking thoughtless of you. I hope you take better care of me.'

'Euphemia!'

'What? What?' I had succeeded at least in making her as exasperated as I was. She flung her microlaser down in irritation. 'God, you give me a pain in the cunt. Why are you so put out, you drippy nob-end? What do you want me to say? What am I supposed to say to your story? Why did you tell it to me? What was the point of it? I really don't understand why you told me.' She suddenly grabbed an upturned beaker and gave a shriek. 'Now look what you've done! My nanobots have escaped all over the carpet and I can't see the little bleeders. It would serve you right if they colonize you and turn you into a ruthless cyborg whining machine.'

'Perhaps I thought I would feel better if I told you!'

She regarded me curiously. 'And do you? It does not appear so, palmfucker.'

'No! I want to beat you to death with a poker!'

'Interesting. And eat me?'

I sighed. 'You weren't moved? You don't see any . . . pathos?'

'The narrative was completely shapeless, you bastard sweatpig. Experience must be redeemed by art. I have no idea why you rebuke me for reciting the episodes of *Doctor Who* socially and then bombard me with anecdotes that are merely droning lists of things that happen to have happened.'

'But I ate my one-time friend!'

'A staple of any zombie movie, beaver-features. Sensationalistic but trite. For true cathartic pity and terror the downfall should come as an inevitable operation of the hero's fatal flaw. A mineshaft accident is not tragic.'

'But . . . he was my friend, and I was forced to eat him!'

'That isn't even ironic, merely unfortunate.' She adjusted her spectacles and added, 'Cockspring.'

'Perhaps I thought you would be inspired and uplifted that I had conquered and overcome it.'

She pursed her lips. 'You endured it, certainly, shitehawk, but conquered? If you had contrived a way out of the mineshaft, yes, but to be utterly powerless like that is just dismal . . . I confess I do not see a lesson unless it is that, as teenage fatalists' T-shirts have it, "shit happens". And as for overcoming it . . . have you really, if you feel the need to harp on about it?'

This time I actually did brandish the poker at her. She regarded me with equanimity. I dimly remembered the care-home woman cautioning me that all five of her previous fosterers had made attempts on her life.

I put the poker down and she went back to her gadget.

'Did you look at him and see a big fuck-off roast chicken?' she asked absently.

'Shut up.'

'Which part did you eat first?'

'I'm not telling you.'

'Did you eat his willy?'

I tried once more to try to explain it to her.

'Euphemia . . . when people trust and feel close to a person . . . when that person is important to them, as you are to me . . . they sometimes like to share private things with them . . . as a way of getting it off their chest . . . not feeling so alone . . . it can feel good to share things.'

'Indeed?' She looked thoughtful. 'Then, my esteemed foster-fuckwit, I am glad not to have stuck my fingers in my ears while you made me the receptacle of your woes, and I hope it has been therapeutic for you.'

She seemed to mean well. 'I . . . thank you, I think.'

'And I would rather the mineshaft incident hadn't happened to you, as utterly frigging futile as that is.'

I nodded. She bowed gravely then went back to tinkering with her machine.

'Euphemia.' I sat near her and spoke gently. 'Would you like to tell me about what your real father did to you?'

'No,' she said absently.

'I would like it if you did,' I pressed.

'Why? Will it arouse you?' she asked interestedly.

'No!'

'Then why the morbid interest, wankshaft?'

'I just thought . . . you might feel better.'

'I shouldn't think so, me old cockwad.'

'It isn't healthy to repress these things.'

'It isn't healthy to brood, nun-muncher, and I prefer to keep private things private.'

'You can't just forget it happened.'

'*Eheu fugaces*, fuckface, I forget nothing I have ever seen, but some things I refuse to dwell on. Onward and upward.'

'But don't you see, unless you confront it you will remain frozen! Perhaps your condition is not genetic but a result of your experiences.'

'Tourette's is not an illness, you bigoted cuntlapper, it is a culture in its own right.'

'I meant—'

'Don't you see, you bollock-sniffing bishop-basher, that I refuse to define myself in terms of a trivial little phenomenon such as being molested by my father? It is not something that I chose but a random contingency that chanced to happen to me and is therefore not a part of who I am. It is something accidental and incidental, such as your being trapped in a mineshaft. If he had died before I was born it would never have happened at all. I do not wish to talk about it, I do not wish to relive it, I do not intend to parade around in a T-shirt printed with "I was raped by my father". Now do me a favour and fuck off and take a running jump at a sweaty buffalo's cock.'

I said, 'I always thought Tourette's was a compulsive verbal tic rather than a fluent outpouring of casual but well-crafted abuse.'

She looked shifty. 'It can be. Fuckshaft.'

Then, one day, just as I was despairing of ever establishing an emotional rapport with her, there was an unexpected breakthrough.

She was working at her chalkboard amusing herself with equations and simultaneously boring me shitless by naming all the counties in England in order of population and reciting some of their principal features: '. . . Cumbria, population 496,223, noted for lakes, pencils, big fuck-off mountains . . . Shropshire, population 494,196, salient features, shrops . . . N-n-Northumberland, population 309,948, noted for prevalence of uncouth agricultural types, menacing walls, horrible absence of latte machines . . . Herefordshire . . .'

Casually I mentioned, 'I was once forced to live in Northumberland.'

Euphemia froze. Her chalk snapped in two. She put it down and came unsteadily over to me. A single tear rolled down her cheek.

'That must have been a cunt,' she whispered huskily, and gave me a hug.

21

Euphemia and I go on television. It ends badly.

In fact, for a while I feared my shocking revelation had had too devastating an effect on Euphemia.

The next day I found her slumped at a table with her head on her arms, morose and broken.

'I can't go on. How can anyone go on living in a world where that can happen to people?' She suddenly flung her arms around me. 'Say it won't happen to me! Say it won't happen to me! Say I won't have to live in Northumberland!'

'Oh Euphemia,' I said sadly, 'there are no guarantees. We just have to be brave and hope we are lucky. But I swear that for as long as I live I will do my utmost to prevent it.'

'Don't ever die! Don't ever die, Daddy!' She sobbed her heart out. 'I dreamed that you died and they took me to Northumberland!'

Every time we got in a car she would whimper, 'Are you taking me to Northumberland? Have I been bad? Oh, Daddy, I promise I'll be good now!' Whenever I turned the car in a northerly direction she screamed, 'No, no, not north! Never go north!' and started to claw frantically at my eyes and wrench at the wheel to try to steer us into the oncoming traffic.

She had problems sleeping, even with the light on. She would lie in bed clutching the covers up to her face, only her terrified eyes visible.

'Northumberland!' she croaked. 'Northumberland is hiding in my wardrobe!'

For some time she became feverish and bedridden. Once when I was putting ice on her burning brow she clutched my wrist with a grip like iron and instructed me to rip 'That Place' out of all her encyclopaedias and atlases.

However a few days later she seemed to be over it.

'Nil desperandum, fuckpig, I am sure even ... The County That Shall Not Be Named has its place in the great scheme of things. Perhaps all the inhabitants of that place were awful in a previous life; although they are undoubtedly more fucking awful in this one.'

Still, it had been a breakthrough in our relationship. For a while she went out of her way to be considerate and tender towards me, as one might be towards an invalid, fetching my slippers and bringing me cups of tea and rushing to help with the household chores. This eventually wore off, and we frequently returned to the old bickering, friction and mutual tantrums, but she was never quite as heartless as before. For my birthday not long after, she gave me a touching little present she had made herself out of household odds and ends, a hand-held device for inducing epilepsy in pigeons. We had a merry old time strolling through the park together watching them spasm and froth.

At this time I had signed a definite contract for my memoirs and was slowly starting to work on them. My editor was keen, even desperate, to sign Euphemia for a book too, especially after, in the interests of understanding her better, I had obtained from the files of her former carers and psychiatrists copies of the pornographic films and pictures her father had made of her as a small child, and showed them to him. The pictures alone, he was sure, could form the basis of a glossy coffee-table book.

I tried to sell her on writing her life story but she was highly conflicted.

'Go and fuck yourself with a moose-head,' she replied absently, not looking up from the gadgets she was tinkering with.

'The equipment for your scientific researches is very costly,' I pressed. 'Santa informs me he can't afford the particle accelerator you asked for for Christmas.'

'That fat cunt. To hell with him then, I shall build my own and never correspond with the fucker again.'

'In fact the way things are going, all we may have for Christmas is a few nuts and oranges.'

'Aiiieeeee!'

'Oh, sorry. Nuts and plums then. Things have been tight since you were banned from the stock exchange for wreaking economic devastation on orange-exporting countries.'

'Aiiiieeee! Those fuckers. Wait until I get my hands on an orbital laser platform. Although better yet might be to effect some shift in the sun's radiation thereby removing the Forbidden Colour from the visible spectrum.'

'Both of which will be expensive. We really could use the money. My publisher thinks your autobiography would be a bestseller.'

'For the love of spunk, why? Who would possibly want to read about the petty tribulations of a girl genius struggling to master time-travel and eradicate a certain colour while having to put up with the interruptions of a nagging cunt with a baboon's-arse face? It's just too kitchen sink.'

I coughed delicately. 'Actually, it's your early life people would be interested in reading about.'

'The gene manipulation years? I refuse to talk about it. It was not my fault my first foster fuckwits turned into giant spiders, and certainly not that they ate the milkman.'

'No, I meant your very earliest years. The things that happened with your real family.'

She blinked. 'The *rape*? The kiddie-porn? That would hardly do, would it? What kind of degraded monster would want to read about that? I'm pretty fucking amoral, Sunny, but if we're that strapped for cash I think it would be much less dubious to dust off my old idea for a chemical weapon that can turn people's brains into gold.'

'People wouldn't read it for prurient reasons. At least, not all of them. The market research is hazy, I gather, people are shy about admitting to getting off on kiddie-rape. But most of them . . . they will enjoy feeling sorry for you.'

'How dare they! I should write this book and coat every page with cholera germs, let them feel sorry for themselves.'

'It may help put their own problems in perspective.'

'So they wish to use my rotten time to feel better about their own wretched lives? Neurolinguistic programming, that's what I'll do, a hidden command word on every page to make them all disembowel themselves.'

I tried to explain, waving an arm. 'It's just . . . diversion. People seem to find these things . . . gripping. Page-turning. Unputdownable. Entertaining. Thrilling.'

'Entertaining? *Thrilling?*' She shook her head. 'I used to worry about changing the timeline too much, when I finally build my chronoporter, but not even waking up to find a London full of commuting dinosaurs with briefcases and umbrellas could be as strange as the fuckverdammt human race.'

'Really, it's just like when people used to read melodramas about heroines being tied to train tracks. Except the heroines are real and five years old and get run over a few times and raped repeatedly before they're untied. It's essentially healthy.'

'I absolutely refuse, you sick bloody pudsucker.'

'Listen,' I pressed, 'you found my tale of living in Nnnn . . . That Place, uplifting, in its way, surely?'

She eyed me. 'Are you mad? It has blighted my young life, you foolish Polo-fucker. I will never be the same carefree girl again.'

'But the fact that I didn't kill myself, that I am here to tell the tale, must be inspiring?'

'If you had fled instantly, triggering a nuclear reactor meltdown behind you, that might have been frigging inspiring. I mean, what of the thousands you selfishly left behind you, who are still there to this day, hmm? Do you ever think of them?'

'Every day,' I admitted, my face buttocks pale and goose-pimpling. 'The survivor-guilt is something awful. But it was every man for himself. I would have climbed over my own grandmother to get out.'

'Is it true that Agas talk to you, There?'

'It's more that you talk to them, to avoid talking to the locals.'

'Quite understandable.'

'About the book. It might be therapeutic for you. You will at least think about it?'

'Go and fuck yourself with the blunt end of a police-man.'

'Very well . . . What exactly are you doing here, any-way?' I asked, nervously eyeing a small swirling purple mass of energy that was hovering just above the carpet.

'Trying to harness a singularity in the pissing space–time continuum, if I could be left in peace.'

'Well, make sure you clean up after yourself,' I said doubtfully.

'Frig a pig! Did Marie bastard Curie have to deal with

the like?' She held up a rather bedraggled laboratory rodent by the tail. 'This mouse has just travelled to Ancient Egypt and back, I'll have you know.'

I frowned. 'Why are its eyes all strange and wide and staring like that?'

She bit her lip. 'A teething problem, while the physical envelope travels instantly its disembodied mind has been suspended in an empty grey limbo between dimensions for a subjective duration of eight thousand years. The fucker is probably just pleased to see me again. Aren't 'oo?' She kissed it. 'Has 'oo missed your mum, cunt?'

'Euphemia, that's terrible! I forbid you to treat your pets like that!'

'Oh, stow it, piss-pants, it's seen the Pyramids being built, hasn't it, that's more than it expected when it got up this morning.'

'I think that glowing thing is singeing the carpet,' I complained.

'Kids! Who'd 'ave 'em, as me old dad used to say.' She went back to her instruments and ignored me.

I clenched my fists. A parent has to learn when to let go, but it is so hard. I scowled at the glowing cosmic singularity. You are my enemy, I thought, you and your kind. If she does not play with you now, she will not one day build a full-blown time tunnel and be trapped in the Pliocene age with dinosaurs chasing her. I'll get you, you little bastard. Then I went out to glare at the cooker.

I continued from time to time to try gently to persuade her to tell her story, playing on the literary aspirations I knew she harboured along with her other ambitions. But when she menacingly noted that spider-mandibles and eight eyes would not work well with my baboon's-arse face, I let it drop.

However a couple of weeks later I came home one day to find her sitting on the couch munching crisps and watching the kiddie-porn videos of her father raping her.

'The camera work is fucking rubbish,' she yawned, 'and absolutely no attention has been paid to the mise-en-scène. Although some of the jump-cuts, you know, are almost Godardian.'

Soon afterwards she announced her decision that she would, after all, write a memoir, and moreover one that would be the last word in the genre. Smugly thinking of my own advancing manuscript I knew that there she was wrong and could not hope to compete. For a time we worked side by side on our separate horror stories every day, scribbling enthusiastically with the fire roaring cosily and her staring-eyed, catatonic mouse slumped on her shoulder.

However, she changed her mind and abandoned her efforts after the first three chapters. Coming across them one day after she had gone to university I found them to be disappointing, amateurish productions with little sense of audience. Still they are not entirely without interest and I have placed them as an appendix at the end of this book.

As my own work progressed my increasingly excited publisher started to arrange advance publicity, beginning to plant my name and features in the public consciousness here and there. I worried it was too soon, but he assured me, to my blushes and modest demurrals, that no one would be likely to forget my face in a hurry. To this end, he put me in touch with a TV producer, who was just as excited as he was to meet me.

'What an embarrassment of riches! Where to begin . . . Let's see, *Me and My Premature Incontinence* is coming up for the BBC. Or we could build a programme around your face, possibly advertise for people with similar conditions . . .

'When Buttocks Go Astray'? 'My Face Is Like An Arse', that might be more . . .'

I coughed. 'My face *is* an arse. I would not wish to be associated with attention-seeking wannabes.'

'Yes, of course.'

But in the end my first (and as it happened last) television appearance was to be on a new live daytime talkshow fearlessly dedicated to exposing social problems.

I still think it could have been the beginning of a TV career if Euphemia hadn't accompanied me. When I mentioned her to the show's researchers their eyes lit up; when the producers urged that the two of us appear together I was somewhat put out, fearing that she would try to upstage me, but I couldn't have foreseen how badly it did turn out.

It was in the make-up room that I should have received my first inkling that she wasn't approaching the experience in the right frame of mind. (When I had asked her if she would be interested, she had first laughed derisively, then called me an arsehole, then watched a couple of editions of the show out of curiosity and suddenly announced she had changed her mind.)

'Do I look pale and wan enough?' she asked the make-up artist now. 'Perhaps I should go in with my dress torn? Shall I take a glycerine bottle in case we need a tear or two? Daddy would sometimes slap me so an artful bruise showed up, perhaps you should try that? I'd better get more close-ups than arse-face. This takes me back to the good old days, you know,' she said conversationally. 'The smell of the greasepaint, the slobbering of the crowd. Born trouper, darling, born in a trunk backstage. And quite often locked in it, actually.'

★

'Euphemia,' said the hostess with a catch in her voice, 'you're going to tell us about the things your father did to you.'

'Yes,' said Euphemia in a wobbly voice, 'if I can.'

'Very painful things,' the hostess prompted.

'Yes.' She lowered her head.

'Something really terrible.'

Euphemia nodded and in a breaking voice said, 'The fucker just stopped my pocket money for chronoporting half an extinct mastodon into the conservatory.' The hostess blinked. Euphemia pointed at me accusingly and cried, 'That man! That man there! He is an enemy of science.'

Automatically but uncertainly, the audience emitted some slightly confused boos and hisses.

'Not me!' I cried.

'No,' said the hostess, 'I don't mean your current adoptive father, I mean your previous—'

'Oh, Spider-Daddy? Yes, he cocooned the milkman and several of my schoolfriends and devoured them slowly over a period of months. It was not my fault.'

The hostess perked up. 'Well that's certainly interesting, I didn't realize – perhaps we could explore that in another programme.'

'You know who she means,' I hissed

'Ohhh, Auteur Daddy. Yes, what a right cunt he was.'

The audience were somewhat taken aback.

The hostess smiled indulgently and said, 'Perhaps I should explain at this point that as well as suffering horrendous abuse at the hands of her father, Euphemia tragically suffers from Tourette's Syndrome.'

'Suffers?' cried Euphemia in outrage. 'It is a culture in its own right, cockbreath.'

'Perhaps we could get on to that later. I'd like to talk

first about your father. Not only did he rape you, he used to film it, didn't he?'

'Ineptly,' nodded Euphemia sorrowfully. 'It was pure schlock. My father was the Ed Wood of underage erotica.' She hid her face in her hands.

The hostess paused uncertainly a second and then said:

'You must have felt betrayed?'

Euphemia looked at her. 'Betrayed? My good woman, I felt utterly shafted. I mean, is betrayed *quite* the word we're looking for? I was raped, you fucktard. I felt betrayed when they changed the origins of the cybermen in the new *Doctor Who*, you vacuous whore, being fucked by your dad is an entirely different order of experience. But I suppose I was a tad let down by the old parental unit, yes.'

The hostess's mouth worked a couple of times. She said, 'Euphemia's being very brave but she's quite obviously distraught by reliving her ordeal for us. We're going to go to a break now.'

Music played. The audience applauded. Make-up artists pounced on us.

'Did they like me?' Euphemia asked the hostess with every appearance of anxiety. 'I think they liked me but I can't tell. I want people to like me but I don't know how to make them. Making them aware of my innate intellectual superiority doesn't seem to do it and threats can backfire.'

The hostess smiled sweetly and said, 'You were fine, but – I thought Tourette's was an involuntary verbal twitch rather than casual abuse that seems to manifest itself pretty much when you please.'

'Oh, so did I!' I exclaimed.

Euphemia glared. 'I didn't come here to be ambushed, you cunts. The Tourette's community is a wide, catholic, all-embracing entity, like a fat fuck of a nun with nymphomania.'

The hostess managed to hold her smile.

'You do know, don't you, that although this show is described as live, there is actually a five-second delay for safety and all your swearing will be bleeped out?'

Euphemia screamed at the top of her lungs.

'GENOCIDE! Bleeping is genocide against the Tourette's culture!'

'Control yourself!' I snapped. 'Behave!'

'Bastards! You have stifled my right to self-expression!'

'Do you have any orange paint on the premises?' I asked the hostess, who looked quizzical.

Euphemia shut up and sat still, wide-eyed with terror. 'I'll be good, Sunny, honest I will.'

The floor-manager cued us. The music played.

'We're back with Sunny and Euphemia, who have both endured horrific abuse as children but are now building a more normal family life together.'

Euphemia threw her head back and laughed. 'Normal? God help us all. Bloody fuck, woman, where were you dragged up? We make the Addams family look like the suburban dream.'

'Perhaps the Addams family should have adopted you, then,' I muttered, stung.

'Oh, don't pout, you morbid fucker.'

Hastily the hostess said, 'We're hoping that now she's composed herself Euphemia will consent to tell us more about her horrific ordeal at the hands of her father.'

Euphemia sighed. 'Jesus. Didn't we already cover this?'

'You didn't really elaborate.'

'You want the full gory details?'

'I think it's important to get the full story.' The woman knelt down and tried to squeeze Euphemia's hand, which was quickly yanked away.

'Do you want me to draw a picture? You know what sexual intercourse is, I presume? It was like that but with more screaming.'

'Yes but . . .' the hostess's voice was solemn and hushed, 'how did it start? What did he do first?'

There was a pause. Euphemia stared at the ceiling.

'I'm not going to force you, of course. But you did agree to come on the show. I think, deep down, perhaps you want to let it out.'

Euphemia sighed again. 'I suspected it would have to come to this, you poxed-up death of a thousand dicks. I gave you a chance,' she said, and pulled out a futuristic-looking mini-disc Walkman and placed the earphones on her head, then closed her eyes.

The hostess turned to me. 'Has she ever opened up to you about it?'

'No, not properly. However I have seen films.'

'Ooh!'

Suddenly Euphemia opened her eyes and stood up, took the Walkman off her head and presented it to the hostess. 'Put this on, please.'

The hostess looked bemused.

'I don't know if I have time to—'

'Well stop fannying around and put it on then, you silly slag.' She suddenly smiled winsomely and fluttered her eyelashes. 'Please? It will help you understand what I went through, since you wanted to know.'

The hostess smiled at her.

'Is this a song that means something to you?' she asked tenderly as she put the headphones on.

'No, it's a downloaded memory of me being shafted by my father which will be injected directly into your loathsome brain, you vapid hogfucker.' She pressed play on the device.

The hostess gave a prolonged hair-raising scream and started to back away and flail at an invisible figure. 'Please – stop – no—'

'Euphemia! How could you!' Appalled, I leapt forward and yanked the headphones off the hostess, who collapsed to the floor in a foetal ball, moaning and shuddering. Technicians and production staff came running up. There were noises of startlement from the audience. 'I'm terribly sorry,' I said.

Euphemia looked down at the woman and said, 'Why were you born, you ghastly fucking ambulance-chasing ghoul? I think I will erase you from history once I have mastered time-travel. I will leave Darwinism to take care of your audience of voyeurs, shut-ins, and doped-up students who wish to feel superior.'

I grabbed her. 'Look what you've done, you little brat!' I yelled. 'I can't take you anywhere! I've told you before about experimenting on live humans! You've broken her brain now! You're grounded for a week!'

'Oh, fuck off, Sunny, they're exploiting you, you silly cunt.'

'You've ruined my TV career! I hate you!' I started to shake her.

'Leave it out, arsehole!'

'All the cute dejected orphans in the world and I had to pick you! I'm taking you back! I'm taking you back to the orphanage! I'm going to swap you for a nice child!'

'Awwww!' said the audience disapprovingly. There were scattered boos.

However Euphemia rounded on them and snarled. 'Stay out of this, you rubbernecking twats, save your sympathy for the people who have to sit behind you on the bus and stare at your fat squat inbred necks.' She bit my hand, darted off and threw a chair at me.

'You little bitch! I'll kill you!'

'Just try it, arse-face!'

'Orange!' I screamed at her. 'Orange!'

She clapped her hands to her ears. 'Aiiieeee!'

'Yes, yes! William of Orange coming to get you, leading a big army of Orange Lodge Oompa-Loompas who pelt you with oranges!'

'Aiiieeee! Stop! Stop!'

'And then they take you to Northumberland and paint a orange stripe around the borders so you can't ever get out!'

'MONSTER! *Monstre indescriptible!* Pigeons! Pigeons, Sunny! Pigeons and doors!'

'Aiiiieeeee!' I shrieked, clapping my hands over my own ears.

The production crew stared at us dumbfounded; the hostess was now shakily on her feet. I was dimly aware of the lead cameraman panning from one to the other of us as we ranted.

'Doors! Doors and pigeons, I tell you! You are trapped forever in a revolving door with pigeons!'

'Aiieee! Orange! Orange! You are drowning in a vat of orange juice in the middle of Northumberland!'

'A giant pigeon pecks your brains out!'

'Zygons painting your eyeballs orange! Orange, orange, all around!'

As we snarled at each other I chased her round and round the studio chairs so I could beat her to death, in turn eluding the security man who was now chasing after me. She changed tack.

'Waterfalls, Sunny! Geysers! Old Faithful! Fire-hoses!'

I felt my prematurely incontinent bladder twinge. 'Stop that!'

'Fountains! Filling baths! Lawn-sprinklers! Riot police spraying crowds!' She started to whistle.

'Stop it! Stop it!' I clutched at my groin.

It was too late. I had to go, now. I started to dash off-set but unfortunately tripped over an electrical cable for one of the cameras, went sprawling and gushed. Even more unfortunately, the cable was frayed and the puddle made contact with it, causing me to scream and writhe in agony as blue lightning writhed around me until a fuse blew offstage with a spectacular shower of sparks.

'Sunny!' Euphemia shrieked in horror and came running over to me, then turned angrily on the hostess, who was standing there with a limp microphone and hanging jaw in a state approaching shell shock. 'Now look what you've made me do! I've electrocuted my esteemed foster-fuckwit! You're for it now!'

She took out a matchbox, brandished it dramatically, then opened it and upended it over the floor. It appeared to be empty.

Euphemia pointed towards the hostess. Her voice rang out commandingly.

'Nanobots – attack!'

We all waited expectantly. The hostess and her team cowered back in alarm.

Seconds passed. By squinting I could just make out a tiny column of microscopic little dots advancing infinitesimally slowly across the floor.

'For fuck's sake, you dozy little bleeders, this week! Oh, I'll do it myself.' Petulantly she stamped on her nanobots and then ran over and kicked the hostess in the shins.

Frantic signals were made. Security grabbed the pair of us.

The end theme tune played. The audience applauded energetically.

*

Not long after that Euphemia successfully applied for early university entry and I was left alone again.

'I don't like long goodbyes,' she said in the car outside her college.

'Me neither,' I said.

She got out of the car and walked off.

I sat there with tears misting my vision.

Thirty seconds later I saw her walking back. I wound down the window.

'Sunny,' she said after a second.

'Yes?' I sobbed.

'Carry my suitcase in, you dozy cunt.'

22

I am finally given a new face. It turns out to be Hitler's.

Over the years I had, as far as is possible, become used to my having a baboon's arse for a face. Other people, however, had not. People passing me in the street would scream, point, faint, vomit, make hurtful remarks, or become so distracted they would walk into walls. People passing me in cars would drive into things, or suddenly slam their brakes on and back up, often quite long distances, to take a second look. A man who had been on his way to work and had spotted me at a taxi rank followed me all the way to the airport and then on to a flight to Tenerife in order to keep staring at me. At the end of my holiday, the entire population of Tenerife followed me to the airport to see me off. People meeting me for the first time would gape frankly and tend to say something like, 'Fucking hell.' Blind dates would go to the toilet very quickly and not come back.

I tried dressing so as to distract attention from my face – wearing a carnation in my buttonhole, T-shirts with amusing slogans, large and jaunty hats, brightly coloured socks, but to little avail.

Nor did it improve my relations with the animal kingdom. Dogs and cats would growl and hiss at me or flee howling. Whenever I went to a zoo the inhabitants would be set in an uproar. The baboons in particular would cling to the bars of their cages and gibber at me as though they were responding to a challenge, as if they thought I was mooning them – or perhaps they were just complimenting me sexually after the manner of human builders – for many times I had consoled myself with the thought that, as baboons' arses go, it was at least a pert and shapely one. Vanity is ineradicable in the human heart.

Of course there were compensations. I at least did not have to shave or worry about spots. A little haemorrhoid cream occasionally (for the donor baboon had led a sedentary life) and I was ready to go. And I never had to pay for Halloween costumes. Still, these were small positives. I would have dreams in which I was handsome and wake up with tear-wet buttocks.

My unique facial challenge had earned me some measure of notoriety by this time: I would be written up in medical journals, or featured at the end of news bulletins in lighthearted 'and finally' items. Occasionally surgeons took an interest in my case but would soon be forced to admit defeat, although there was a ray of hope once when one suggested that if I could learn to suck my cheeks in it wouldn't look so bad.

I was told that the first full human face graft could be no more than a couple of years away, but I treated this with scepticism. But in fact it would be I, and not the woman who subsequently got into the history books, who was to be the first recipient of a human face transplant. My operation, which preceded hers by quite some time, was conducted in utmost secrecy and thereafter hushed up, for reasons which will soon become apparent.

Alas, I was to learn there are far worse things than having a rump on your face.

*

'I am Herr Doktor Himmelmann, originally from Frankfurt, later practising at Ausch – that is, the Mayo Clinic, and for many years past ze head of a small research laboratory in ze Paraguayan jungle. I believe I can give you a face zat you vill be proud to valk down ze street vith.'

The man who was to change my life was tall, stooped and white-haired, walking with the aid of a cane whose silver top was worked into a striking death's head motif. Although I was later to learn he was at least ninety, he moved with the carriage of a sprightly seventy-five and was animated with an unmistakable life-force which showed itself in an intense, almost manic gleam in the eye and, when he really felt passionate, a slight frothing at the mouth. He wore a monocle and had a jagged white shrapnel scar on one cheek and dressed in stylish black leather. He clicked his heels on my doorstep and presented me with a business card printed in a Gothic typeface and embossed with little eagles.

He was smiling a broad and merry smile and I trusted him immediately. 'Please come in,' I said.

As he entered, to my astonishment, a thuggish young man carrying a machine gun barged past both of us and charged into the kitchen and then out into the back yard.

'Clear exit at the back,' he called upon his return, before disappearing up the stairs.

'Please excuse my assistant,' said Dr Himmelmann genially, daintily dusting a chair with a handkerchief and sitting. 'I have another appointment soon and may have to leave in a hurry, it is well to be prepared.'

Before I could close the door a second young thug barged in too and saluted the Doktor. 'There's a family with a semitic name in a flat two houses down.'

Himmelmann twitched his leather-gloved fingers. 'Could zey remember me from – ze Mayo Clinic?'

'The ones I saw were too young.'

'Go to the window and keep dixie.'

The doctor smiled at me.

'Now, my friend,' said this remarkable man, 'are you happy to go through life with the face of a simian's posterior?'

'I am not.'

'Then will you place yourself in my hands?'

'Forgive me,' I said, 'but I know nothing of your bona fides and I have had many disappointments at the hands of medics – starting perhaps with the one who gave me my current face, whom I now understand to have been a mad scientist.'

'You ingrate!' he screamed, rising and threatening me with his cane so that I instinctively flinched. 'He was a great man, my most brilliant student! Mad? He was ahead of his time. Why I myself have been called – ahead of my time, several times. Without his work—'

He calmed himself and sat. 'But it is certainly true,' he said with a resumption of his former genial manner, 'that we can now do better for you than transplanting a crude monkey's backside. I have now reached the point where I can graft on to you – you, you lucky, blessed man' – he lowered his voice reverently – 'a human face.'

When I expressed my doubt he passed over some photographs. 'So that you may believe, some of my early attempts at face transplant, using the jungle natives.'

I regarded the pictures: a sequence of unhappy-looking Indians, with noses, lips and eyebrows placed haphazardly, almost at random, over their faces.

'This doesn't look quite right,' I pointed out diffidently, indicating one particularly unfortunate-looking subject with eyebrows halfway up his forehead at different levels and angles and a nose jutting wildly, and upside down, out of his left cheekbone.

He shrugged. 'Yes, noses in particular are real bastards to do. My hand trembles somewhat nowadays and ze blasted superglue is very quick to set. Do not be alarmed. I have now abandoned what I termed the Mr Potato Head paradigm of facial reconstruction and gone for tacking on the whole face in one go as one might a carpet.'

'I see.' I considered. 'But even if you can succeed at that – where are we to find a face to transplant?'

A faraway look came into his eye. 'I have had one lying around for – qvite some time.' He studied me thoughtfully. 'You have lost some hair, I perceive,' he said casually. 'I will also throw in a follicle transplant, and . . . a haircut. I have become rather good at that.'

He passed over some more pictures of natives. They all seemed to have had the same hairdo – a nice neat short back and sides with a long fringe on one side falling almost over one eye. It seemed to ring a bell vaguely.

'They all have hair over one eye,' I chuckled. 'Why, it is almost as if you have a fixation on, er . . . who am I thinking of . . . Bryan Ferry, is it?'

'Bryan Ferry!?' he screamed, jumping up and beating me violently about the head with his cane. 'I vill give you Bryan Ferry, arse-faced *untermensch!*' His assistant came from the window and forcibly restrained him.

'Forgive me,' I said hastily, 'I meant no aspersions on your hairdressing skills. It is a lovely haircut.'

'With a haircut such as that a man could rule the world!'

'I am sure,' I said as he sat and with an effort controlled himself. I swallowed. 'Would this be – a painful operation?'

'Immensely,' he said with satisfaction. 'I have always regarded anaesthetic as for weaklings and it is entirely inappropriate for this operation, which depends on tautness of the facial muscles, and besides screams help steady my hand, I find. I have made careful enquiries into your . . . heritage before approaching you. You are of a healthy stock and your father – a great man – strengthened you to the endurance of pain, even in fact to the pounding of nails into your face. Even so, frankly there is a chance of death. I believe the face may reject you if you are . . . in any way impure. But you, you with the face of Bosse-de-Nage, you have nothing to lose. And if I succeed . . . a great new destiny awaits you. You will do it, yes?'

I tried and failed to keep my voice from breaking. 'Yes,' I sobbed, tears coursing down my arse cheeks. 'Gladly.'

He sighed. 'Zank you. You vill not regret it.'

I felt ashamed to ask. Nevertheless I stammered:

'Will I be – good looking?'

He reached over and squeezed my hand. There appeared to be tears in his eyes too. With emotion he said:

'I vill give you ze most beautiful face in human history!'

*

Himmelmann took me in his car, an antique open-topped limousine painted grey with crosses on the doors and a machine-gun quaintly mounted on the boot, and drove me to a remote manor house deep in the countryside. For the first few miles he and his confederates kept glancing nervously in the mirror, but he finally relaxed as we drew up to the gate.

A sign on the gate declared the property the HORST WESSEL MEMORIAL HIGH-SECURITY RETIREMENT CASTLE. An aged man doddered from the gatehouse to open it to us and saluted as we drove past. He wore a round grey helmet and a medal in the shape of a Maltese cross.

I found the inhabitants of the nursing home a genial bunch of old men, fondly fighting old battles and reliving ancient massacres in the tranquil calm of their twilight years. The place was full of German army memorabilia I imagined they had captured during the war.

The nurses all wore a strange insignia on their uniforms, a sort of twisty cross that vaguely rang a bell – a new, non-faith-specific, politically correct version of the traditional first-aid cross, I assumed. (The same motif, I noticed, was repeated on the long red drapes lining a ballroom, which also featured a raised podium and gleaming eagle standards.) There was something else odd about the nurses – most of them carried firearms of some sort, and they seemed to have had some sort of martial arts training. At any rate, I once saw one of them wrestle a delivery boy to the ground and deftly twist his arm behind his back while another frisked him for ID. Himmelmann explained that security was important at a residence for feeble and entirely harmless old men armed only with a few machine guns and mortars and that many of the nurses had been trained as ninjas. (On this head, I later witnessed a very efficient nurse administer ten enemas in half as many seconds by whirling round in the middle of a room and flinging them, like shurikens, with deadly accuracy into ten upturned old bottoms.)

The whole place was run with martial precision. The gardeners wore smart black uniforms and carried their rakes at a military slope-arms, or pushed wheelbarrows with a brisk goose-step. There was a strict regimen of exercise and every afternoon the inmates would go marching in lock-step about the grounds to the sounds of stirring music, or keep their hand-eye co-ordination spry by firing some howitzers across the back lawn into a mock-up of a Polish shtetl. They practised a form of callisthenics by standing in a crowd keeping their right arms extended into the air at a forty-five degree angle for ages at a time while making rousing and jolly cries. Meanwhile Himmelmann or a fierce old man in a bathchair would address them from a dais – some sort of political lecture which was lost on me but which I imagined would keep their brains active.

On weekends parties of younger men whom I took to be their sons and grandchildren would visit. They represented a wide variety of professions although men in the uniforms of traffic wardens and car-park attendants seemed to be in great supply, and quite a number of teachers. They too attended the free lectures and exercise drill.

I was there for two weeks while Himmelmann prepared for the intricate and pioneering operation – mainly he was waiting for a nail-gun to be delivered – and I was strengthened for my ordeal. Everyone was very pleasant to me – indeed, I was treated as guest of honour, and many appeared to stare at me with a wonder and admiration that startled me. I endeavoured to join in their callisthenics and was told that the arm-extension was actually a form of salute. I tried to emulate it but my injured, floppy wrist let me down. Himmelmann, however, was excited by this.

'See here – stand on the podium, in the box, return the salute – keep your hand close to your body, look – forget extending the arm – so, yes. Now, let your hand flop upwards from the wrist instead of down – Mein Gott! It is perfect! See, he can do His floppy hand salute!'

'It is a sign,' breathed the fierce old man in the bath chair wide-eyed, making the sign of the cross over himself, although in a twisty way like the nurses' insignia. 'He is worthy to bear The Face.'

At last came the day of the operation. I was strapped to an operating table in a small clinic. Himmelmann was masked and in his butcher apron and a nurse stood by to mop his brow and load the nail-gun. His two male assistants were on hand to set fire to my feet for distraction if the pain in my face became too much to bear.

'Und so ve commence. Scalpel.'

'Scalpel.'

'Carving knife.'

'Carving knife.'

'Junior hacksaw.'

'Junior hacksaw.'

'Are you getting much golf in at the moment?' Himmelmann asked his assistant calmly as he sawed my old face off. It was at that point that I passed out.

I was wakened by a blowtorch being applied to my foot. The baboon's arse had been removed and I must now be conscious for the face-fitting procedure. Solemnly, they opened a refrigerated cooling box and took what looked like a mask from within; I couldn't see it properly for clouds of dry ice.

I lapsed in and out of consciousness as the agonizing operation proceeded. The sound of Himmelmann's relaxed voice surged and ebbed above me like waves on a misty shore.

'... most appalling divot on the seventeeth ... the greenskeeper should be liquidated ... and members of the chosen race wanting to play through every two minutes ... I had my caddy bury landmines before we left ... nearly there, Sunny, stay with us ... ah ... why does he have a goatee rather than a moustache ... *Scheisse!* I have put it on upside down, haven't I? The nose points downwards, Himmelmann, you *Dummkopf*, otherwise the snot collects, and ze people drown when it rains, when will you learn!' He tutted. 'There is always one little thing, isn't there? Perhaps if I was to wrench his head round – no, no, rip it off, boys, we must start again . . .'

The pain went on and on.

Finally Himmelmann was satisfied. 'One last one . . . keep it nice and taut at the temples there . . . tauter than it was, what the hell, we give the old boy a face-lift . . .' A final stab of the nail-gun and it was over and I was allowed to sink into oblivion.

The next day, face swathed in layers of bandages, I went through a similar but slightly less painful procedure for the hair transplant, Himmelmann this time in a barber's smock.

'Whose is the scalp?' I wondered.

'Picked it up in South America some time ago. Trade Union leader.'

'Died?'

'Eventually.'

'Didn't his family object? I mean . . . are scalps covered on donor cards?'

'You really are the most extraordinary fellow. I do hope we haven't made a mistake in choosing you.' He started to cut and groom. 'Did you see the match on Saturday?' he asked as he worked.

When he had finished he tweaked the bandages so there was a gap around my eyes and showed it to me in the mirror. Although I had asked him to leave it long around the ears, he had given me the same old short back and sides with lopsided Bryan Ferry fringe. Except – no, if it looked like Bryan Ferry in the mirror, in real life it must be reversed. Whose haircut could I be thinking of?

The bandages stayed on for a week. Himmelmann changed them twice and seemed to gloat over his handiwork but wouldn't let me see it.

There was to be a grand unveiling ceremony in the

ballroom with everyone present. But I couldn't wait. The morning of the seventh day I leapt out of bed before the nurses came round and dashed to the bathroom. Impetuously, fumble-fingered with impatience and excitement and a slight apprehension, I started to unwind the bandages from myself. Soon, soon, any moment now, I would be able to start to confront the world with a new dignity, without shame, no longer shunned, feared and hated by my neighbours. I would no longer scurry but walk with head held high, a man not a monster, an object of respect, even envy, someone people would like, and want to spend time with, and . . .

The bandages were gone. I surveyed myself in the mirror.

At first the face struck me as unremarkable, although certainly a miraculous contrast to the one I had had before, even an improvement on the ordinarily misshapen one I had been born with. It was an average face really. No, not average – it had a certain pathos to it. The face, you would have said, of an underdog, the face of a man with a grievance against the universe, suffering under intolerable wrongs, a victim, a human sacrifice, a martyr, but one who was resolved to fight back against impossible odds. The lopsided fringe made a striking effect, and sort of worked with the face, I had to admit, although I wasn't sure if I would keep it. And that ridiculous little toothbrush moustache definitely had to go.

That was when I realized that I knew the face. I had seen it before, many times, although never in pyjamas and dressing gown.

'Oh, for fuck's sake, isn't that just my sodding luck,' I think I said.

For a moment I toyed with a remote hope that it was

not Bryan Ferry whom Himmelmann was fixated on but the keyboard player out of the Sparks.

But no. There was no way around it.

I had been given the face of the man born Adolf Schicklgruber, otherwise known as Hitler.

23

*My fortunes seem to improve somewhat: I am installed as
the god-emperor of a heavily armed Nazi-revival movement and
my every whim is gratified. But there are hidden drawbacks,
and my arm hurts with all the saluting.*

I burst into Himmelmann's room and shook him furiously.

'Look what you've done to me, you bastard!'

He gazed at me in rapture, a big happy smile on his face.
'O joyous day! It is better, better than I dared to dream . . .
and the hair, the hair . . . let me touch the hair . . .'

I slapped his hand away. 'Look at me! I . . . I look like
. . . you have given me Hitler's face!'

He blushed and dimpled. 'Please, there is no need to
thank me. To gaze on those saintly features once more is all
the reward I ask. Yes, my friend, it is true. I saved the
Führer's face. It has been lying around in my junk room all
these years. Many times my wife nagged me to throw it out
but I knew one day it would come in useful. At one point I
despaired and thought to sell it on eBay. But now, now it
has risen again to inspire us and he is reborn in you! Now
you will lead us in a new and glorious Fifth Reich!'

'Then . . . you are Nazis?' I was appalled. 'Wait, though
– *Fifth* Reich?'

He waved a hand. 'The Fourth was a small affair, not
well-publicized, just me and a few close friends marching
round the jungle.'

'You're a maniac! What's to become of me now? How will I ever dare to leave the house looking like this?'

'No, no – you must not think of it, not yet. There are those who would stop our great work before it has begun. But we are strong, Führer, strong! We have been building our strength in secret. We have people in all walks of life – schools, academia, ze government, ze judiciary, local councils, social services, ze police, everywhere. We are united and disciplined and we are growing all ze time. All we lack is a leader, for what is power without purpose?'

'What do you want from me?'

'Order us! Tell us what to do! To take orders and force others to obey them is what we live for! Tell us who to persecute! Tell us who to shoot! Tell us who to push around! The righteous pushing around, zat is the breath of life for a Nazi!'

'You're insane! I want no part of this! Give me my old face back and let me go!'

'I regret zat is not possible.' He went to a bureau and pulled out a Luger and levelled it at me. 'You bear The Face. You are bigger than yourself now. You vill be our new Führer or I vill shoot you like a dog.'

He marched me to the ballroom where the rest of them, old and young alike, were gathered in ranks and files in an expectant hush. At my first appearance they burst out into rapturous cries of '*Sieg Heil*' doing their salute. The hall thundered with it. Himmelmann had put his gun away but pushed me firmly to the lectern that had been set up.

'What am I supposed to say?' I hissed as I struggled against him.

'Whatever you wish, my Führer. If you get stuck throw in some salutes.'

He shoved me forward. The joyous cries rose to a peak

and then died down respectfully as I picked up the microphone that had been set up for the benefit of those at the back. I fumbled and dropped it, setting up a squeal of feedback. 'Shit, sorry,' I mumbled as I retrieved it.

I gazed out across their expectant faces.

'Um, hello,' I said.

The crowd went wild. It took five minutes for the cheers to die down.

'It's great to be here,' I said. 'Um . . . *Sieg Heil.*'

They went berserk, the response was deafening.

I decided to milk it. 'Yeah, you like that one, hey? *Sieg Heil! Sieg Heil!*'

Again they erupted.

'Yeah, the old ones are the good ones . . . This is a great room, isn't it? You're a lovely crowd. There's a lot of warmth here, I can tell. I . . . can you hear me OK at the back? I . . . the thing is . . . *Sieg Heil! Sieg Heil*, yeah!'

I felt a metallic prod in my back.

'You are fumfering,' Himmelmann whispered. 'Ze Führer never fumfered. Deliver ze material and get off. And *Sieg Heil* only works as a punchline, not punctuation, don't overdo it, it's not clever.'

As the cheers died down I stared at them in a panic, flop sweat trickling down my back.

As the silence lengthened an old Nazi at the front waved his walking stick and implored, 'Give us orders, Führer, tell us what to do!'

'Yes, yes!' they cried.

'I . . . I'll get back to you on that. This is very strange for me. For now, just . . . relax.' They looked at each other in bafflement. 'You've been great. Keep it up. Thanks for . . . bye.' I did a final salute and fled.

The upper echelons of the Nazis pursued me into the corridor.

'Führer, Führer! You will give us instructions soon? What are your plans?'

'I'll let you know. Don't badger me, OK? Just . . . I'm ordering three days of celebration, all right? Now leave me alone.'

'How may we celebrate, Führer?' the old man in the bathchair asked eagerly, propelling himself along after me. 'May we burn down some villages?'

'No!' He seemed crestfallen. 'All right, just one, then,' I relented. 'But no massacres, understand?'

'Thank you, my Führer!'

I fled to my room and slammed the door. Himmelmann followed me.

'Not bad for your first time. You vill learn.'

'I order you to piss off!' I yelled.

'See, you are getting it.' He saluted and pissed off smartly.

For three days I lurked in my room, mostly lying in bed with the sheet pulled over my head brooding. I turned all the mirrors to face the wall to avoid screaming when I caught sight of myself. When I asked for a razor Himmelmann informed me that if I touched the sacred moustache he would kill me. There seemed no way out of my predicament. Whenever I emerged from the room to get food or go to the toilet, slouching through the back corridors in my ratty dressing gown and slippers and my old pyjamas with little unicorns on, eventually stealing some dark glasses in a futile attempt not to be recognized, I would be besieged by Nazis begging me to tell them what to do. Irritably I would set them a few pointless chores about the house or garden, or tell them to go and do some sit-ups or collect some flowers or something, and they would bustle off happily.

Eventually Himmelmann prevailed on me to address them in the ballroom again. I gradually grew more confident with it, but only set them tasks of the utmost banality, instructing them to organize games of hide-and-seek or hunt-the-thimble just to keep them out of my cute lopsided hair. I reflected that I was at least keeping them out of mischief. Once when an elderly Nazi dared question my order that they should all go out into the garden and play hopscotch he was dragged out and shot. I had to admit that the constant cheering and the crowd hanging on my every word grew heady. A couple of times I decided since I had the audience and the microphone I might as well do some karaoke and regaled them with 'My Way' and 'MacArthur Park' to thunderous applause.

'He is testing us,' I would overhear the older Nazis muttering sadly as they shuffled about the corridors on Zimmer frames.

'Yes, we have not proved worthy to hear his real plans yet.'

Himmelmann was disappointed with my orders so far, but patient, confident my new position would come to grow on me. 'Is there anywhere you would like us to conquer, Führer?' he would murmur in my ear temptingly. 'Who do you hate? We will kill them.'

'Knock it off.'

'Come on, let's invade just a small country', he held his fingers an inch apart to demonstrate how small – 'just a little tiny one to start with, you'll like it.'

He would coach me on the public speaking.

'You are getting by on the charisma of the Face. But

your voice needs work. For one thing it is a bit too rural at times. Have you lived in Cornwall, for example?'

'For a while.'

'You need to lose the burr. And stop calling people "My haandsome", it doesn't fit the image.'

'OK.'

'And . . . Northumberland?'

'Unfortunately.'

The Nazi shuddered. 'How can such cruelty be permitted? Anyway, lose the "Marrer". And you are too . . . matter of fact, level-headed. There should be more rage and hysteria. Ideally you should growl and shriek and really carry on. Work on the snarl and the aggrieved whine. Hitler's whipped-dog whining was worth ten panzer divisions.'

I couldn't deny it was fun to be saluted and deferred to all the time and stared at worshipfully as I passed. I decided I might as well make the most of it until I worked out a way to extricate myself from the situation. I let them pamper me and surround me with various kinds of luxury and came to get used to it.

There was one big torment. Some of the Nazi ninja nurses were highly attractive and they were quite plainly taken with my new air of authority and world-beating haircut. But due to my tragic injury there was not a lot I could do about it.

Once when Himmelmann had come in to ask if I had any orders for the day, I ruefully eyed the nubile young Nazi ninja nurse who was bustling about tidying the room after having brought my breakfast in bed and idly said, 'I don't suppose you could make me a new penis?'

He stared at me wild-eyed.

'Penis?' he shrieked. 'Penis! You ask me to make you a penis?'

'Well, I thought . . .'

He bent and kissed my hand. 'My Führer! I am honoured! I vill make for you a penis the likes of vhich the vorld has not seen! It will be the V3! Frankly, you know, the original was not much to write home about . . . This time, you will *need* the baggy pants!' He paced the room gesticulating. 'I will get twelve of our strongest men to sacrifice their right arms to provide the flesh for it! It will be reinforced with the iron of a melted cannon! We will engrave it with runes and sigils! It will glow! It will glow and whirr and hum!'

'Just something normal will do.'

'Normal? Normal? What are you giving me with normal? It must be a penis worthy of you! The foreskin will be of pure silk . . . rolling back majestically to reveal a cupola of beaten gold, decorated with swastikas, eagles, little Aryan cherubim . . .'

'Yeah, whatever. Just hurry up,' I said as the Nazi ninja nurse bent over to tuck in the bed.

'It will fire anti-tank shells, or phosphorus . . . the bollocks alone will be the size of a man's head . . . you will have to keep it in a Zeppelin hangar . . . if only Von Braun was here to help, or Speer . . . marble, there must be marble . . . searchlights will be mounted on the base, playing about the column as it pierces the sky . . .' Eyes alight with the fire of creation, Himmelmann went out raving, followed by the slinky nurse, and I was left alone to contemplate my situation in gloom.

Then one morning I woke up with my great idea. Leaping out of bed, I threw on a dressing gown and excitedly called a rally in the ballroom.

'Nazis!' I harangued them exaltedly. 'My people! My haandsomes, my marrers. I mean, my valiant Aryan hordes.

I have come to a momentous decision! Do you still want my instructions?'

'Yes, Führer, yes!'

'And will you obey me unquestioningly?'

'Always!' 'Unto death!' 'Forever!'

'Then I will lead you as you ask.'

'Thank you, thank you!' There were tumultuous cheers and salutes.

I held up a hand. 'But there will be a big difference. This time, I want you to do good in the world!'

They looked nonplussed, even shocked, although not in the way I had expected.

'But of course, my Führer!'

'Don't we always?'

'We are Nazis, that is what we are for.'

'We just want to leave the world better than we found it.'

'But how? How? Tell us how, my Führer!'

I hadn't really thought about this clearly. I started some more salutes to buy time, they liked that.

'You know, just . . . be nice. Friendly. Smile at people. Be helpful.'

'How? How? Tell us what to do.'

I frowned for a moment. 'Oh! I know! Today, all go into town and help old women across the road. And, you know, help them with their shopping. And take an interest, talk to them, listen to their stories.'

'At once, my Führer!'

'Everyone – to a town!'

'Last one to help an old woman is a Jewboy!'

Within moments the hall was deserted as they turned as one and dashed out to obey me. Well pleased with myself, I went back to bed.

However, things did not turn out quite as I expected.

Next day I was appalled to read newspaper headlines along the lines of:

MYSTERIOUS GOOSE-STEPPING MANIACS TERRORIZE THE ELDERLY

and

NURSING HOME RESIDENTS MARCHED ACROSS ROAD AT GUNPOINT

They had prowled high streets in regimented platoons dragging protesting old women across the road whether they wanted to go or not. They had seized their shopping lists and looted shops for them. Down in the cellar I found one of them shining a lamp into the eyes of a terrified old lady and saying:

'You vill tell me all your stories and I vill listen. Tell me again in more detail ze one about what your grandson said about your budgerigar or you vill not leave here alive.'

'No!' I said. 'No! This isn't what I meant!'

They were coming up to me eagerly to regale me with tales of their exploits.

'I ferried seventy-two of them across the street, Führer. I rounded them up and formed them into a crocodile for greater efficiency.'

'And I utilized a large catapult.'

'I put burning petrol across the road so the cars would have to stop.'

'I smiled at a man, Führer, repeatedly and without provocation.'

'I saw a man who was not being friendly to people, so I beat him and extracted some teeth.'

'Erm ... great ...' I said half-heartedly. 'It's not quite what I had in mind, though.'

But clearly their hearts had been in the right place and their devotion to me was unquestioning. The thing had possibilities. I retired to my room for a while to think it out.

The first thing that had to go was their horrendous racialism. So I sent them all on diversity training courses, and had people come in and lecture them on tolerance and equality and multiculturalism and racial awareness and social inclusiveness, while they all sat obediently in the hall with heads bent diligently taking notes.

'From this day forth,' I declaimed, 'let all good Nazis work tirelessly to stamp out the evils of bigotry and prejudice!'

'*Sieg Heil!*'

'Surely he can't include the Jews in that?' muttered one unregenerate old Nazi disconsolately as they filed out of the hall.

'Silence, *Schweinhund*, you will be sent to the Northumberland front!' He paled and later shot himself.

('But it's still all right to hate the Israelis, right?' another mumbled to a comrade stealthily. 'Yes, that appears to be almost mandatory.')

But the diversity retraining and my orders to fight prejudice did not work out quite as I expected either.

Several days later I found the interrogation rooms in the cellars filled with beaten and bloody men chained to the wall.

'Who are these blokes?' I asked.

'They are comedians, Führer, or people we overheard in public making inappropriate or offensive remarks.'

'Jokes?' I gaped as someone had a charge of electricity sent through his gonads. 'You dragged them here for making jokes?'

'They can be very dangerous, Führer, when they are in poor taste.'

'Not just jokes, Führer, nasty opinions too.'

'This one is a Christian preacher. In expounding his beliefs on sin he was guilty of homophobia.'

'That one is a homosexual. In defending his beliefs he was guilty of Islamophobia.'

'While that woman is a secular Muslim, also guilty of Islamophobia.'

'That one there told a knock-knock joke. That may be offensive to battered wives.'

'And this one?'

'He denied the Holocaust,' said a young Nazi shaking his head sadly.

'Yes, Führer,' said a more unreconstructed older Nazi eagerly, 'he dared cast doubt on your great achievement!' His comrade nudged him warningly and whispered. 'Oh, right, I forgot.'

'I have to say, Führer,' said the fierce old Nazi in the bathchair, face lit up with enthusiasm, 'in my unworthy heart I questioned you, but your new directives are genius, genius! A whole new world has opened up to us. It is worth giving up persecuting the You-Know-Who's and so on – really, why limit yourself? Here there are infinite possibilities.'

I was uneasy. This wasn't really what I had intended.

'Well . . . make sure you only pull in real shits, OK? And don't go too far.'

'Oh, no, Führer,' the bathchair warrior assured me as he heated up a poker, 'we take very good care of our clients. They will emerge sadder but nicer men from re-education.'

Really, it wasn't what I had meant at all. But I told myself it was for the best. I refused to be discouraged.

The next week I called another assembly and said:

'So I heard the world is heating up dramatically and we're all going to drown or burn, and the only habitable place left will be Antarctica, where the ice is increasing, I don't understand that bit, but it's all mankind's fault and it's the exhaust fumes from cars and so on that are doing it. It is clearly our duty to stop this.'

'At once, my Führer!'

Unquestioningly they dispersed to set to work. I smiled with satisfaction at their zeal and went off to pinch some nurses and see how Himmelmann was coming along with my new penis.

Again, however, the results were alarming.

'We have confiscated or destroyed almost 500 cars so far,' a secretary announced in the briefing room a couple of days later. 'Drivers were dragged out and beaten and their vehicles set on fire. Or we would simply drive them off the road with our armoured cars, and we set up a couple of field guns commanding the trunk road and shelled them as they slowed down for the corner. There was one bastard in a 4x4 and we strung him up from a lamp post.'

'No!' I said. 'No, no, no! That isn't what I meant!'

'Don't worry, my Führer, we were careful only to target the less well off. Rich people will not be discouraged from running cars.'

'What?' I cried. 'Why? That's outrageous! How could you? What are you, fascists?' Someone nudged me and whispered.

'It is regrettable but necessary,' said an adjutant apologetically. 'Poor people and the middle class make up by far the bulk of the polluters. The elite need not be inconvenienced. The middle class can be propagandized into going along with it out of guilt and will help us browbeat the workers. The measure is of course for the good of all.'

'Then all should suffer for it equally. We could ration mileage or something.'

Several pairs of eyes lit up and heads were put together as they excitedly discussed this. I instantly regretted saying it; they'd love the possibilities for control and bureaucracy involved there. 'Excellent idea, Führer! A rationing system is always great fun. Of course it would be the case that important and wealthy people would need to be granted extra rations or exemptions, due to their important work for the common good.'

'No, no, forget it, forget I spoke. I'm . . . going to have to rethink this whole thing.'

But they had established their own momentum. Down in the cellars with the tasteless comedians and the rest I found a new crop of prisoners, scientists who had expressed doubts that there was a warming or that man was to blame for it. I talked with one or two of them idly as their feet were roasted and my troops abused them and they said it was more possibly, I forget exactly what now, something to do with the earth going round the sun or something heretical like that. I shrugged it off and went back to the nurses but continued to feel uneasy.

Soon those of them with influence in government were drawing up plans to stop people from ever going on a plane except for Very Important business or showbiz reasons. Meanwhile they had discovered that cows emitting methane was a problem, and the troops had a merry old time zealously blowing up all the cows nearby with bazookas.

Then one day one of the very efficient planners said, 'We have realized that CO_2 is carbon dioxide, which humans breathe out.' A gleam came into his eye. 'There must be – fewer people in the world.'

I didn't like where he was heading with that so I called a halt to the whole campaign.

One day I was reminiscing and I said, 'My wife used to

blow smoke in my face, and I hate the smell and I was born with a tickly lung and it made me cough. That shouldn't be allowed to happen.'

'Say no more, my Führer.'

So they went round all the pubs and other public places in gangs, and broke them up and threw all the smokers out, and ransacked the tills and grabbed the owners by the balls and said if they allowed anyone to smoke any more they would come back and burn the place down. And that while they were at it, they should serve less alcohol too, especially to wine drinkers.

'That isn't what I wanted!' I protested. 'At least, I don't think so.'

'It is for the public health, my Führer, strength through hygiene.'

'But – you might as well persecute people for eating cream cakes or too many pies!'

They looked at each other in admiration. 'See, that is why he is the Führer and we are just lowly minions.' And by dawn there was not a single pastry shop in the area with its window intact, and every fatty they could lay their hands on was mugged and ducked in a river and tied to an exercise treadmill.

'Being fat isn't so bad,' I said in exasperation. 'I had anorexia, that was far worse. There's a disease I would cure if I could.'

The word spread and the top brains put their heads together. The next day every supermodel in the country had been kidnapped and was down in our cellars being force-fed lard.

I became scared to ever say anything in front of them. When I fondly reminisced about old Skip's daring circus antics and how they had almost cost him his life later on, they were outraged that a dog could be used in that way and went round closing down all the circuses they could get their hands on. When I mentioned my fear of doors (actually greatly lessened these days, especially now I had a squad of crack bodyguards who could kick them open for me, and toss grenades through any I was especially scared of) and the problems they had caused at work, they went round ordering all the offices in the district to take all their doors off their hinges on pain of reprisals. When I told of Gerald's tragic demise, they mounted a campaign forcing all land-owners with abandoned mineworkings on their property to erect large warning signs in their fields and eventually fill in the shafts at their own expense.

'That isn't necessary!' I protested. 'It was a freak million to one accident!'

'There are sixty million people in the country, Führer,' I was piously chided. 'Although by no means all of them and not nearly enough ethnic minorities get out into the fields.'

From being an eternal victim I had become the wielder of extraordinary, despotic power. Surely there must be some good I could put it to.

I told them of my dismal childhood, my stepfather pounding nails into my head. Perhaps they could do some-thing to stop that sort of thing?

'Yes, yes! Of course, Führer, we will stamp that right out! We will stop people ever chastising their children in any way again. If they so much as smack they will be hauled to our cellars.'

'Isn't that a bit too much?' I said doubtfully.

'You cannot take half-measures.' There were excited mutterings around the conference table. 'Parents must not be allowed to abuse their children. Therefore we will establish targets for a certain number of children to be taken into care each year.'

'Targets? That can't be . . .'

'Oh, they will be easy to meet, Führer, we will take them from the *untermenschen*, the slow, the retarded.'

'Perhaps it would be safer to break up the family unit altogether?' another suggested. 'Statistically most child-abuse incidents happen within the home.'

'Yes, children are better raised by the state and freed of bad influences anyway.'

'You always go too far!' I cried.

I was becoming quite downhearted now. I was starting to consider the quite surprising possibility that no good could ever come of pushing people around.

Glumly I toured the punishment cells in the dungeons, filled with people who had smoked in bus-shelters, people who had smacked their children, retards who had loved their children, waddling supermodels fattened up like foie gras geese, muzzled fatties tied to treadmills, people who held unfashionable opinions, people who drove the wrong sort of cars or who liked to go abroad, publicans who had sold alcohol to people who were drunk, people who had been deemed to mistreat animals, a priest who had said it was wrong to have sex with animals thereby infringing the rights of people who liked to have sex with animals, people who had sold fruit with imperial weights thereby infringing the rights of foreigners not to have to do maths . . . I wondered what all these people had in common and decided it was, they happened to live here and they happened to have no power.

Desperately I tried to think of an area where their draconian methods might actually do some good.

Then I read that over in the next town there was an epidemic of muggings, burglaries and vicious assaults directed against old people. Although they were undoubtedly reactionary, we had not yet officially come out as disapproving of old people, although we had issued communiqués saying they were suspect and should bloody shape up, so it probably wasn't us doing it. And the Nazis had enjoyed the initial bout of helping old ladies.

'Crime!' I said in the conference room, pounding the table dramatically. 'There's a crimewave! We will do something about the problem of crime!'

I looked at them expectantly. They looked back at me.

'Yes, my Führer?' they said carefully.

'Well . . . go to it!'

'How, my Führer?'

'I don't know, do what you normally do!' I flailed an arm. 'Overkill, espionage, intimidation, property confiscation, overwhelming force, dawn raids, kick some doors in, drag them to the cells and punish the little toerags.'

They looked shocked.

'But my Führer, these poor criminals are obviously from deprived backgrounds and have had unsatisfactory upbringings. If anyone is the victim here, it is them.' They all nodded.

'And what about their rights, Führer?' said another virtuously. 'The rights of the individual must always be respected.'

'Besides we are overstretched as it is and our cellars are full.'

'You cannot fight a war on two fronts, Führer, you ought to have learned that by now.'

I moped around the garden brooding. I should escape somehow rather than be part of this, but I had become used to the deference and privilege and ticklish nurses. It would be hard to give it all up and I reflected that after all I deserved it, I was doing good, or trying to.

I came up with one last idea of how our power could be useful.

'I know one thing we can do! All my life I've had crappy jobs, when I've had any job at all. You National Socialists, you're all about the state planning, right? Why don't you arrange it so you can provide all the people of this country with good jobs, I mean ones that last, useful jobs with security and dignity?'

They looked even more shocked than before.

'That was the old days, Führer, those ideas are long discredited.'

'We are not Neanderthals, you know.'

'You cannot interfere with The Market, my Führer, not even a superman like you.'

'But you know goods and services are cheaper, so pay goes further when they are working, and there's more entertainment when they're on the dole.'

Defeated, I started to slouch out of the room.

I had one last thought and came back.

'Public transport—'

'The market, my Führer.'

So that was that. They couldn't even make the trains run on time.

I had had enough. I went out to the workshop, a large converted barn, where Himmelmann had been shut up for the past few weeks working day and night on my splendid new Führer-penis. He had scarcely emerged save to issue orders requisitioning materiel for his great work – iron, copper, basalt, microchips, plutonium, sheep and oxen by the hundreds to be sacrificed to propitiate the old Teutonic gods. You could often hear him hammering and singing and in the night strange crackling energies could be glimpsed from within.

As I started to walk in now he shrieked, 'No! It is not ready,' thrusting me out and slamming the door. I heard the sound of him fumbling with ropes.

When he finally let me in I saw behind him nothing but a huge tarpaulin draped over an object approximately the length and width of three long caravans placed one behind the other with two huge spheres at the bottom. It hummed and throbbed beneath its cover and an eerie light pulsated from the gaps between tarpaulin and floor. The cover was roped down and I got the impression the object within was floating slightly off the ground.

He indicated three comatose nurses in a corner. 'Test subjects. They faint at the mere sight of it.'

'But how are they expected to—'

'It will take a hundred of them, I estimate, climbing all over it and writhing in concert to stimulate it to climax. That can be arranged. We will arrange a test-firing next week, when I can think of a suitable target city for demolition.'

I sighed. That hadn't been what I wanted either.

'I won't be here next week. I'm leaving.'

'But your penis, Führer! Once I have solved the nose-cone re-entry problem and grind down the guidance fins it is ready to be sewn on.'

'I don't care.'

'I am not sure what to name it. Perhaps *Notung*, after Siegfried's sword, or perhaps Lulubelle, after my mother.'

'I really do not care.'

'It has quadrophonic stereo, you know, and a built-in MP3 player.'

'Himmelmann. Listen to me, please. It's over. You can take your face back. Shoot me if you want to. I'm not being your Führer any more.'

'Himmelmann. Listen to me, please. It's over. You can take your face back. Shoot me if you want to. I'm not being your Führer any more.'

He raged and expostulated. 'Your destiny—'

'You made a mistake! You'll be glad to be rid of me when you know.' I grabbed him by the arm and dragged him out. 'Come and see what I've done with them.'

I pointed to the flagpole where a swastika had used to fly. There was now a flag with a smiley face on and the slogan 'Caring, Sharing, Inclusive!' We had outlawed the swastika not long before, shortly after prohibiting the Union Jack, and anyone who still used it was now down in the cellars.

I showed him some of our new propaganda literature and told him what we had been doing. A couple of times he yelped in disbelief.

At the end, though, he smiled and shrugged.

'Well, I am an old man, and it is not my style of thing. But they are clearly having fun.' He clapped me on the shoulder. 'I did not make a mistake. You have done very well for us. I told you, we just needed someone to tell us who to push around.' He sighed. 'We had lost the faith. Capitalism had won and we did not dare to fight it. We could not see how to achieve anything grand or meaningful or worthwhile. But in this new road of pettiness you have shown us the way ahead.'

He gazed fondly across the park to where panting fatties where being whipped around a racetrack.

'The human instinct to tyrannize adapts and evolves. It is a marvel of nature. You teach at the schools of the witch-burnings, and the children are shocked and think, "Oh, zhose squares! I would not have been like that. I would have stood apart." They learn of McCarthy and are righteous in disgust, never realizing they will do similar in their way. Because it is hard to step aside from what is accepted by your time, and people do not learn to think for themselves. They all think they have been taught to think for themselves, but they have not learned to reason philosophically, they have only learned to reject what their teachers tell them is oppression. The few who do rebel, if they survive, may gain their own acolytes and perhaps one day enforce a conformism of their own. And so it goes on and on and it is good, because the weak must be squashed, minorities must be downtrodden, and power must be exercised, always.'

'You nasty old bastard. Take your face back or don't, I'm going.'

'I will take it. I will take it and keep it safe for future generations, for it may be needed again one day. And for you, I will find you a brand spanking new baboon's arse to wear, you will like that, yes? But it is a shame about The Penis. Come, at least let me show you what it looks like erect.'

24

The end of my tale: reconciliation with my family

I must now bring my memoir to a close. Although there have been other awful things that have happened to me which I have not yet related, time and space are against me. (Euphemia, who is staying here at the moment and is currently reading this over my shoulder, has just snorted with laughter at the phrase 'time and space are against me', saying it sounds like the ultimate recrimination against the universe and should be the title of this book. Orange.)

But there is one last chapter in my life I must briefly mention, particular as it enables me to end on a happy note, namely the reconciliation of sorts I was finally able to effect with my family.

This came about largely thanks to my editor, who took it upon himself to get in touch with my mother in order to commission a memoir from her, which he thinks cannot help but be inspiring to paralysed dick-technicians everywhere and also has a solid chance of bringing in film and TV rights. This she agreed to, even promising to name names, which will apparently include prominent figures in the leper community.

Not long after, though, a momentous message was conveyed to me: my stepfather was on his deathbed and wanted to see me.

My heart was heavy within me as I made my way to the

hospital. So much remained unresolved from my childhood. Though years had passed and I was a grown man who could no longer be hurt by him, some of the wounds he had inflicted had never healed (particularly a festering one at the base of my skull) and there was so much I wanted to say to him. This could be our last chance for a rapprochement, and the thought that he might die before we had reached some sort of understanding and resolution frightened me.

His room was darkened. Grave-faced medics attended him. 'You only have a few minutes,' warned a nurse. 'Try not to excite him too much.' They left us alone with the beep of the monitors.

He drew a ragged breath. 'Come here, son,' he whispered.

I sat on the edge of the bed.

'Closer.' I obeyed. I could barely hear his voice. 'I want to . . .' He beckoned. 'Lean closer.'

I put my ear close to his mouth.

P-tunk.

The nail-gun he had had concealed under the covers shot a seven-incher straight through my eardrum.

He sniggered and died.

I am glad that we had that final moment together.

Postscript

One final hideous accident

Several days ago, I gazed proudly at the advance review copies of this my life story being printed off, the first of many thousands that will be launched into the world for the inspiration and uplift of mankind.

Beside me my editor beamed happily. 'Well, Sunny,' he said, 'you've come a long way. The bad times are behind you now. Stick with me and we'll be farting through silk.' And he clapped me amiably on the shoulder.

Alas, I was unprepared for this and overbalanced, and fell off the factory gantry we were standing on and into the printing press below.

The pain was excruciating and every bone in my body was broken. I am dictating this postscript to a nurse, and even that hurts my mouth. On the plus side, the doctors assure me that the text which was printed over my entire body will fade with time.

Most people, I suppose, are able to hear the phrase 'Sticks and stones may break my bones but words will never hurt me' and think it very true; but from now on I will laugh hollowly. Or I would, if that didn't hurt me too.

August–November '07

Appendix

Euphemia's unfinished memoir

The Rape of the Tot

or

Daddy, You Give Me a Pain in the Cunt

*being a monograph on the experience and after-effects
of a young girl being fucked ragged by her own dear pater,
dildo that he was, from a very early age and often before
a paying audience; with digressions on the matter of
being born mentally different to every other cunt,
and sundry matters related thereto*

by

Euphemia Fucking McCreary, aged 12¾

I

Horas non numero nisi serenas

I was a porn star at the age of three: to have peaked so early is depressing, and it will all be downhill from here. It strikes me as both insufferably precocious and unbearably poignant to write my memoirs at the age of twelve.

I understand it is common for child stars to have difficulty adjusting to normal life. Not merely common but vulgar, I should say; as far as I am concerned normal life can adjust to me.

Watching those early triumphs now, lamenting, yet again, my utter lack of residuals (child stars of the future, the first time a nice man offers you a lollipop, *phone an agent*), I am ravished by my natural charisma. I am the undoubted star of the scene, the babe in the cot surrounded by her toys. Daddy, in singlet and scowl, slouching towards Bethlehem, has delusions of Brando, but he has forgotten the adage 'Never work with children or animals' and I upstage him effortlessly.

As I study those grainy stills, that creaky footage, I admire my luminous screen presence. My hair was baby-blonde then, a fluffy halo of innocence which seems to have a built-in backlighting, and I am like a young, a very young, Harlow, a more ingenuous Monroe, Fay Wray in the hand of a huge hairy ape.

The freeze-frame flickers; I slip into memory and the ghastly movement starts as he inserts his throbbing cock into my cunt.

Are you shocked? Revolted? Well what did you fucking expect upon buying such a book? Isn't that what you paid for, shithead? To be shocked and revolted and to cry on my behalf? I really don't know what you want. Maybe you want to be excited.

Sunny's publisher is excited, particularly by the stash of photos and films Sunny obtained from my case worker. They are to be turned into a lavishly illustrated deluxe coffee-table version of my life story, to be available from this publisher and stocked in all good bookshops and supermarkets soon. Later, perhaps, a film of the films? With myself to be impersonated by the chameleonic _____, no doubt, shrunk to crotch-height by the miracle of CGI. No: she is a star: the rest of the cast will stand on boxes. If I was somewhat younger they could get me to reprise my starring role, simulating, of course, faking what were once genuine screams and moans.

(I toy with your emotions: I never once cried out, save for the prompt when I had forgotten my lines.)

(Again I toy. That is a joke, one of the ones for which they tried to lock me up once and may do again.)

But all true sexual reverists know the word is supreme and worth a thousand pictures. The theatre of the mind, the studio within, where we are all perfectionist De Milles brandishing riding crops at the actors until we get things just right. The word pornography itself, of course, comes from the Greek for 'writings of a whore'. Porn, ubiquitous and unassailable, has become the defining commodity of our time. It has become a universal modifier: food-porn, misery-porn, emotional-porn, redemption-porn. Is this porn? Am I being a whore now? Perhaps at best it resembles some experience-substitute from *Brave New World*.

I am unfamiliar with this genre. Am I supposed to save the moneyshots for later on in the book so we don't peak too early? Or do I dole them out regularly and often to keep your interest from flagging, give the narrative a shot of adrenaline, provide you with your sympathy fix? Do you need a climax at the end of every chapter? I was raised to be an obliging girl and will do my best to please.

Diligently researching, here are some Amazon reviews of works in the field: 'Despite feeling sympathy, it's possible to rate a horrible childhood as mediocre.' 'Keeps you at a distance', too evasive and euphemistic; 'never really piercing the core of the reader . . . it doesn't move me as much as other books have'.

How photogenic all the cover stars are! Do ugly children never get raped? I suppose paedophiles, like photographers, can afford to be choosy. None of them are as pretty as I was, however. I find myself almost tempted to become the queen of this genre. I'll give them graphic, Sunny can ghostwrite the emotion. Or maybe there's software that can do it, a Word application. 'As he thrust his tool into my five-year-old vagina I remember feeling distinctly put-out / dismayed / overcome with ennui / sore / violated to the core of my being / his taut wobbly bollocks.'

Sunny's publisher has big plans for both of us. I do not pretend to understand all of his publishing argot but he has used the words 'goldmine' and 'ka-ching'. With a history like mine one seems distressingly destined to attract both predators and publishers.

I suppose there is a remote chance that, performed with all my intelligence and art, this may after all be cathartic for me, but it will surely tend to debase you. I advise you to close the book now, and if you want thrills and a gripping read buy a nice Robert Ludlum. If you wish to wallow in depravity, go to the political memoirs section. If you need to feel sorry for someone, look in the fucking mirror.

No? Still avidly reading? Well, I tried. This will not, anyway, be what Sunny or his pimp expects or hopes for. This will be art, not reportage. I will use it to do what I want. But fear not, dear reader, I promise you healthy lashings of incest and brutality to keep you entertained.

II

We must also talk about my Terrible Afflictions. I am a monster: because I am a perfect being, sufficient unto myself. That is the first thing to know about me, and it is why they will never lock me up.

To have been born Autistic is to have won first prize in the lottery of life. To have Tourette's on top of that is merely the icing on the cack.

The freedom! The freedom! You poor trammelled normals, you cannot conceive how I bless my diagnoses for the freedom they have won me. This is not merely a figure of speech, nor does it just refer to the latitude I am permitted in polite society. I believe the fact that my quirks have been officially approved and sanctioned has literally kept me at liberty in a situation where an ordinary person would have been locked away.

As Tourette's is a licence to swear (and, I have joyously found, to the horror of the po-faced, say far worse things which are not permitted nowadays), so autism has proved a get-out-of-jail-free card. Except it is not jail I specifically fear but mental hospitals; although I suppose it is possible that sooner or later they will start to jail as well as hospitalize people for the crime of Not Giving a Fuck. Provided we can feed and clothe ourselves, it is not currently the fashion to institutionalize my people on a large scale. Indeed it would appear the only types currently less at risk of ever seeing the inside of a nuthouse (pardon the solecism, my fucking Tourette's, you know) are hallucinating schizophrenics who are liable to kill some poor cunt: these are being kicked out on to the streets as it is thought the fresh air does them a power of good.

What am I talking about? I will tell you what I am cunting well talking about. You, dear reader, poor normal-brained nob-gob, are more at risk of being carted off to an asylum than me with my Autistic Excuse card or a psycho with a bloody axe. You could go to the GP feeling mopey or lethargic, you could have a bad day at work and yell at someone or hit the photocopier or break down in tears, and they could suck you into the system, and haul you off to lose ten years of your life shuffling round a brightly painted ward in slippers and paper panties listening to Mantovani. *You could be committed for not showing the emotions they expect you to show.*

Did you know that laughing at your misfortunes can be taken for a sign of bipolar disorder? Did you know that showing a stiff upper lip over bad experiences can be taken for a sign of lack of affect indicative of a serious psychosis? I know because I was there.

I do not wish to dwell on it. Of all the things I wish to forget, that shrink who thought I was mad for wanting to forget things is among the first. The eternal toy-like nod to show she was listening, the automatically glazing eyes as she dismissed the words I said because they did not fit her preconceived theory . . . theirs is the true psychosis. She did not like my jokes about my father's inadequate sexual technique, or the fact I was never given my own trailer on set and they would get the colour of jelly-babies in my backstage rider wrong. They do not like jokes. She did not care for the way I shrugged and yawned when she asked me how I felt about it. She was positively suspicious of the fact that I preferred not to think about it rather than dig it all up again. She thought I was *repressing* something. Repressing *what*? My dad and his mates were fucking me nightly and there were films to prove it. What was there left to repress? Perhaps the cat had also had a go and that had thrown me over the edge . . . And very soon I saw that every tramline conversation, every baited question, every note eagerly scribbled on her pad at my most innocent remark was leading towards one prearranged destination: me being prescribed unneeded medication (which would itself have turned me batty) and filed away for life with the completely bugfuck.

How I bless those medical journals in the waiting room! How thankful I am for that inspired moment of self-diagnosis! I suppose for all I know it may even have been true . . . There had been high-profile cases of misdiagnosed Auts turned psychotic by anti-psycho medication I knew she'd be familiar with; I can still remember the paling of her already pallid face as I carefully laid my clues . . . But what would you have done in my place?

I say again: they can hospitalize people for not showing the accepted feelings and soon they may be jailing them . . . At the very least, the police have already arrested people for ill-considered jokes.

Consider my people: my glorious, geeky, badly socialized people. Are they not a bona fide modern bogeyman? Are we not authentic, balls-out, honest-to-fuckery media stars? (I mean of course the Autistic now, although the same applies to a lesser extent to Tourette's sufferers, who may soon be the only jesters left licensed.) The ultimate object of horror and pity for this age, they who do not show or pick up Feelings.

The coy neutrality of the word 'neurotypical' to describe you ordinary weepy-heads apart, there is relatively little relativism, I find, directed towards our affliction compared with some I could name. Less of 'Who are we to judge what is normal?' Less consideration of us as noble savages or *Artistes Naïfs* with our own unique vision than is often accorded to more dramatic and destructive mental conditions. By and large we are seen as something alien and pitiable and terribly tragic. The kids who prefer not to hug! We may as well wear fucking antennae. Any parent would rather have a three-legged dwarf with a shrivelled warty penis growing out of his forehead. Mind you, I'll wager there are thousands of the fuckers up and down the country who have gleefully, gratefully misdiagnosed their surly teenagers as having Asperger's simply because they are rude or awkward little shits who prefer books to suburbia.

And I note, with wry amusement, and some alarm on your behalf, that the word 'autistic', shorn of any strict medical connotations and in startling contravention of prevailing pieties, is passing into usage as a term of disparagement or abuse, meaning 'one who does not pay the required tribute of compassion', 'one who does not emote on cue', 'one whose social or political opinions or philosophy of life do not accord with my own and who is therefore lacking in feelings'.

Camus wrote that a man who did not cry at his mother's funeral would be sentenced to death. Nowadays if you fail to cry at a princess's funeral (or indeed a polar bear's drowning) you are at the very least shunned. Prefer not to talk about your own mother's death or your father shafting you and you will be thought heartless and inhuman and cold. To fail to show pity to others is looked on as unforgivable; to fail to pity yourself is almost as much so.

We are all Coriolanus now, forced to make show of our wounds or risk being turned upon by the mob. In happier times film stars, pop stars, sports stars were allowed to project a godlike glamour and invulnerable insouciance. Now, democratically, they must demonstrate they have been as hemmed about by misery and henpecked by tragedy as we; and also confess their sins, which were often in simpler ages known as 'having a jolly good time of it, all in all', and hope for absolution.

Over at the next table Sunny is writing his book. The publisher thirsts for his every paragraph. I have no doubt it will be a bestseller. A hero of our times! A passive victim, a prostitute, a drug addict, a drunk, a drudge, a drag. We live in an age of the fuck-up as culture hero; and in the not-too-distant future, everyone will be a victim for fifteen minutes.

On an afternoon TV show chaired by a couple of conjoined mongoloids they are running a competition to find the person who's had the most painful experience. This is true and not satire, which went out at about the same time that record-players did and is far more obsolete. The viewers have to vote for who's had the most tragic life. The winner will get a book contract.

Victims vying with victims! A voyeuristic gladiatorial arena where he with the most wounds wins. Not merely obscene in itself but a perfect metaphor for modern society.

Whoever can claim to have suffered the most bags the sympathy vote and the moral high-ground and all the indulgence they want. Who gets your vote? The fundamentalist Islamic homophobes or the open lesbians next door? Does not compute, guilt overload, ignore dilemma or find scapegoat. In actuality the radical Muslims win: they're foreign, and so by definition downtrodden by us, even if they're oil rich or were never part of the Empire or were born here, and their violence and bigotry are seen as concrete evidence of how much they're hurting. The muggee or the criminal with the sad upbringing? That one's too easy, and besides jails are too expensive. The raped or the rapist who was raped, or who comes from a poverty-stricken country, poor dear? Share the love, spare the blame. When blacks kill blacks or poor kids kill poor kids the murderer is as much a victim as the murdered. *Und so weiter*. Behind them all, Mother Earth, being touted as the biggest rape victim of all, when I suspect the truth is she would shrug in her slumbers and annihilate us all if she even felt the pathetic tickling of our tiny tools. She is the ultimate anointed sufferer, outranking even the Islamists. How to get the left on board the war on terror: calculate the carbon footprint of 9–11.

Society carved up into a pie-chart with smaller and smaller slices, bisected over and over by ever-proliferating Venn diagram circles, people divided into tribes, lobby groups, support groups, fetishes, marketing demographics rather than nations or classes . . .

Since shortly after my eleventh birthday I have been meditating a novel, *The Body Politic*. A group of characters in a place that was once a nation, who between them represent – literally – every organ of the human body, and who brought together (which they never are) would make up a whole and complete person. The celebrity who is the new Face of Urethritis; a lawyer for the Bog-Eye Anti-Defamation Front; a woman whose life revolves around an Inverted Navel Support Group; a girl whose ears alone are famous as she is a model for earlobe fetishists, another who is a Hollywood arse stand-in; lobbyists and campaigners for heart, lungs, kidney, bowel and brain diseases, and so on and so forth, a collage of fracture, obsession, and inane over-specialization. Jostling for revenue and influence, the charities and lobby groups, who have the budgets of small countries and employ the populations of entire towns, indulge in corporate espionage against one another, blind assassins battling ninja spastics, Aspie spies slipping killer peanuts to allergy spokesmen – but no, what good would it do to harm the opposition? Instead, they embark on campaigns to make their rivals look really happy and healthy and deprecate the effects of their disabilities. Bulimics doctor photos of Stephen Hawking ski-ing in his chair; claustrophobics kidnap the Face of Face Cancer, fatten him up and give him a makeover; the Alopecia Foundation fakes a study showing that psoriasis is a surefire babe-magnet; Save the Lemur puts out brochures full of smiling Sudanese whooping it up entitled 'Darfur? It's a fucking paradise, give them nothing'.

For myself I choose not to go down that route. I have refused all Sunny's eager offers to take me to support groups and clubs. I will not be defined in that way. I am not a set of symptoms. I am not a syndrome. I am not a victim.

It is true I once daydreamed of making myself the Queen of the Auts and leading my nerdy and emotionally reserved hordes in a jihad against our weepy-brain oppressors – I am embarrassed to say there are those of my fellows who think in those overemotional terms, although I suspect them of being wannabes or agents-provocateur from the Emotionalist hegemony. Protest marches with very long chants beginning '2–4–6–8, 16–32–64–128, 256–512–1024–2048' and going on and on for a very long time without ever getting round to saying who it is we really hate. – Except we hate no one, we merely find them distressingly irrational. Our demands simple at first, free K-Mart underwear of course, compulsory Qantas flights to science-fiction conventions, the immediate resumption of Alan Moore's *Big Numbers*. Then the terrorist outrages: logic-bombs, fractal grenades, fiendishly irresolvable equations chalked in public areas intended to cause mental paralysis in passers-by. Or the simple removing of our services – we jam the TV to smugly announce our complete withdrawal to a world of pure maths, and let's see how civilization copes with a sudden absence of *Star Trek* fanlistings and Samurai Sudoku.

Far from wiping out the weepy-brains upon assuming power, it would actually be my mission to save them from themselves . . .

I watched a documentary some normal-brains made about my people. It was hilarious. The programme-makers played sad music to indicate when people should feel sorry for us. Maybe humans were not always like these normals, but I find them lacking in dignity and as machine-like as we are supposed to be. 'We will press a button and you will go "Ahhh".'

But no, I will enter no ghetto, I will have no group. Any time I use 'us' or 'you' or 'my people' or especially 'my culture' is tongue-in-cheek. I will be a gang of one, a tribe of I and I and I suppose Sunny if he behaves. All the same, I am grateful to belong when it counts. My serene detachment is officially approved, and I have an excuse to be really snotty.

I have a letter from my doctor excusing me from emotionalism. Envy me, weepy-brains. I have another saying I can call you a cunt and you're not allowed to hit me, or a slovenly overweight underachieving transsexual whore and you're not allowed to call the police. (Conversely, insult me or my mindset and you will go straight to prison.) Do thou likewise if you would stay sane. Get affiliated! Find your own lobby group! Start your own religion! Claim the blessed sanctuary of victimhood!

For soon it will be a crime not to emote or empathize, the Compulsory Pity Orders will start being sent out . . .

No, but I believe we are almost reaching a point where everyone should practise being a shit for ten minutes a day simply to build strength of character, for the biggest form of social control is now, 'You're a nice person, aren't you? Only an utter bastard could possibly oppose such-and-such a measure.' And all too often they hide behind some poor unfortunate and one does feel an absolute cunt if one guiltily mumbles, 'Yes, but hang on, think of the consequences.'

And yet . . . glacial Aut-Queen or self-sufficient little shit though I be, I am passionately devoted to the Aristotelian mean, and I also fear compassion burn-out and the inevitable eventual reaction to these excesses of spurious emotionalism almost as much as I dislike the excesses themselves. The pendulum must one day swing back – and then the results of the mushy thinking of today will be used to justify the most appalling callousness in the name of reason and logic and the rules of algebra. Then, the one who appears the most hard-headed and unsentimental in an argument will gain the upper hand, and what larks will follow.

. . . But enough. I promised myself I wouldn't do this, or at least not all at once. I rant and ramble. Perhaps I contradict myself. (Do I? Well, I contain multitudes. – No, I will scribble that out. Contain multitudes nowadays and you will be diagnosed with multiple personality disorder.) I will not be as hysterical as they. I am becoming emotional and unworthy of my chosen People, who will one day supplant you.

And rereading the above, perhaps I am trying too strenuously to construct a unified field theory of moping. The world never suffers from just one disease at once and 'Only connect' can be taken too far. But still one inclines to think of these various phenomena as symptoms of the same illness or at the very least books in the same genre.

Appendix

I am forgetting my audience. I am in danger of committing the ultimate sin and boring you. ('This book was boring compared to some I have read' – Amazon reviewer commenting on abuse memoir.) Time for some paydirt for the diligent reader, methinks.

Let us by all means return to the rape and related jolliness!

III

'Thou shalt not gaze on thy father's nakedness' is an excellent injunction, especially when your father is as unattractive and out of shape as mine was and is coming towards you with a lob-on. But I had nowhere else to look.

I recall noting interestedly, at perhaps the age of five, that one of father's bollocks was smaller than the other, making his scrotal sac resemble the sign for infinity. Will this happen infinitely, I thought? If time is circular, will this happen again and again, my irritation and annoyance growing with every iteration? Will I remember? Will I somehow, on one of my circles of this particular hell, manage to change the record and stop it happening again? Or will it just come round and round eternally and I'll be trapped forever in some Hedayat-like loop as he makes me smoke the blind owl? And no I said no I won't No!

Perhaps this was the beginning of my obsession with time travel . . . One of the therapists obsessed with making me relive the past once regressed me to one of those primal scenes of outrage, in a semi-hypnotic state or willed imagining – Picture the scene, I am – and had the older me step back into it. All right, I'm back there, then. Now what? Give your younger self a hug. I do not hug, I told her, and I would have enjoyed it no more than I would. Secondly, to hug the girl on the bed just then would have constituted troilism, not to mention a form of incest more incestuous than the one she was currently undergoing. What she needed was not a hug but an ice-pick and the knowledge of where to stick it.

Remembrance, remembrance, relive and regress, over and over . . . I suggested we just sit and watch the films, we could have brought popcorn. But maybe repetition does inure you to horror, as it is said to kill the force of eternal truths, and maybe that is not healthy.

The abyss gazes also . . . Yes, I'm talking about you now, constant reader. Patently one cannot turn one's back on suffering altogether. But as I told Sunny, it don't do to dwell.

The worst is not, so long as we can say, this is the worst. But when that becomes a positive enticement, an endorsement to put on the back of a book? When we cry, 'Roll up, roll up, this is the worst, come and buy your tickets to see the worst?' What cunts we are . . . And always in search of a stronger and stronger fix, the race to the bottom. But the ramp effect kicks in, the law of diminishing returns; sadly I've found this holds true even of swearing and smutty jokes. Shock effect not repetition, me old fucktards.

Me dear dead dad could have told you all about it, I imagine, just before 'e went and topped 'is silly self, the boredom and deadness that sets in when there's no stronger kick, nowhere fouler left to go. ('This childhood was not as painful as some I have read.' 'You call that a rape? That was barely a tickle.' 'Four people do not constitute a gangbang! I want my money back.' 'She don't get my sympathy that easy.' Cunts.) He only wanted entertainment, I reckon, same as what you do (no, I don't say you'll end up like him, unless you're that way inclined already, I'm only setting up a bleeding parallel, enni?) and he lived in a world where entertainment was the highest good and anything people found entertaining was an acceptable form of it. (I make no excuses for anyone as I will offer none for myself. Some people are wicked and there's an end to 'em.) And as he never found out in time, sooner or later the brakes must be applied. Censorship, of the self–variety always being much the classier option, the old taste and restraint and common decency.

But bollocks to that, *I* says. And Sunny's publisher would throw a fuck-fit.

As he doubtless will when he sees this. But bollocks to him, too, says I. I toyed, you know, with giving him what he wanted – or what he didn't know he wanted but secretly yearns for, what he and his drooling readers certainly deserve, and I'm the girl could do it, too: the last word in the genre, the *dernier cri de coeur*, the abuse memoir to end all of them, the culmination of the movement, the destination it must one day reach, a book so revolting it finally makes them cry Stop, finis, enough, we have supped full of horrors, a litany of filth and degradation that would eat their rotten brains out so they would be left staring and catatonic and old before their time. That last word will be reached sooner or later, I suppose, but someone else must do it for I find I can't be fucked.

Or will it be reached? Or will we just go on and on into darker and darker depths? Spengler wrote that our Faustian age is characterized by a reaching for the infinite – which I find noble and inspiring in some ways, but dispiriting when applied to such things as greed, material possessions, power, unnecessary refinements (a better mousetrap, a better razor, a better rape scene), our appetite for distraction, for sensation, for degradation. Maybe we will never cry Hold, enough.

But this will not be a catalogue of crimes. This will not be reportage such as Sunny and his shark want, where one is strapped down passive and helpless for a ride on the ghost train. This is art, where I am allowed to reshape and improve the past rather than merely relive it, and by reshaping, conquer. One is forced to admit the supremacy of art not only over journalism but also over life and, alas, science, at least until I can lick the quantum stabilizer problem. For now, this is my only time machine, my only way to go back and change things.

I watch the scene again, no longer passive. I break the fourth dimension, I break the fourth wall. I step into the past, I step into the room with them. I do not hug her, no room, but we pull chummy tongues at each other behind his back. I hand her an ice-pick and watch her put her arms around him and embed it in his brain.

Of course it didn't happen like that, and ice-picks are so messy anyway. She would have to endure another six months of it before she finally succeeded in synthesizing a suitable poison from handy household items and watched him die in agonizing pain. Matching his handwriting for the suicide note was a simple exercise in applied shape recognition, which I was very good at. I was not, at that time, able to keep the bastard old Tourette's from spilling over into my writing with any degree of success, but once the facts were out everyone who read his billet-adieux was forced to agree that 'I am a fucking cunt and deserve to die slowly' pretty much met the case perfectly.

I suppose that was not what you expected. Are you disappointed by my abrupt happy ending, reader? Shocked? Shocked that I killed him and got away with it and have felt not a second of remorse? And if you found out I had, over the years, killed off the whole shagging ring of them and made it look like accidents . . . ?

Is he now the victim, have your sympathies shifted? I

know if he had lived but been caught you would have given him treatment and locked him away from vengeance with every human comfort. Do not mistake me: I am above anger and hatred and all useless emotion. But I have a keen sense of the shape of things and the laws of moral justice fit together as sweetly as a mathematical proof or a piece of aesthetically pleasing art.

Ah, but there's my cop-out, cops and soothing syringe-wielders and guardians of the morals: this is art. I need admit nothing. I may be reshaping the past to my own satisfaction. The punishment of the villain, so satisfying in art, so forbidden to us in life. You will never know; you may have it as you prefer. Maybe I only choose that it happened that way. It may only be my time-machine.

I can go further back, further, kill him before I am born, before he drives my mother to death, and I grow up happy and none of it ever happened.

Or even further, kill him before they meet, for he was not, I serenely decide, can *not* have been my father, my father was a time-traveller, a spaceman, a slumming Vulcan, Zeus in the form of a milkman, that man whose picture I found her clutching, I bring the two of them together, they die in each other's arms, I cut him out of my timeline, and none of it ever happened and I will never think of it again.

That is what I choose. If you could create an alternate timeline a girl would grow up to whom that had never happened and I choose I already am that girl. I choose we start again tabulae fucking rasae each morning if we want to and I am the victim of no one.

I will do many things in my life. I will perfect my time-machine and use it to journey to the exciting eras of the past rather than just revisit the sordid dullness of my own life. (Perhaps I will take Sunny back to meet the Spanish Inquisition; he will like that, it will give him a whole new chapter. He can compare notes with Candide and Pangloss.) I will write my novel, and give it a happy ending in which the characters learn to be whole, rounded individuals in themselves and come together in the body of a nation. I will produce proofs for Riemann's Hypothesis. For an encore I will attempt to reconcile the existence of God with the existence of N--------land. But one thing I will not do is write this book. I will not relive those times again and I will not be defined by things beyond my control that happen to have happened to me. I will never complain, explain, or let them see me bleed.

I have burned the pictures, I have burned the films. I will keep this to show Sunny, to study his reactions, but if I have any say in the matter they will have no permission to publish. Another country; the wench is dead. I will write my memoirs when I win the Nobel Prize and they will open, with no hint of what has gone before, on the day I am born, the day when I am finally able to live life on my own terms and under no one's power but my own.

Daddy, Not On My Hair! I Just Washed It
*The Memoir of an Abused Girl with a
Poor Sense of Perspective*

Daddy, Slow Down! Let Me Finish For Once
A Memoir of Incest and Sexual Ineptitude

Who's Better in the Sack, Me or Mummy?
Surviving Incest and an Overcompetitive Streak

Daddy, Pots!
A Memoir of Incest and Dyslexia

Also

Grandma, I Love You . . . But Not In That Way!

That Isn't a Lollipop, Uncle!

Nice Tits, Aunty, But This Isn't Devon, You Know

Bless, Me, Father, For I Have Gurble Wurble Furble

**Daddy, Why Can't We Just Buy a Cage? My Hamster
Gets Lonely Up Your Bum**

Mummy Hogged the Crack-Pipe

COMING SOON TO A BOOKSHOP NEAR YOU

Indexed Under C for Child
The True Story of the Boy Raised in a Filing Cabinet

When You Close the Door the Light Goes Out of My World
The Tragic Tale of a Girl Who was Kept in a Fridge

Spare
The Story of a Child Kept in a Car Boot

Flowers in the Coal-Bunker

Angels in the Cistern

Moppets in the Tumble Dryer

Don't Tell Mum the Babysitter's Dead
Lord Lucan was My Father

**An Endless Scream of Despair from the
Bleeding Stump-End of the World**
Memoirs of a Northumberland Childhood
(not for sale to minors or those with heart conditions)

COMING SOON TO A BOOKSHOP NEAR YOU

POP-UP MISERY MEMOIRS

A new range for younger children!

Because they're never too young to learn
how grim the world is

It's never too early to teach kids to be concerned, or worried about what will happen to them if you die. With our new range of colourful Pop-up Painful Lives you can do just that.

Watch the expression on their faces as they pull a tab and make Uncle Bernard's cock slide into Sally's mouth!

Or open a page and see a multicolour 3D tableau of child soldiers butchering villagers – with fully detachable heads!

These absorbing books are guaranteed to keep your children soberly preoccupied for hours on end. A traumatized child is a quiet child.

POLITICAL MISERY MEMOIRS

Please Tony, Stop!

The Memoir of a Labour Minister Betrayed

To the world outside, they were just like any other cabinet.

But behind closed doors, it was a unending nightmare of bullying, intimidation, and broken promises.

Young and idealistic, Clementina Bevan went into politics to make a difference.

But what can she do when the man she has pledged her soul to is interested only in unnatural liaisons with big business and sadistic acts of nanny-statism?

He made her do terrible things, things that shocked and appalled her.

And yet he was her leader and she couldn't stop loving him, and obeying like a robot.

Complicit in his crimes, haunted by a legacy of guilt and shame, she finally escapes to what she thinks is a happy ending in the care of an avuncular Scotsman . . . only to be pimped out again.

Gasp . . . as she learns the real meaning of an ethical foreign policy
Shudder . . . as she is verbally abused by his press secretary
Swoon . . . as you realise what your taxes have been pissed away on

Coming next year

No, Dave, No! I Won't Wear a Baseball Cap on 'Newsnight'

COMING SOON TO A BOOKSHOP NEAR YOU

The Painful Life Cookbook

Bestselling misery-memoir author Phil Gultree, kept locked in the cellar by his parents for the first ten years of his life, finally shares the heart-warming recipes that helped pull him through.

Including:

Earwig Surprise

Woodchip Flapjack

Mouse à la Urine

Earwig à la Urine

Woodchip à la Mouse

Open-Topped Woodchip and Earwig Sandwich

Frozen Urine Sorbet

and many more.

SLIGHTLY PAINFUL LIVES

A new range of Misery Memoirs for readers who want to feel compassion but can't take *too* much suffering

Imperfect

The Tragic Tale of a Woman Who Knew She Was Really, Really Fit . . . Apart from Her Elbows

Filomena Silk was set apart from every other woman on earth by a freak one-in-a-billion syndrome: she was completely happy with her body. Until, that is, the tragic day when she started worrying her elbows were a bit too pointy.

From then on she descended into a living hell, wracked by the suspicion that she was a freak with pointy elbows and the slow realization that no one gave a flying fuck. Refusing to bend her arms, she went through life unable to nudge people and so was thought cold and distant by her merry Cockney family. Or something.

He Shot, He Missed

Garry Garrack was the great footballing hope of his generation. Instead of running round a park like an overgrown child and showering with other men, however, he spent all his time drinking, drugging, and having orgies with models. 'I regret nothing,' he says.

SLIGHTLY PAINFUL LIVES

My Slut of a Mother Abandoned Me

The Tale of a Surly Twenty-Something Slacker
Whose Mum Went Round to Visit Her Friend Janet
Without Leaving Him Anything for Tea

'Just Popping Round to Janet's.' It was with these innocent words that Roland Balt's nightmare ordeal began. Only that morning the future had looked bright for pompous, overweight Ignatius Reilly wannabe Roland, with a top-1000-ranked weblog and a timid dole officer he had almost browbeaten into accepting his innate genius. But all that changed when, succumbing to hunger pangs shortly after his mother left, he looked in the microwave – and found it bare.

There was some uncooked chicken in the fridge but it might as well have been a vagina for all he knew what to do with it. In all, his heartless mother was at Janet's for almost three hours. As he told her in no uncertain terms on her return, if it hadn't been for his brainwave of ordering a dozen pizzas on her credit card, he would unquestionably have starved to death while she was doubtless comparing vibrators with the harlot Janet, and it would have served her right if he had called the NSPCC.

This startling tale is guaranteed to move no one.

SLIGHTLY PAINFUL LIVES

Minted

The Painful Story of a Boy Born Filthy Stinking Rich

From earliest childhood Lucius was suffocatingly pampered with material possessions. The only way his father could show him affection was by buying him cars and yachts. Every opportunity in life was his for the taking. Then he discovered the one thing that money couldn't buy: the cachet of a tough upbringing. But he learned how to fake it, so that was OK. Then he started drinking heavily, and he couldn't handle his drugs, but that's his look-out really. Your best chance of a snivel is when he rolls his Porsche in chapter ten, it was a fucking nice one.

Also

My Dad Wore Espadrilles To Open Night

My Parents Bought Betamax

They Said My Rabbit Had Gone On Holiday
Memoir of a Child Deceived

Wasted
The Girl Who Dropped Her Ice Cream

I Did Floretta Without Knickers On and a Boy Saw My Bum

MySpace Whore
*The Shocking Story of a Girl Who Couldn't Say No
to Friendship Requests*

www.ingramcontent.com/pod-product-compliance
Ingram Content Group UK Ltd.
Pitfield, Milton Keynes, MK11 3LW, UK
UKHW040640280225
455688UK00002B/45